ECONOMICS

3rd edition

OTHER ECONOMIST BOOKS

Guide to Analysing Companies
Guide to Business Modelling
Guide to Business Planning
Guide to Economic Indicators
Guide to the European Union
Guide to Financial Management
Guide to Financial Markets
Guide to Hedge Funds
Guide to Investment Strategy
Guide to Management Ideas and Gurus
Guide to Organisation Design
Guide to Project Management
Guide to Supply Chain Management
Numbers Guide
Style Guide

Book of Obituaries
Brands and Branding
Business Consulting
Business Strategy
Buying Professional Services
The City
Coaching and Mentoring
Doing Business in China
Emerging Markets
Headhunters and How to Use Them
Mapping the Markets
Marketing
Organisation Culture
Successful Strategy Execution
The World of Business

Directors: an A–Z Guide
Economics: an A–Z Guide
Investment: an A–Z Guide
Negotiation: an A–Z Guide

Pocket World in Figures

The
Economist

ECONOMICS

Making Sense of the Modern Economy

3rd edition

Edited by Saugato Datta

WILEY

John Wiley & Sons, Inc.

ISBN 978-1-118-01042-6

Printed in the United States of America
10 9 8 7 6 5 4 3 2 1

Contents

Contributors

Matthew Bishop is *The Economist*'s US business editor. He contributed articles to Chapters 1, 9 and 10.

Simon Cox is *The Economist*'s Asia economics editor. He contributed to Chapters 1, 2, 8 and 9, and wrote Chapter 11.

Saugato Datta is *The Economist*'s economics correspondent. He wrote some of the articles in Chapters 1, 2, 3, 4, 6 and 10. He is also the editor of this book.

Greg Ip is *The Economist*'s US economics editor. He contributed articles to Chapters 3 and 8.

Patrick Lane is deputy business affairs editor at *The Economist*. He wrote parts of Chapters 1, 4 and 10.

Zanny Minton-Beddoes is *The Economist*'s economics editor. She wrote some of the articles in Chapters 2, 3, 6, 7, 8 and 9.

John O'Sullivan is Britain economics editor at *The Economist*. He contributed to Chapters 4, 7 and 8

John Parker is *The Economist*'s globalisation editor. He contributed to Chapters 2 and 10.

John Smutniak was economics correspondent at *The Economist*. Chapter 10 includes an article written by him.

Henry Tricks is *The Economist*'s Tokyo bureau chief. Chapter 8 includes an article written by him.

Paul Wallace is *The Economist*'s European economics editor. He contributed to Chapter 10.

Pam Woodall is senior economics writer at *The Economist*. Articles she wrote are part of Chapters 1, 2, 5 and 8.

Introduction

Discussions about economic affairs have acquired a rare immediacy in the aftermath of the worst global recession since the Great Depression. After several years of robust global growth, what began as a meltdown in America's housing market developed first into a deep financial crisis and eventually into a fully fledged global recession. Output shrank, trade collapsed, industrial production fell off a cliff, and many millions of people around the world found themselves out of work. For a while, the world economy seemed in danger of ending up in a slump like that of the 1930s. That it did not was largely the result of government intervention on a massive scale. All this has ensured that the minutiae of fiscal and monetary policy no longer seem impossibly arcane or far removed from daily life, and debates about economic policy have challenged many deeply held beliefs.

Every week, *The Economist* wades into these waters with its mix of reportage, analysis and opinion. Making use of the best evidence available and thinking matters through from first principles, its writers take a stand on the issues of the moment. While the impetus for the articles the newspaper publishes is usually found in the news of the week, many of the things that provoke *The Economist*'s writers to enter the fray are also questions – or aspects of questions – of enduring importance. This means that much of what is published in the newspaper remains interesting well beyond the precise context in which it was originally written.

Such are the articles collected in this book, which seeks to provide curious readers with a sort of guided tour of the many areas to which economists apply the tools of their trade. Some of these are recognisably the provinces of economics: fiscal and monetary policy, ways to promote economic growth, or how to measure a country's standard of living. Many of the articles concern the roots and effects of the global economic crisis of 2008–09, the defining economic event of the first decade of the 21st century. Others explore the challenges that economic policymakers face in the years ahead as they struggle to kick start growth in places where it is still sluggish or deal with imbalances in the global economy. Yet others discuss issues that may strike the reader, at least at first, as "not quite economics".

Why do people give money to charity? What are the causes and consequences of the all-too-familiar human tendency to put things off for "later"? Is politically slanted reporting a sign of a dysfunctional news media? What determines how much prostitutes are paid? All these turn out to be areas where the tools of economic analysis have something useful to say. The answers that economists have provided to the wide range of questions they have turned their attention to may not always convince, but they rarely fail to provoke discussion and debate. Ultimately, economics' greatest utility lies not so much in its answers to particular questions, but rather in its providing a coherent framework that can be used to think about a vast variety of issues. This book opens a window into this enormous versatility.

PART 1

What economics is about

Angus Maddison, the economist profiled in the first article in this section, devoted his life to the task of economic measurement. He called himself a "chiffrephile", or a lover of figures. An unfamiliar word, perhaps; but many economists, who are rarely content with words where figures are an option, will nevertheless see a reflection of their own interests in Mr Maddison's labours. This quest to quantify is the subject of the first chapter of this section, which discusses the debates that surround the definition and measurement of ideas like well-being and poverty. These concepts are the nuts and bolts of the discipline, and the articles here are a window into the way in which economists think about them.

As the articles in Chapter 1 argue, economists use GDP as a useful (if imperfect) measure of a country's standard of living. Not surprisingly, therefore, they spend a lot of time thinking about what determines how fast GDP grows and why some economies grow much faster than others. ("Once you start thinking about growth", Robert Lucas, a Nobel-prize-winning economist, once said, "it's hard to think of anything else.") The articles in Chapter 2 discuss some of the fruits of their thinking about factors that affect economic growth. Some of these will seem familiar: how much economies save and invest, the quality of their workforce, how good they are at developing new technologies, and how open they are to trade, for example. But other less obvious factors, such as the quality of a country's institutions and how much its people trust each other, may also play an important role in determining economic performance in the long run, even if pinning down the way in which they do so is not always straightforward.

Institutions, trust and even savings rates change only in the long term. On a more immediate basis, economic policymakers spend a great deal of time dealing with the ups and downs of the economic cycle. Chapter 3 explains how this is done, delving into the role of monetary and fiscal policy. It discusses, among other things, how policymakers use instruments like the interest rate and money supply to fine tune the working of the economy, as well as how their established ways of going about their business have been challenged by the global recession. Articles describe what countries' tax systems look like at the moment as well as what economists think they ought to look like. You will notice that the former sometimes diverges enormously from the latter. Economic policy is sometimes best thought of as economic analysis mediated by a large dose of politics.

But economics is not all about the size of economies or policies designed to make them grow faster or with fewer ups and downs; it is a way of thinking about the world. The range of problems to which economic analysis can be applied is immense. Is skewed news reporting a sign of a dysfunctional media? Why don't farmers in rural Africa use enough fertiliser on their crops? These are all questions that economists have analysed using the tools of their trade. The insights that their analyses have yielded – sometimes provocative, invariably interesting – are the subject of Chapter 4.

1 Debates about the basics

Maddison counting

A long, passionate affair with numbers has finally come to an end

ANGUS MADDISON, who died on April 24th 2010 at the age of 83, described himself as a chiffrephile – a lover of figures. Like many men, he had his first serious crush at the age of 13. He read "How to Pay for the War", by John Maynard Keynes; it was the annex on national income that most tickled his fancy. For the next 70 years he pursued ever more elusive numbers, estimating GDP for a growing range of countries over a lengthening span of time. In 1995 he published GDP estimates for 56 countries as far back as 1820. In 2001 his romantic adventures culminated in an estimate for world output in the year 1AD: $105.4 billion at 1990 prices.

GDP is a modern term, but the urge to count the nation's produce and compare countries' standards of living predates Adam Smith. Maddison saw himself as heir to a tradition that began with William Petty, the pioneer of "political arithmetick", who in 1665 estimated the income of England and Wales at £40m. That calculation was of pressing concern to Petty, who wanted to show the king how to pay for the war against the Dutch. But why did Maddison care about the GDP of the distant past?

He believed that the "pace and pattern" of economic activity had deep historical roots. Economies, he thought, do not "take off", as if from nowhere. Even the industrial revolution was too gradual to warrant the term revolution and too broad to be considered merely industrial. Take, for example, the progress of maritime technology. By 1773, John Harrison was claiming a £20,000 prize from the British Parliament for inventing a seaworthy chronometer. Captain James Cook had reached Australia's east coast, and thanks to sauerkraut and citrus juice, he had lost none of his crew to scurvy.

Even scholars who believed there was a lot of economic progress to measure before the 19th century doubted there was enough data to measure it. Maddison made the most of whatever was available. He drew on one scholar's work on probate inventories in 17th and 18th century England, which showed that each generation passed on more property, furniture and houselinen to its descendants than the last. His economic portrait of Mughal India was influenced by a 16th-century survey by Abu Fazl, vizier to Emperor Akbar. His estimates of Japan's population relied on the annual register of religious affiliation, brought in after the Portuguese were expelled and Christianity outlawed in 1587. One of his students, Bart van Ark, now chief economist of the Conference Board, says Maddison urged him to venture beyond libraries and statistical offices. Even a painting in a museum might provide some clue to a country's standard of living centuries before.

"There is room for two or three economic theorists in each generation, not more," wrote Colin Clark, one of Maddison's heroes. Every other economist, he added, should be content to build knowledge by steadily laying "stone on stone". Maddison laid the foundations for many big thoughts. Ten days before his death he was cited in a speech by Robert Zoellick, president of the World Bank, declaring the end of the "third world". Maddison's figures show that Asia accounted for more than half of world output for 18 of the last 20 centuries. Its growing clout in the world economy is, therefore, a "restoration" not a revolution.

Even as they foreshadow the rise of Asia, his numbers also help explain the historical rise of Europe. His estimates of per head GDP provide a useful empirical crosscheck for a grand thesis proposed by Daron Acemoglu, Simon Johnson and James Robinson in 2005. They argued that European countries prospered after 1500 in so far as they imposed checks on monarchical power and enjoyed access to the Atlantic Ocean, with its lucrative trade in commodities and slaves. Maddison's estimates also appear in their work explaining why poor colonies became rich, and rich colonies became poor. They conclude that sparsely populated colonies benefited over the long run from the property rights that European settlers brought with them. Richer, well-populated colonies suffered from efforts to suck them dry.

Messrs Acemoglu, Johnson and Robinson caution that Maddison's figures for the years before 1820 are "no more than educated guesses". Maddison freely conceded that the further back he went, the more he had to rely on "clues and conjecture". In an intemperate article in 2009, Gregory Clark of the University of California, Davis, described these numbers as "fictions, as real as the relics peddled around Europe in the Middle Ages". Credulous economists demanded numbers, "however dubious their provenance", and Maddison supplied them.

Go figure

Quantification can create the illusion of precision. For example, Maddison assumes that African GDP before 1820 remained more or less at subsistence levels. If that is all that can be said, does it add anything to put a number on it ($400–425 per head)? But he was not selling comforts to the credulous. He believed that numbers sharpened debate. Quantification, he wrote, "is more readily contestable and likely to be contested." In disputing his figures, scholars would be inspired to provide their own. Even those who disagreed with his work would be influenced by it.

Given the length and depth of his career, it is tempting to say that this intellectual influence is impossible to measure. But that would be contrary to his faith in quantification. His curriculum vitae counts 20 books and 130 articles, plus another 19 volumes that he edited or co-authored. His work has been translated into 12 languages and two books have racked up more than 2,000 citations, according to Google Scholar. He supervised 13 doctoral students, as well as co-founding the Groningen Growth and Development Centre at the University of Groningen, which he joined in 1978, and the Club des Chiffrephiles in 1990. But as even Maddison admitted, "no sensible person would claim that [quantification] can tell the whole story." He was deeply fond of numbers. And a large number were deeply fond of him.

Measuring what matters

Man does not live by GDP alone. A new report urges statisticians to capture what people do live by

HOW WELL OFF are Americans? Frenchmen? Indians? Ghanaians? An economist's simplest answer is the gross domestic product, or GDP, per person of each country. To help you compare the figures, he will convert them into dollars, either at market exchange rates or (better) at purchasing-power-parity rates, which allow for the cheapness of, say, haircuts and taxi rides in poorer parts of the world.

To be sure, this will give you a fair guide to material standards of living: the Americans and the French, on average, are much richer than Indians and Ghanaians. But you may suspect, and the economist should know, that this is not the whole truth. America's GDP per head is higher than France's, but the French spend less time at work, so are they really worse off? An Indian may be desperately poor and yet say he is happy; an American may be well fed yet fed up. GDP was designed to measure only the value of goods and services produced in a country, and it does not even do that precisely. How well off people feel also depends on things GDP does not capture, such as their health or whether they have a job. Environmentalists have long complained that GDP treats the despoliation of the planet as a plus (via the resulting economic output) rather than a minus (forests destroyed).

In recent years economists have therefore been looking at other measures of well-being – even "happiness", a notion that it once seemed absurd to quantify. Among those convinced that official statisticians should join in is Nicolas Sarkozy, the French president. On September 14th 2009 a commission he appointed in 2008, comprising 25 prominent social scientists, five with Nobel prizes in economics, presented its findings.[1] Joseph Stiglitz, the group's chairman and one of the laureates, said the 292-page report was a call to abandon "GDP fetishism". France's national statistics agency, Mr Sarkozy declared, should broaden its purview.

The commission divided its work into three parts. The first deals with familiar criticisms of GDP as a measure of well-being. It takes no account of the depreciation of capital goods, and so overstates the value of production. Moreover, the value of production is based on market prices, but not everything has a price. The list of such things includes more than the environment. The worth of services not supplied through markets, such as state health care or education, owner-occupied housing or unpaid child care by parents, is "imputed" – estimated, using often rickety assumptions – or left out, even though private health care and schooling, renting and child-minding are directly measured.

The report also argues that official statisticians should concentrate on households' incomes, consumption and wealth rather than total production. All these adjustments make a difference. In 2005, the commission found, France's real GDP per person was 73% of America's. But once government services, household production and leisure are added in, the gap narrows: French households had 87% of the adjusted income of their American counterparts. No wonder Mr Sarkozy is so keen.

Sizing up the good life

Next the commission turns to measures of the "quality of life". These attempt to capture well-being beyond a mere command of economic resources. One approach quantifies people's subjective well-being – divided into an overall judgment about their lives (a "ladder of life" score) and moment-by-moment flows of positive and negative feelings. For many years researchers had been spurred on by an apparent paradox: that rising incomes did not make people happier in the long run. Recent studies suggest, though, that countries with higher GDP per person do tend to have higher ladder-of-life scores. Exactly what, beyond income, affects subjective well-being – from health, marital status and age to perceptions of corruption – is much pored over. The unemployed report lower scores, even allowing for their lower incomes. Joblessness hits more than your wallet.

Third, the report examines the well-being of future generations. People alive today will pass on a stock of exhaustible and other natural resources as well as machines, buildings and social institutions. Their children's human capital (skills and so forth) will depend on investment in education and research today. Economic activity is sustainable if future generations can expect to be at least as well off as today's. Finding a single measure that captures all this, the report concludes, seems too ambitious. That sounds right. For one thing, statisticians would have to make assumptions about the relative value of, say, the environment and new buildings – not just today, but many years from now. It is probably wiser to look at a wide range of figures.

Some members of the commission believe that the financial crisis and the recession have made a broadening of official statistics more urgent. They think there might have been less euphoria had financial markets and policymakers been less fixated on GDP. That seems far-fetched. Stockmarket indices, soaring house prices and low inflation surely did more to feed bankers' and borrowers' exaggerated sense of well-being.

Broadening official statistics is a good idea in its own right. Some countries have already started – notably, tiny Bhutan. There are pitfalls, though. The report justifies wider measures of well-being partly by noting that the public must have trust in official statistics. Quite so; which makes it all the more important that the statisticians are independent of government. The thought of grinning politicians telling people how happy they are is truly Orwellian. Another risk is that a proliferation of measures could be a gift to interest groups, letting them pick numbers that amplify their misery in order to demand a bigger share of the national pie. But these are early days. Meanwhile, get measuring.

Note

1 "Report by the Commission on the Measurement of Economic Performance and Social Progress", available at www.stiglitz-sen-fitoussi.

Light relief

Data about light emitted into space may help improve growth estimates

HOW RAPIDLY DID Equatorial Guinea's GDP grow between 1975 and 1999? According to the latest version of the Penn World Table (PWT), the most comprehensive source of figures about countries' GDP since 1950, the answer is 4% a year. But the data in the 2002 version suggest an annual rate of -2.7%. As Arvind Subramanian, an economist who worked on the sums, points out, Equatorial Guinea may therefore have had the second-fastest economy in Africa. Unless, that is, it was the slowest.

This may be an extreme case but the PWT reckons that data for all 43 sub-Saharan African countries have margins of error of 30-40%. Much of this is due to the underfunding and overstretching of their statistical agencies. Some researchers have tried to use things like changes in electricity consumption as proxies for GDP growth. But these numbers also come from official agencies.

In a working paper, Vernon Henderson, Adam Storeygard and David Weil of Brown University suggest an alternative source of data: outer space. In particular they track changes in the intensity of artificial light over a country at night, which should increase with incomes. American military weather satellites collect these data every night for the entire world.

It is hard to know exactly how much weight to put on extraterrestrial brightness. Changes in the efficiency of electricity transmission, for example, may cause countries to look brighter from outer space, even if economic activity has not increased much. But errors in its measurement are unlikely to be correlated with errors in the calculation of official GDP, since they arise for different reasons. A weighted average of the growth implied by changes in the intensity of artificial light and official GDP growth rates ought to improve the accuracy of estimates of economic growth. Poor countries in particular may have dodgy GDP numbers but their night-light data are as reliable as anyone else's.

Take Myanmar's economy, which grew at an official but improbable 8.3% a year between 1993 and 2003; adjusting for brightness suggests a more modest 5.8%. But night-light data suggest that official figures may be understating growth in places like Tajikistan or the Congo, perhaps because of rising informal economic activity.

Grossly distorted picture

If you look at GDP per head, the world is a different – and, by and large, a better – place

WHICH ECONOMY ENJOYED the best economic performance between 2003 and 2007: America's or Japan's? Most people will pick America. The popular perception is that America's vibrant economy was sprinting ahead (albeit fuelled by credit and housing bubbles that have now painfully burst), whereas Japan crawled along at a snail's pace. And it is true that America's average annual real GDP growth of 2.9% was much faster than Japan's 2.1%. However, the single best gauge of economic performance is not growth in GDP, but GDP per person, which is a rough guide to average living standards. It tells a completely different story.

GDP growth figures flatter America's relative performance, because its population is rising much faster, by 1% a year, thanks to immigration and a higher birth rate. In contrast, the number of Japanese citizens has been shrinking since 2005. Once you take account of this, Japan's GDP per head increased at an annual rate of 2.1% between 2003 and 2007, slightly faster than America's 1.9% and much better than Germany's 1.4%. In other words, contrary to the popular pessimism about Japan's economy, it has actually enjoyed the biggest gain in average income among the big three rich economies. Among all the G7 economies it ranks second only to Britain (see Figure 1.1, left-hand side).

Using growth in GDP per head rather than crude GDP growth reveals a strikingly different picture of other countries' economic health. For example, Australian politicians often boast that their economy has had one of the fastest growth rates among the major developed nations – an average of 3.3% over the five years to 2007. But Australia has also had one of the biggest increases in population; its GDP per head grew no faster than Japan's over this period. Likewise, Spain has been one of the euro area's star performers in terms of GDP growth, but over the three years to 2007 output per person

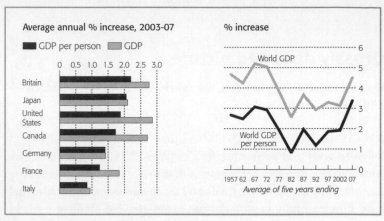

Sources: IMF; Angus Maddison; Economist Intelligence Unit; National statistics

FIG 1.1 Looking through a di erent lens

grew more slowly than in Germany, which like Japan, has a shrinking population.

Some emerging economies also look less impressive when growth is compared on a per-person basis. One of the supposedly booming BRIC countries, Brazil, has seen its GDP per head increase by only 2.3% per year since 2003, barely any faster than Japan's. Russia, by contrast, enjoyed annual average growth in GDP per head of 7.4% because the population is falling faster than in any other large country (by 0.5% a year). Indians love to boast that their economy's growth rate has almost caught up with China's, but its population is also expanding much faster. Over the five years to 2007, the 10.2% average increase in China's income per head dwarfed India's 6.8% gain.

Focusing on GDP per person also affects comparisons of economic health over time. During the five years to 2007, world GDP grew by an average of 4.5% a year, its fastest for more than three decades, though not as fast as during the golden age of the 1960s when annual growth exceeded 5%. But the world's population is now growing at half of its pace in the 1960s, and so world income per head has increased by more over the five years to 2007 than during any other period on record (see Figure 1.1, right-hand side). Mankind has never had it so good.

Redefining recession

Once you accept that growth in GDP per head is the best way to measure economic performance, the standard definition of a recession – a decline in real GDP over some period (eg, two consecutive quarters or year on year) – also seems flawed. For example, zero GDP growth in Japan, where the population is declining, would still leave the average citizen better off. But in America, the average person would be worse off. A better definition of recession, surely, is a fall in average income per person. On this basis, America has been in recession since the fourth quarter of 2007 when its GDP rose by an annualised 0.6%, implying that real income per head fell by 0.4%.

Many Americans will shrug this off, especially those politicians who believe that the prime goal of policy is to retain their economic and military dominance over the world. They see the size of a country's GDP as the best measure of its economic clout, in which case the absolute rate of GDP growth matters more than growth in income per head.

There are several other reasons Americans can quibble over the use of GDP per head, especially with reference to Japan. Firstly, its shrinking population is also an ageing one in which the labour force will decline as a share of the population. Unless this is offset by more rapid productivity growth, this could make it harder to maintain the same growth in output per person in future and so harder to pay pension bills. Secondly, slower GDP growth makes it more difficult to reduce the ratio of existing public-sector debt to GDP, which by 2010 was nearing 200% in Japan. Last, but not least, investors care about GDP growth. Corporate profits depend upon the absolute rate of growth of an economy. And companies wanting to invest abroad will favour markets that are expanding more rapidly.

If GDP per head is nevertheless a superior measure of people's prosperity, why do governments not publish such figures each quarter along with their standard GDP figures? Population statistics tend to be less up-to-date than GDP figures and are generally not available on a quarterly basis. But that is a lame excuse: it should be much easier to count bodies than to put a value on diverse sorts of economic output. Not only do people have a right to know whether average living standards are rising or falling, but publishing such numbers could also benefit some countries. If Japan's government had drawn attention to the sprightlier growth in income per head in recent years, in contrast to endless reports about its "underperforming" economy, consumers may have felt cheerier and spent more – in other words, its GDP growth would have been stronger.

On the poverty line

Has "a dollar a day" had its day?

IN DECEMBER 2007 the World Bank unveiled the results of the biggest exercise in window shopping in history. Scouts in 146 countries scoured stalls, supermarkets and mail-order catalogues, recording the price of more than 1,000 items, from 500-gram packets of durum spaghetti to low-heeled ladies' shoes.

This vast enterprise enabled the bank to compare the purchasing power of many countries in 2005. It uncovered some statistical surprises. Prices in China, for example, were much higher than earlier estimates had indicated, which meant the Chinese income in 2005 of 18.4 trillion yuan ($2.2 trillion at then-market exchange rates) could buy less than previously thought. At a stroke, the Chinese economy shrank, in real terms, by 40%.

Since then, many scholars have wondered what this economic demotion means for the bank's global poverty counts. It famously draws the poverty line at "a dollar a day", or more precisely $1.08 at 1993 purchasing-power parity (PPP). In other words, a person is poor if they consume less than an American spending $1.08 per day in 1993. By this yardstick 969m people suffered from absolute poverty in 2004, a drop of over 270m since 1990. The world owed this progress largely to China, where poverty fell by almost 250m from 1990 to 2004.

But if the Chinese economy was 40% smaller than previously thought, surely its poverty count must be correspondingly higher. Surjit Bhalla, of Oxus Investments, speculated that China's toll would increase by more than 300m. He mischievously accused the bank's number-crunchers of conspiring to lift the poverty count so as to keep their employer in business beyond its natural life.

Give a quarter, take a quarter

The dollar-a-day definition of global destitution made its debut in the bank's 1990 *World Development Report*. It was largely the discovery of Martin Ravallion, a researcher at the bank, and two co-authors, who noticed that the national poverty lines of half-a-dozen developing countries clustered around that amount. In two working papers[2] published in May 2008, Mr Ravallion and two colleagues, Shaohua Chen and Prem Sangraula, revisit the dollar-a-day line in light of the bank's new estimates of purchasing power. They also provide a new count of China's poor.

Thanks to American inflation, $1.08 in 1993 was worth about $1.45 in 2005 money. In principle, the researchers could count the number of people living on less than this amount, converted into local money using the bank's new PPP rates. But $1.45 a day strikes the authors as a bit high. Rather than update their poverty line, they propose to abandon it. It is time, they say, to return to first principles, repeating the exercise Mr Ravallion performed almost two decades ago, using the better, more abundant data available now.

They gather 75 national poverty lines, ranging from Senegal's severe $0.63 a day to Uruguay's more generous measure of just over $9. From this collection, they pick the 15 lowest (Nepal, Tajikistan and 13 sub-Saharan countries) and split the difference between them. The result is a new international poverty line of $1.25 a day.

Why those 15? The answer is philosophical, as well as practical. In setting their poverty lines, most developing countries aim to count people who are poor in an absolute sense. The line is supposed to mark the minimum a person needs to feed, clothe and shelter himself. In Zambia, say, a poor person is defined as someone who cannot afford to buy at least two to three plates of *nshima* (a kind of porridge), a sweet potato, a few spoonfuls of oil, a handful of groundnuts and a couple of teaspoons of sugar each day, plus a banana and a chicken twice a week.

But even in quite poor countries, a different concept of poverty also seems to creep in, the authors argue. It begins to matter whether a person is poor relative to his countrymen; whether he can appear in public without shame, as Adam Smith put it.

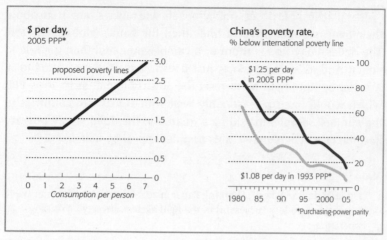

Source: Shaohua Chen and Martin Ravallion

FIG 1.2 Lines, damned lines and statistics

This notion of relative deprivation seems to carry weight in countries once they grow past a consumption of $1.95 per person a day. Beyond this threshold, a country that is $1 richer will tend to have a poverty line that is $0.33 higher (see Figure 1.2). The authors thus base their absolute poverty line on the 15 countries in their sample below this threshold.

How many people in the world are poor by this new definition? The authors are not yet ready to say. But they have taken another look at China. By their new standard, they find that 204m Chinese people were poor in 2005, about 130m more than previously thought.

That is the bad news. The brighter news is that China's progress against poverty is no less impressive than previously advertised. By Mr Ravallion's and Ms Chen's new standard, the number of poor in China fell by almost 407m from 1990 to 2004, compared with the previous estimate of almost 250m.

China's economic co-ordinates may be different than thought, but its trajectory is much the same. And therein lies a lesson. Give or take a dime or two, it matters little where a poverty line is drawn. Like a line in the sand, an absolute poverty standard shows whether the economic tide is moving in or out. It does not matter too much where on the beach it is drawn.

For practical purposes, policymakers will always care more about their own national poverty lines than the bank's global standard. The dollar-a-day line is more of a campaigning tool than a guide to policy. And as a slogan, $1.25 just doesn't have the same ring to it. A better option might be to reset the poverty line at $1 in 2005 PPP, which would line up reasonably well with at least ten countries in the authors' sample. In adding a quarter to the dollar-a-day poverty line, the researchers may cut its popular appeal by half.

Note

1   "Dollar a day revisited", Working Paper 4620. "China is poorer than we thought, but no less successful in the fight against poverty", Working Paper 4621.

Redefining recession

A new yardstick for measuring slumps is long overdue

THERE HAS BEEN a nasty outbreak of R-worditis. Newspapers are full of stories about which of the big economies will be first to dip into recession as a result of the credit crunch. The answer depends largely on what you mean by "recession". Most economists assume that it implies a fall in real GDP. But this has created a lot of confusion: the standard definition of recession needs rethinking.

In the second quarter of 2008, America's GDP rose at a surprisingly robust annualised rate of 3.3%, while output in the euro area and Japan fell, and Britain's was flat. Many economists reckon that both Japan and the euro area could see a second quarter of decline in the three months to September. This, according to a widely used rule of thumb, would put them in recession, a fate which America has so far avoided. But on measures other than GDP, America has been the economic laggard over the past year.

Figure 1.3 looks at several different ways to judge the severity of the economic slowdown since the start of the credit crunch in August 2007. On GDP growth, America has outperformed Europe and Japan. Unemployment, however, tells a very different tale. America's jobless rate hit 6.1% in August, up from 4.7% a year earlier, and within spitting distance of its peak of 6.3% during the previous recession after the dotcom bust. Other countries have so far published figures only for July, but their jobless rates have barely moved over the past year: Japan's has risen by only 0.2%, the euro area's has fallen slightly (though in absolute terms it is still a bit higher than America's). Another yardstick, GDP per head, takes account of the fact that America's population is rising rapidly, whereas Japan's has started to shrink. Since the third quarter of 2007 America's average income per person has barely increased; Japan's has enjoyed the biggest gain.

To the average person, a large rise in unemployment means a recession. By contrast, the economists' rule that a recession is defined by two consecutive quarters of falling GDP is silly. If an economy grows by 2% in one quarter and then contracts by 0.5% in each of the next two quarters, it is deemed to be in recession. But if GDP contracts by 2% in one quarter, rises by 0.5% in the next, then falls by 2% in the third, it escapes, even though the economy is obviously weaker. In fact, America's GDP did not decline for two consecutive quarters during the 2001 recession.

However, it is not just the "two-quarter" rule that is flawed; GDP figures themselves can be misleading. The first problem is that they are subject to large revisions. An analysis by Kevin Daly, an economist at Goldman Sachs, finds that since 1999, America's quarterly GDP growth has on average been revised down by an annualised 0.4 percentage points between the first and final estimates. In contrast, figures in the euro area and Britain have been revised up by an average of 0.5 percentage points. Indeed, there is good reason to believe that America's recent growth will be revised down. An alternative measure, gross domestic income (GDI), should, in theory, be identical to GDP. Yet real GDI has risen by a mere 0.1% since the third quarter of 2007, well below the 1% gain in GDP. A study by economists at the Federal Reserve found that GDI is often more reliable than GDP in spotting the start of a recession.

Tapping the slumpometer

These are good reasons not to place too much weight on GDP in trying to spot recessions or when comparing slowdowns across economies. The Business Cycle Dating Committee of the National Bureau of Economic Research (NBER), America's official arbiter of recessions, instead makes its judgments based on monthly data for industrial production, employment, real income, and wholesale and retail trade. It has not yet decided whether a recession has begun. But even the NBER's more sophisticated approach is too simplistic in that it defines a recession as an absolute decline in economic activity. This can cause problems when trying to compare the depth of downturns in different cycles or across different countries. Suppose country A has a long-term potential (trend) growth rate of 3% and country B one of only 1.5%, due to slower labour-force growth. Annual GDP growth of 2% will cause unemployment to rise in country A (making it feel

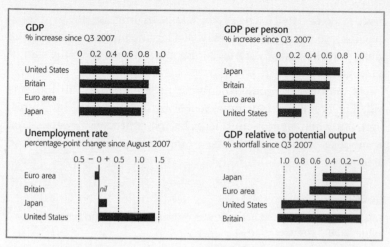

Sources: Thomson Datastream; IMF; *The Economist*

FIG 1.3 Don't say "R"

like a recession), but to fall in country B. Likewise, if faster productivity growth pushes up a country's trend rate of growth, as it has in America since the mid-1990s, an economic downturn is less likely to cause an absolute drop in output.

This suggests that it makes more sense to define a recession as a period when growth falls significantly below its potential rate. The IMF estimates that America and Britain have faster trend growth rates than Japan or the euro area. The bottom-right chart in Figure 1.3 shows that since the third quarter of 2007, growth has been below trend in all four economies, but Britain, closely followed by America, has seen the biggest drop relative to potential.

But even if this is a better definition of recession, potential growth rates are devilishly hard to measure and revisions to GDP statistics are still a problem. One solution is to pay much more attention to unemployment numbers, which, though not perfect, are generally not subject to revision and are more timely. A rise in unemployment is a good signal that growth has fallen below potential. Better still, it matches the definition of recession that ordinary people use. During the past half-century, whenever America's unemployment rate has risen by half a percentage point or more the NBER has later (often much later) declared it a recession. European firms are slower at shedding jobs, so unemployment may be a lagging indicator. Even so, the jobless rate has usually started to rise a few months after the start of a recession.

As the old joke goes: when your neighbour loses his job, it is called an economic slowdown. When you lose your job, it is a recession. But when an economist loses his job, it becomes a depression. Economists who ignore the rise in unemployment deserve to lose their jobs.

Note

This piece was published before it was certain that the world economy as a whole would contract in 2009.

Paul Samuelson

The last of the great general economists died on December 13th 2009, aged 94

"I WAS REBORN, born as an economist, at 8.00am on January 2nd 1932, in the University of Chicago classroom," wrote Paul Samuelson in a memoir published at the beginning of December 2009. He became probably the most influential economist of the second half of the 20th century. For his work in several branches of the dismal science he became the first American economics Nobel laureate. Through his bestselling textbook, he introduced millions of people to the subject. And right to the end he kept on mentoring the profession's brightest stars.

His actual birth took place almost 17 years earlier in the steel town of Gary, Indiana, to a family of upwardly mobile Polish immigrants. His earliest memories – of the recession of 1919–21 and strikebreaking immigrant workers from Mexico, and of the boom and bust that followed – shaped Mr Samuelson's macroeconomic views throughout his life. He approved of massive government spending to help an economy escape from recession when monetary policy can do no more. When the Obama administration introduced just that sort of stimulus in 2009, partly on the advice of Mr Samuelson's nephew, Larry Summers, who is Mr Obama's chief economic adviser, he was quick to approve.

Though regarded as America's leading standard-bearer for Keynesian economics, he called himself a "cafeteria Keynesian", just picking the bits he liked. His combination of Keynesian and classical economic ideas became known as the "neoclassical synthesis". From his chair at the Massachusetts Institute of Technology and in his column in *Newsweek*, the self-described "dull centrist" became a fierce critic of the libertarian Chicago School, and especially of Milton Friedman (writer of a rival *Newsweek* column). Markets are not perfect, he believed, and dire warnings from Friedman, and earlier from Friedrich von Hayek, about the regulation of markets "tells us something about them rather than something about Genghis Khan or Franklin Roosevelt. It is paranoid to warn against inevitable slippery slopes ... once individual commercial freedoms are in any way infringed upon."

As for Mr Samuelson's friend of 50 years, Alan Greenspan, once chairman of the Federal Reserve, "the trouble is that he had been an Ayn Rander" – a devotee of laissez-faire capitalism. "You can take the boy out of the cult but you can't take the cult out of the boy," Mr Samuelson told the *Atlantic* in summer 2009. "He actually had [an] instruction, probably pinned on the wall: 'Nothing from this office should go forth which discredits the capitalist system. Greed is good'."

The huge sales of Mr Samuelson's textbook, "Economics", first published in 1948 and updated every three years, owed much to his lively writing. (The abstract of his memoir ended with the words: "Boo hoo.") The book transformed how economics was – and is – taught around the world. If the earlier editions too readily believed that an economy could achieve equilibrium, that may have stemmed from the author's conviction that mathematics could be a useful tool for economists, and that economics had much to learn from physics and the laws of thermodynamics. Today it is fashionable to argue that economics was led astray by "physics envy", which blinded it to the subtleties of human behaviour, yet after winning his Nobel prize in 1970 Mr Samuelson anticipated economists' current interest in biological systems by writing several papers on Mendelian dynamics.

The inefficient market

He was the last of the great general economists, making important contributions on trade, macroeconomics, public finance and consumer behaviour. Yet he decided, at around 50, that to remain academically competitive he had to specialise. Perhaps because it was close to his beloved mathematics, the specialist field he chose was financial economics.

His work helped lay the foundations for two of the field's biggest ideas: the efficient-market hypothesis and options pricing. In 1965 he published a paper explaining that in well-informed and competitive speculative markets, price movements over time will be essentially random – a concept at the heart of the efficient-market hypothesis later described in its full majesty by Eugene Fama, whom Mr Samuelson believed ought to win a Nobel prize. In the 1950s it was Mr Samuelson who had rediscovered the pioneering early work of Louis Bachelier, a French mathematician whose insights would later underpin the Black-Scholes option-pricing model; and it was Mr Samuelson who suggested the assumption, that share prices move according to geometric Brownian motion, which makes this model workable. Mr Samuelson remained close to Robert Merton, who won a Nobel prize for his work with Fischer Black and Myron Scholes on options pricing.

Yet Mr Samuelson also understood that beyond the ivory tower the conditions necessary for efficient markets rarely existed; they needed regulating. "To understand economics you need to know not only fundamentals but also its nuances," Mr Samuelson would explain. "When someone preaches 'Economics in one lesson' I advise: Go back for the second lesson." The latest crisis (for which he felt some responsibility, since he had helped develop financial derivatives that company executives did not understand) proved that "free markets do not stabilise themselves. Zero regulating is vastly suboptimal to rational regulating. Libertarianism is its own worst enemy!"

Mr Samuelson was happy to be "linked with such Methuselah masters as Verdi" who did some of their best work in old age. He was able to do so, not least, because of his interest in evidence-based medicine. For decades he read the *New England Journal of Medicine*, and – noting a weakness in his male ancestors – he was an early adopter of cholesterol-reducing statin pills, as well as skimmed milk. His passion for "looking for theoretical understandings of empirical reality" may help explain his long life, as well as his lengthy list of achievements.

The material on pages 3–25 was first published in *The Economist* in April 2010 (pages 3–5), September 2009 (pages 6–8), August 2009 (pages 9–10), March 2008 (pages 11–14), May 2008 (pages 15–18), September 2008 (pages 19–22) and December 2009 (pages 23–5).

2 How economies grow

Reserve army of underemployed

Is China's pool of surplus labour drying up?

WHAT IS THE SINGLE most important price in the world? Popular answers are the price of oil, American interest rates or the dollar. Yet Chinese wages are, arguably, more important. China has by far the world's biggest labour force, of around 800m – almost twice that of America, the European Union and Japan combined. Thus recent claims that it is running short of cheap labour would, if true, have huge consequences not just for China, but also for the rest of the world.

A seemingly unlimited supply of cheap workers has been one of the main forces behind China's rapid economic growth. But over the past couple of years, factory owners have complained of labour shortages and wages have risen more rapidly, leading some to conclude that China's "surplus" labour has been used up. The country's one-child policy, introduced in 1979, has caused the growth in its labour supply to slow sharply (see Figure 2.1). After rising by 1.3% a year during the decade to 2005, the population of working age is expected to increase at an annual rate of 0.7% until 2015, and then shrink by 0.1% a year until 2025. At the same time, the shift of workers from agriculture to industry, which has been an important source of productivity gains, will also slow. Jonathan Anderson, an economist at UBS, reckons that these two trends will reduce China's sustainable growth rate from 9–9.5% today to 7–7.5% by 2025.

But as well as boosting growth, the flow of workers from farms to factories has held down manufacturing wages – not only in China, but also throughout the world. The theory behind this was first expounded by Sir Arthur Lewis, an economist from St Lucia, who

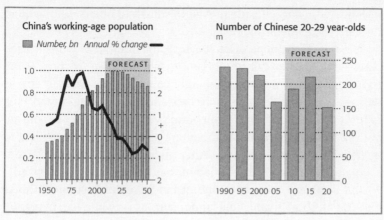

Sources: UN Population Division; Standard Chartered

FIG 2.1 The great fall

won the Nobel prize for economics in 1979. He argued that a developing country with "surplus" (ie, underemployed) rural labour could expand industrial employment for many years without causing wage inflation, because employers enjoy such a large supply of labour. During the first 50 years of Britain's industrial revolution, real wages remained more or less flat while profits soared. Likewise in China, as millions of migrants have quit the countryside for urban factories and construction sites, the real wages of low-skilled workers barely rose during the 1980s and 1990s, despite big productivity gains; only recently have they increased rapidly.

This acceleration of wages has prompted some to conclude that China's surplus labour in the countryside has been used up. In 2007 Cai Fang, the director of the Institute of Population and Labour Economics at the Chinese Academy of Social Sciences, argued that China has reached the "Lewis turning point". By 2009, he predicted, there would be a widespread shortage of workers, pushing up industrial wages.[1] Does this mean the death of China's growth model?

As so often in China, this debate is clouded by the poor data. Until recently, most estimates of surplus labour varied between 150m and 200m people. But the true figure is probably much smaller, because government figures for the rural labour force include millions of migrants who have already moved to cities and others who work in rural industry, not farming.

In addition the population is ageing: the number of workers aged between 20 and 29 fell from 233m in 1990 to 165m in 2005. Many textile and electronics firms hire only young women in their 20s, as they are thought to be less troublesome and more willing to work long hours. Construction firms favour young single men. Older people are not only less employable, but they are also typically less willing to migrate if they have children. After taking account of this, Mr Cai estimates that China's surplus labour has been virtually exhausted.

But Stephen Green, an economist at Standard Chartered, thinks that talk of China's vanishing labour surplus is premature. In a 2008 report he argued that the surplus would not run out for another decade. Although the number aged between 20 and 29 fell over the past decade, their ranks are now rising again. Using the 2005 census, Mr Green estimates that the 20-something group will increase by a third in the ten years to 2015, as baby-boomers' children join the workforce (see Figure 2.1, right-hand side); only then will it start shrinking sharply.

What is more, the recent spurt in urban wages is not necessarily proof that the surplus has gone. Mr Green argues that to attract migrant workers, urban employers have to pay more than rural income, which has increased in recent years, thanks to government policies and higher food prices. The temporary increase in the age group between 20 and 29 over the next few years will also ease the upward pressure on urban pay.

Go East, young women

The World Bank agrees that China's labour surplus has not yet run out. Even when the number of young people drops, the labour supply is determined by more than demographics. Migrant workers are usually excluded from urban social-security schemes and have to pay more for education and health care. The bank suggests that phasing out the household-registration system would encourage more people to move to the city. Vocational training for rural residents aged over 30 would equip them better for jobs in industry. And financial incentives to encourage workers to retire later could also boost the labour supply: only 60% of men and 30% of women aged over 50 have jobs.

Moreover, Mr Cai's estimate of China's labour surplus assumes that 180m workers, or 24% of total employment, are needed for farming. But that is based on today's agriculture. Mechanisation and the consolidation of land plots will boost productivity, meaning that fewer farmers will be needed. That will in turn release more workers for industry. In developed countries only 3% of workers till the land.

China's surplus labour will eventually dry up, but it still seems some years away. In any case, that moment should be cause for cheer not fear in China and elsewhere, because it will lead to bigger gains in income and consumption. That, after all, is the whole point of development.

Note

1   Although this did not happen, in 2009 and 2010 there was a great deal of labour unrest in China, with workers agitating for (and in some cases succeeding in obtaining) higher wages.

Health and wealth

Improved health does not always make countries richer

JEFFREY SACHS, a development economist, writes in his book "The End of Poverty" of a telling phrase by Gro Harlem Brundtland, then the director-general of the World Health Organisation (WHO). "If you want to get someone's attention about the health crises in Africa, 'show them the money'," she once remarked to him. This is something that governments and international agencies have long known: emphasising that an idea is good for economic growth makes it easier to sell. The WHO has used the same argument to press for more investment in health.

The link between health and income seems pretty uncontroversial. After all, healthy people can work longer and harder than sick people. Healthier children are likely to stay in school longer and learn more, earning more when they enter the workforce. Even across countries the relationship seems clear: those with better health are generally richer, and those that improve their citizens' health grow faster. So the conclusions of two papers that improving life expectancy at birth (a common indicator of better health) can depress income per head for as long as two generations may come as a shock.

Correlation or causation?

Daron Acemoglu and Simon Johnson, both of the Massachusetts Institute of Technology (Mr Johnson is a former chief economist of the IMF), are sceptical[1] about the notion that healthier countries are richer, because it is not clear where the causality lies: countries with higher incomes may simply spend more on health. To investigate, they needed to study health improvements that were not driven by economic growth in the countries concerned. The expansion of the international public-health system after 1940, the researchers found, fitted the bill.

Beginning in the 1940s, several medical innovations involving penicillin, streptomycin and DDT made it easier to treat diseases – such as tuberculosis, malaria and yellow fever – that disproportionately affected people in developing countries. Because these ideas originated in the rich world and were spread by organisations such as the WHO, any improvements in health they led to would have been unconnected with prior improvements in the economic circumstances of poor countries.

This international revolution in public health did lead to substantial increases in life expectancy in poor countries by the 1950s. However, the researchers found that income per head actually declined when life expectancy went up and did not recover for up to an astonishing 60 years.

The reason was that increased life expectancy led to a higher population using a limited stock of things like land and capital, thus depressing income per person. Over time, reduced fertility, more investment and the entrepreneurial benefits of having more people could reverse some of this, but the data suggested that reductions in fertility in particular took a long time.

Researchers at Brown University reached a similar conclusion.[2] They used estimates of how various health improvements affected different economic variables, such as schooling, and how schooling in turn affected adult wages, in a model of the economy to work out the broader impact of an increase in life expectancy. Their results looked forward and confirmed what Messrs Acemoglu and Johnson had found by looking back: increased population would more than wipe out any productivity benefits of better health. For the first 30 years after an increase in life expectancy from 40 to 60, income per person would be lower than it would have been if life expectancy had not improved.

Hoyt Bleakley of the University of Chicago thinks these results may be too pessimistic.[3] He argues that the Malthusian spectre of diminishing returns as more people crowd on to the same plot of farm land is less relevant in a fast-urbanising developing world, as well as in one more open to trade and capital flows.

Mr Bleakley also argues that focusing on life expectancy may miss the point. Some health improvements may not lead to a longer life, but may nonetheless make people more productive. Hookworm infection, whose eradication from the American South Mr Bleakley has studied, is a case in point. Getting rid of hookworm disease made children quicker learners in school, and increased their incomes when they started working. However, it did not increase life expectancy since the infection was not fatal and so did not lead to a rise in population, which could have prevented individual benefits from carrying over to the economy as a whole. Policies that improve health without affecting the length of life may well be the ones that have a bigger economic pay-off, and a focus on life expectancy may miss this.

Some of Mr Bleakley's other work points in this direction. Studying the impact of the eradication of malaria in Colombia, he noted that parts of the country were affected by a species of the malarial parasite called *Plasmodium vivax*, which led to very poor health but was rarely fatal. The more lethal version, *P. falciparum*, affected other areas. He found that eliminating *P. vivax* led to significant gains in human capital and income; eliminating *P. falciparum* did not.

So even if the researchers at Brown and MIT are correct that increasing life expectancy does not quickly increase income per head, particular health improvements may well do so. Meanwhile, the lesson is that careful analysis should precede any sweeping statements about the economic benefits of specific policies. It may be best to make a case for improving health because it is a good thing in itself, rather than on the basis of presumed economic benefits that may not appear for generations.

Notes

1   "Disease and Development: The Effect of Life Expectancy on Economic Growth".
2   Qamurul Ashraf, Ashley Lester and David Weil, "When Does Improving Health Raise GDP?"
3   "Comments on Acemoglu and Johnson (2006)"; and "Comments on Ashraf, Lester and Weil (2008)".

The in-betweeners

A lot is expected of the middle class in emerging economies. But they just want a quiet life

TWO JARS OF CHICKPEAS, 20 bars of soap, three packs of cigarettes and six sachets of shampoo – all these items and more are in stock at a village store five hours away from the Indian city of Hyderabad. It is the leanest of inventories, and yet it supports great hopes. Combined with a scrap-metal business, the store is just enough to lift its owners into the ranks of India's fabled middle class. They and their comrades in Latin America, Africa and emerging Asia belong to a vague demographic that no one can define precisely, but which everyone agrees is vital to stability and prosperity in the developing world.

"The virtues of a middle class are those which conduce to getting rich – integrity, economy, and enterprise," observed John Stuart Mill after the industrial revolution. Do the new middle classes share those virtues? In a 2007 paper[1] Abhijit Banerjee and Esther Duflo, two economists at the Massachusetts Institute of Technology, tried to find out. As well as visiting village stores outside Hyderabad, they drew on household surveys in 13 developing countries, from Mexico and Panama to Tanzania, South Africa and East Timor. The result is a sequel to their 2006 portrait of the lives of those living on about $1 a day.

The two authors define the middle class abstemiously, as those who spend $2–10 a day, measured in 1993 purchasing-power-parity dollars. In other words they have about the same command over goods and services as Americans spending $1,050–5,200 a year in today's money. If this seems too austere a standard, note that 88% of the rural Indians in their surveys lived on less than this, and that the middle-class Britons who won Mill's praise earned little more.

Do the emerging middle classes exhibit the temperance and economy that Mill celebrated? Like good burghers everywhere, they invest in their health and their homes, the surveys show. Most also spring for a television, and the share of their spending devoted to entertainment rises steadily with income. To be middle class is to have licence to indulge more freely in creature comforts. To the very poor, on the other hand, even drinking tea is a wasteful extravagance.

And what of enterprise? Does the spirit of capitalism burn in the new middle classes? They are often portrayed as "entrepreneurs in waiting", the authors note, ready to transform their lives and their economies if only they can get secure title and ready capital to underwrite their businesses. "It is impressive how pervasive is the view that the poor are sitting at the cusp of a huge opportunity to get much richer – by now it's almost an axiom," says Mr Banerjee.

A nation of shopkeepers

In fact, the urban middle classes are no more likely to own a business than the poor. (In the countryside, the pattern is mixed.) And even when they own one, their hearts are not really in it. Their ventures are tiny, often one-person operations doing mostly what their neighbours do. In Hyderabad and its environs, 21% of the middle class run general stores, 17% tailor-shops, 8.5% telephone booths and 8% sell fruit and vegetables. Others sift through rubbish for items of value, sell milk or collect dung. The businesses turn a modest profit, but only if the value of the owner's own time is not counted.

The businesses are short of capital. The threadbare inventory the authors discovered in the village store outside Hyderabad is only one example. Few businesses own machinery, or even a bicycle. The two economists cite an experiment, sponsored by the World Bank, which randomly bestowed about $100–200 of extra capital on tiny businesses in Sri Lanka. The annualised return on the money was an impressive 94% on average.

If their businesses are so starved of capital, why do the middle classes not invest more in them? Borrowing, as the proponents of microcredit point out, is expensive. But there is nothing to stop households accumulating capital by saving. After all, they defer gratification enough to "invest" in their homes and TV sets, so why not in their enterprises?

The authors speculate that the new middle class is not an aspiring bourgeoisie of petty businessmen. They are, instead, aspiring salarymen. To be middle class is to draw a pay packet weekly or monthly, rather than daily or hourly. An hour from Udaipur, another Indian city, the authors spotted well-tended homes with motorcycles in the courtyard and children in starched school uniforms. Sure enough, a zinc factory was operating nearby.

For those who cannot get such regular jobs, a petty business is the next best thing. The hours are long, but not very intense. The store-owner outside Hyderabad chatted happily with the pair of inquisitive economists for two hours. Only two customers showed up in that time. One bought a cigarette, the other a stick of incense.

This segment of the middle class may lack the gumption to expand their businesses, or perhaps they know something about their prospects that their cheerleaders do not. Their businesses might benefit from a little more capital: some extra jars of chickpeas or sticks of incense. But once such businesses get beyond a certain size, the authors argue, the returns to scale diminish quickly. A village can support several identical stores, but not if they get too big.

Adam Smith, who described Britain as a nation of shopkeepers, had a keen sense of what could be expected of the middle class. The prudent man, he wrote, "does not go in quest of new enterprises and adventures, which might endanger, but could not well increase, the secure tranquillity which he actually enjoys." Cup of tea, anyone?

Note

1   Available at econ-www.mit.edu/files/2081

Anatomy of thrift

What causes people to save and invest?

ACCORDING TO THE ECONOMICS TEXTBOOKS, saving and invest-ment are always equal. People cannot save without investing their money somewhere, and they cannot invest without using some-body's savings. Saving and investment are two sides of the same coin.

And indeed that is true for the world as a whole, but it is not true for individual countries. Capital can flow across borders, so the amount an individual country saves does not have to be the same as the amount it invests. The difference between the two is the amount borrowed from or lent to foreigners; this is called the current-account deficit or surplus. If a country's current-account surplus rises, it means that either its saving has increased or its investment has fallen, or both. Either way, that country has generated an excess of saving which it has exported.

Moreover, whereas it is true that at a global level saving must equal investment, the fact that saving and investment end up in balance does not mean that millions of households and individuals spontaneously desire to save and invest in equal measure. To use the language of economics, saving and investment are an "ex-post" iden-tity, but the world's "ex-ante" appetite to save and invest may well be out of balance. Actual saving and investment must be equal. Desired saving and investment may not be.

Most of the time, mismatches between the desired levels of saving and investment are brought into line fairly easily through the inter-est-rate mechanism. If people's desire to save exceeds their desire to invest, interest rates will fall so that the incentive to save goes down and the willingness to invest goes up. Across borders, exchange rates have a similar effect. If a country has a saving deficit, its currency will fall to the point where its assets are cheap enough to lure foreign savings in.

But there is some uncertainty about how smoothly these adjust-ments are made. Classical economic theory suggests that interest rates automatically bring saving and investment into a productive balance. The central principle of Keynesianism, however, is that this alignment between saving and investment is not always automatic, and that a misalignment can have serious consequences.

If an economy is not running at full capacity, John Maynard Keynes wrote in his "General Theory" in 1936, more saving might, paradoxically, result in less output rather than more. Companies' decisions to produce depend on the demand they expect for their products. More saving means less spending and hence less demand. Hence the idea that you can have too much thrift, and that there is a place for "Keynesian" government spending policies to boost demand.

It's all true

The modern consensus is that both classical and Keynesian theory can be right, but over different time frames. In the long term, saving and investment will be brought into line by the cost of capital. But in the short term, firms' appetite to invest is volatile, and policymakers may need to step in to shore up demand. Thus, although saving and investment are equal ex-post, economic theory leaves plenty of room for an ex-ante saving glut. This glut could be caused by long-term changes in people's desire to save or firms' desire to invest, or it might be caused by short-term cyclical deviations from normal saving and investment patterns. In either case, the size and duration of mismatches can be influenced by government policy.

What might change people's desire to save or invest? That is a question about human behaviour which economists cannot answer with total confidence. Still, they have made some progress in explaining what motivates investment, and a little more in explaining what drives saving.

The most influential theory of household saving is the "life-cycle hypothesis", pioneered by Franco Modigliani, an Italian economist. It suggests that people try to smooth consumption over their lifetime: they save little or nothing when young but more in their middle years if they have a good income. They then draw down those savings in retirement. It follows that demographic shifts and economic growth are the most important drivers of thrift.

Another theory suggests that people save for "precautionary reasons", in case they need the money for a rainy day. This implies that people will save more if their income is variable. It also suggests that they will be more inclined to save if they have no access to credit.

A third possibility is that people save because they want to leave assets to their children, either because they love them or as a way to bribe the children to look after their parents in old age. (Economists are always reluctant to believe in altruism.) Whatever the motive, the bequest theory of thrift suggests that savings might not actually be drawn down in retirement.

A final possibility is that people save in response to their government's actions. This theory, known as "Ricardian equivalence", suggests that people save more if government saves less because they expect higher taxes later on.

How well do these theories fit with what has actually happened in the past? Saving rates differ dramatically between countries and over time, giving economists plenty of statistical ammunition with which to test their theses. Inevitably, there are differences among academics about which hypotheses are best supported by the data. But, in general, the following factors seem to play a role:

■ **Demographics**. Although it is hard to confirm Modigliani's hypothesis by studying individual households, it seems to hold for entire countries. Saving rates do rise when the ratio of children in the population falls (as in China), and decline when the proportion of pensioners rises (as in Japan). Given that the world's population as a whole is ageing but, in most countries, most people are still working, global saving should currently be rising.

■ **Economic growth**. Especially in poorer countries, saving rates rise as economies grow. That is probably because people do not adjust their consumption patterns as quickly as their income rises. Rapid growth was an important reason behind the big rise in saving rates in East Asia in the 1970 and 1980s. It may account for much of the rise in saving by emerging economies today.

■ **Terms-of-trade shock**. If a country's exports suddenly go up in price, its saving rate tends to go up too, at least temporarily. Oil exporters, for example, put on a saving spurt if oil prices rise. This effect also helps to explain the recent increase in saving in many emerging economies.

- **Financial development.** As an economy's financial system becomes more developed, saving rates tend to fall because people find it easier to borrow. This seems to be true for both rich and poor countries. It suggests that saving rates may be lower in countries with more sophisticated financial systems, such as America.
- **Capital gains.** In rich countries there is increasing evidence that capital gains influence saving rates. If the stockmarket or house prices rise, people feel richer and save less. A study by the OECD published in 2004 suggests that housing wealth has a bigger effect on saving than financial wealth, and that this effect is stronger in economies with flexible mortgage markets and high rates of home ownership.
- **Fiscal policy.** In some countries, people do appear to behave as Ricardian equivalence theory suggests: they save more when budget deficits expand, perhaps because they expect higher taxes in the future, although private-sector saving rises by less than the rise in budget deficits. The big exception is America, where the impact of fiscal deficits on private saving appears to be weakest.

Some of these factors work in opposite directions, and gauging which matters most is difficult. But there are indications that in rich countries the biggest disincentives to saving have been capital gains and the ability to borrow. National saving rates in rich countries have been falling gradually for more than two decades, and particularly steeply since the mid-1990s (see Figure 2.2). In a study for the 2005 *World Economic Outlook*, Marco Terrones and Roberto Cardarelli, two economists at the IMF, looked at saving patterns in 46 countries between 1972 and 2004 and found that easier credit (thanks, probably, to higher house prices), along with bigger budget deficits, were the most important reasons for the overall drop in saving in rich countries since 1997.

In emerging markets, on the other hand, the most powerful factors pushed in the opposite direction. Fast economic growth and increases

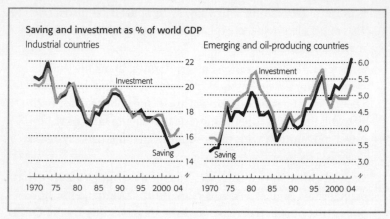

Source: IMF

FIG 22 Spot the di erence

in government saving, thanks partly to terms-of-trade shocks, have increased total national saving.

These opposing movements show up clearly in global statistics. Over the past 35 years, the emerging economies' share of global saving has doubled, from 15% to 30%. In 2004, emerging economies saved the equivalent of 6% of global GDP. If there is a glut of saving, it is likely to be found in emerging economies and oil-exporting countries.

The investment puzzle

If it is hard to find out why people save, it is even harder to discover why they invest. In theory, firms should invest if the expected return on their investment exceeds the cost of the capital they are using. In the short term, firms need to worry about the state of overall demand. But in the long term, returns on capital depend on how much capital an economy already has, how productively it is used, and how fast the workforce is growing. If there is little capital available or the workforce is growing rapidly, firms would usually expect a high return on investment.

The evidence supports these theories, up to a point. Statistical analyses suggest that investment rises when economies grow, when productivity increases or when the share of workers in the population goes up, and that it slows when capital becomes more expensive. The IMF's analysis, for instance, suggests that a 1% increase in the cost of capital in rich countries will lead to a drop in investment rates of 0.4% of GDP.

However, in recent years these statistical relationships have failed to hold. Both in rich countries and in emerging economies (except China), investment levels have been lower than economists had expected at the levels of interest and growth rates prevailing at the time. This shortfall could simply be the unwinding of earlier excesses as firms repair their balance-sheets, but several "structural" explanations have gained support:

- **Demographics.** A young and growing workforce boosts the level of investment, just like a mature workforce boosts the saving rate. So the world economy is likely to move through a cycle in which investment peaks first and saving peaks a bit later. With rising life expectancy and falling birth rates, the world economy may be moving into the high-saving phase. But although demographics are important, they change slowly. It is hard to ascribe the recent sharp drop in investment demand in regions such as Japan or East Asia to demographic change alone.

- **Declining capital intensity.** Firms in rich countries may not need to invest as much as they used to because the share of capital-intensive industries in their economies is shrinking. Economists at UBS, a bank, have pointed out that in America the share of corporate profits that is generated by investment-heavy industries (oil, gas and chemicals, for instance) had fallen from 55% of the total in 1948 to 21% in 2004. This long-term trend may have accelerated in recent years. But it does not explain investment busts in poor countries.

- **Deflation of capital-goods prices.** In recent years prices of capital goods have fallen sharply relative to prices of other goods and services, thanks largely to cheaper computers, so companies are able to achieve the desired level of real investment for a smaller outlay. Calculations in the IMF's *World Economic Outlook* show that in real terms, the fall in average investment rates in industrial countries has been much more modest than it appears at first sight. This may help to explain some of the recent weakness in investment, particularly in rich countries. But it is unlikely to last. Relative price shifts tend to run their course and then stop. More important, computers depreciate more quickly than other capital goods, so eventually firms will need to invest more to maintain the same level of net investment.

■ **The rise of China.** This may have prompted a geographic shift in global investment patterns. As firms move their production to China to take advantage of its huge pool of untapped labour, investment elsewhere slackens. But investment flows to China from America, Europe and Japan are not yet big enough to explain the sluggish investment in those countries. Besides, the rise-of-China thesis is about the location of investment more than about changes in its global level.

In sum, none of these explanations for a structural, global decline in investment is altogether convincing. To understand the pattern of global saving and investment properly, you have to look in detail at what is going on within the world's main saving and borrowing countries. The best place to start is the biggest net saver of all, Japan.

Building BRICs of growth

Record spending on infrastructure will help to sustain rapid growth in emerging economies

THE BIGGEST INVESTMENT BOOM in history is under way. Over half of the world's infrastructure investment is now taking place in emerging economies, where sales of excavators have risen more than fivefold since 2000. In total, emerging economies are likely to spend an estimated $1.2 trillion on roads, railways, electricity, telecommunications and other projects this year, equivalent to 6% of their combined GDPs – twice the average infrastructure-investment ratio in developed economies. Largely as a result, total fixed investment in emerging economies was predicted to increase by a staggering 16% in real terms in 2008, according to HSBC, whereas in rich economies it was forecast to be flat. Such investment would help support economic growth as America's economy stalls – and for many years to come.

Compounding the 2008 figure, Morgan Stanley predicted that emerging economies would spend $22 trillion (in today's prices) on infrastructure over the next ten years, of which China would account for 43% (see Figure 2.3, left-hand side). China is already spending around 12% of its GDP on infrastructure. Indeed, China spent more (in real terms) between 2004 and 2008 than in the whole of the 20th century. In 2007 Brazil launched a four-year plan to spend $300 billion to modernise its road network, power plants and ports. The Indian government's latest five-year plan has ambitiously pencilled in nearly $500 billion in infrastructure projects. Russia, the Gulf states and other oil exporters are all pouring part of their higher oil revenues into fixed investment.

Good infrastructure has always played a leading role in economic development, from the roads and aqueducts of ancient Rome to Britain's railway boom in the mid-19th century. But never before has infrastructure spending been so large as a share of world GDP. This is partly because more countries are now industrialising than ever before, but also because China and others are investing at a much brisker pace than rich economies ever did. Even at the peak of Britain's railway mania in the 1840s, total infrastructure investment was only around 5% of GDP.

Infrastructure investment can yield big economic gains. Building roads or railways immediately boosts output and jobs, but it also helps to spur future growth – provided the money is spent wisely. Better transport helps farmers to get their produce to cities, and manufacturers to export their goods overseas. Countries with the lowest transport costs tend to be more open to foreign trade and so enjoy faster growth. Clean water and sanitation also raise the quality of human capital, thereby lifting labour productivity. The World Bank estimates that a 1% increase in a country's infrastructure stock is associated with a 1% increase in the level of GDP. Other studies have concluded that East Asia's much higher investment in infrastructure explains a large part of its faster growth than Latin America.

A report by Goldman Sachs argues that infrastructure spending is not just a cause of economic growth, but a consequence of it. As people get richer and more of them live in towns, the demand for electricity, transport, sanitation and housing increases. This mutually reinforcing relationship leads to higher investment and growth. The bank has developed a model that uses expected growth in income, urbanisation and population to forecast future infrastructure demands.

Urbanisation has the biggest impact on electricity requirements. Goldman calculates that a 1% increase in the share of people living in cities leads to a 1.8% increase in demand for installed capacity. A 1% rise in income per head leads to a 0.5% increase in demand. Putting this together, electricity capacity may have to surge by 140% in China and by 80% in India over the next decade (Figure 2.3, right-hand side). Air travel – and hence airports – will see the fastest growth in demand, because it is by far the most sensitive to income: a 1% increase in income per person leads to a 1.4% increase in the number of passengers travelling by air. The number of air passengers could jump by more than 350% in China and by 200% in India over the next decade.

China's faster growth in income per head and its more rapid pace

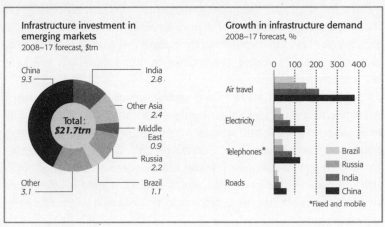

Sources: Morgan Stanley; Goldman Sachs; *The Economist*

FIG 23 A bridge to the future

of urbanisation mean that it is likely to pull even further ahead of India on most infrastructure measures. China could add 13 times as many fixed-line phones as India over the decade, seven times as many air passengers and six times as much electricity capacity. Brazil and Russia, which are already much more urbanised and relatively richer (implying slower growth in income), will also see more modest growth in infrastructure.

A boom in fumes

How will emerging economies finance all this spending? The fiscal finances of most emerging economies are in good shape. As a group, they are close to having a balanced budget, although a few, notably India, have large deficits. Even so, the vast scale of investment will require more private-sector money. To attract that, emerging economies will need to offer investors a decent return and that will require reform of their regulatory systems and a move towards market pricing. In India only about half of all electricity generated is paid for, because power is stolen and bills are left unpaid. In turn, the financing needs of massive infrastructure investment could encourage the development of domestic bond markets, bringing additional long-term benefits.

The infrastructure boom has global implications. Increased investment means more imports of capital equipment, which will help to slim current-account surpluses in China and elsewhere, and so reduce global imbalances. Rising demand for building materials will keep commodity prices high.

Last, but not least, will be the negative impact on the environment. An expected 75% increase in emerging economies' electricity demand over the next decade will worsen air pollution and global warming. Many fear that China's Three Gorges Dam, the world's largest hydro-electric project, could cause massive environmental damage. China's national bird, the red-crowned crane, is an endangered species. Some people may wish that the construction crane was also breeding less rapidly.

Secret sauce

China's rapid growth is due not just to heavy investment, but also to the world's fastest productivity gains

PRODUCTIVITY GROWTH is perhaps the single most important gauge of an economy's health. Nothing matters more for long-term living standards than improvements in the efficiency with which an economy combines capital and labour. Unfortunately, productivity growth is itself often inefficiently measured. Most analysts focus on labour productivity, which is usually calculated by dividing total output by the number of workers, or the number of hours worked. According to figures published on November 5th 2009, America's output per hour worked had increased by 4.3% over the previous year, thanks to big job cuts. Even more impressive was China, where labour productivity had risen by 7-8%.

The snag is that labour productivity is an incomplete gauge of efficiency. Firms can boost output per man-hour by investing more and equipping workers with better machinery. But once the extra capital spending is taken into account there may be little or no gain in overall economic efficiency. Part of the jump in America's labour productivity during the "new economy" era of the late 1990s reflected a rise in investment as a share of GDP. The huge increase in China's labour productivity in recent years is partly due to heavy investment rather than true efficiency gains.

A better gauge of an economy's use of resources is "total factor productivity" (TFP), which tries to assess the efficiency with which both capital and labour are used. Once a country's labour force stops growing and an increasing capital stock causes the return on new investment to decline, TFP becomes the main source of future economic growth. Unfortunately TFP is much harder to measure than labour productivity. It is calculated as the percentage increase in output that is not accounted for by changes in the volume of inputs of capital and labour. So if the capital stock and the workforce both rise by 2% and output rises by 3%, TFP goes up by 1%. Measuring hours worked is

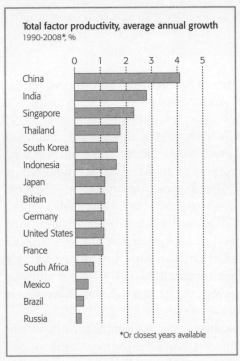

Total factor productivity, average annual growth 1990-2008*, %

China
India
Singapore
Thailand
South Korea
Indonesia
Japan
Britain
Germany
United States
France
South Africa
Mexico
Brazil
Russia

*Or closest years available

Sources: UBS; OECD

FIG 2.4 More e cient chopsticks

fairly easy, but different ways of valuing a country's capital stock can produce different results.

The OECD publishes figures for its rich-country members. These show that since 1990, average TFP growth has been remarkably similar in America, Japan, Germany, Britain and France, at around 1% a year. A report by Andrew Cates, an economist at UBS, attempts to estimate TFP growth in emerging economies over the two decades 1990–2008 (see Figure 2.4). He calculates that China has had by far the fastest annual rate of TFP growth, at around 4%. Probably no other country in history has enjoyed such rapid efficiency gains. India and other Asian emerging economies have also enjoyed faster productivity growth than other developing or developed regions. In contrast, productivity in Brazil and Russia has risen more slowly than in rich economies.

These figures undermine a common claim – that China's rapid growth has been based solely on overinvestment. Sceptics like to compare China with the Soviet Union, where heavy investment also produced rapid rates of growth for many years before it collapsed. But the big difference is that TFP in the Soviet Union actually fell by an annual average of 1% over 30 years to 1988. In contrast China's productivity has been lifted by a massive expansion of private enterprise, and a shift of labour out of agricultural work and into more productive jobs in industry. China's average return on physical capital is now well above the global average, according to Goldman Sachs. A decade ago it was less than half the world average.

Why have the Asian economies led the pack? The most important determinants of longer-term productivity growth are the rate of adoption of existing and new technologies, the pace of domestic scientific innovation and changes in the organisation of production. These, in turn, depend on factors such as the openness of an economy to foreign direct investment and trade, education and the flexibility of labour markets.

Using a composite index of technology penetration and innovation (including, for instance, computers and mobile phones per head), Mr Cates finds a strong link between the rate of increase in an economy's technological progress and its productivity growth. China's level of technology is still well behind that in America, but it has seen by far the fastest rate of improvement over the past decade. This is not just because China started from such a low base but also because it is more open to foreign investment than many other emerging economies, including Japan and South Korea when they were at similar stages of development. China's TFP growth is almost twice as fast as that of Japan and South Korea during their periods of peak economic growth.

An emerging advantage

UBS's analysis suggests that the financial health of firms and governments also matters for productivity growth. Although TFP measures the extra gain in economic efficiency after taking account of the direct impact of a larger capital stock, weak balance-sheets constrain the availability of capital for new technology and innovation. The financial crisis may therefore reduce TFP growth in many rich countries. Some analysts also worry that future productivity growth in emerging economies will be curbed by slower growth in world trade and capital flows. But Mr Cates argues that healthier domestic balance-sheets in most emerging economies, along with continued rapid adoption of old and new technologies, should support robust productivity gains. He thinks that China, India, Indonesia and Brazil look particularly well placed. China's surge in infrastructure spending will also help.

That said, even if China's productivity growth remains faster than that of the developed world, it is likely to slow unless the government pushes ahead with bolder reforms. China's growth is still too capital-intensive. Opening up the service sector to private firms and making it easier for workers to shift from rural to urban areas would result in a better allocation of labour and capital. That would help sustain rapid growth but would also make it more job-intensive. The resulting fall in labour-productivity growth might cause alarm among some analysts, but TFP would remain strong.

Of internet cafés and power cuts

Emerging economies are better at adopting new technologies than at putting them into widespread use

DURING 2008 CHINA overtook America as the country with the world's largest number of internet users. Even when you factor in China's size and its astonishing rate of GDP growth, this was a remarkable achievement for what remains a poor economy. Since 2005 China has also been the world's largest exporter of information and communications technology (ICT). By mid-2007 it already had the same number of mobile-phone users (500m) as the whole of Europe.

China is by no means the only emerging economy in which new technology is being eagerly embraced. In frenetic Mumbai, everyone seems to be jabbering non-stop on their mobile phones: according to India's telecoms regulator, half of all urban dwellers have mobile- or fixed-telephone subscriptions and the number is growing by 8m a month. The India of internet cafés and internet tycoons produces more engineering graduates than America, makes software for racing cars and jet engines and is one of the top four pharmaceutical producers in the world. In a different manifestation of technological progress, the country's largest private enterprise, Tata, in January 2008 unveiled the "one lakh car"; priced at the equivalent of $2,500, it is the world's cheapest. Meanwhile, in Africa, people who live in mud huts use mobile phones to pay bills or to check fish prices and find the best market for their catch.

Yet this picture of emerging-market technarcadia is belied by parallel accounts of misery and incompetence. In 2007 ants ate the hard drive of a photographer in Thailand. In 2008 internet usage from Cairo to Kolkata was disrupted after something – probably an earthquake – sliced through two undersea cables. Personal computers have spread slowly in most emerging economies: three-quarters of low-income countries have fewer than 15 PCs per 1,000 people – and many of those computers are gathering dust.

And the feting of prominent technology projects in emerging economies is sometimes premature. Nicholas Negroponte, of the Massachusetts Institute of Technology, has long been championing a $100 laptop computer, presented with great fanfare at the World Economic Forum in Davos in 2006. The laptop was supposed to sweep through poor countries, scattering knowledge and connectivity all around. But two years later the project was behind schedule, the computer did not work properly and one prominent backer, Intel, a chipmaker, had pulled out.

So how well are emerging economies using new technology, really? Hitherto, judgments have had to be based largely on anecdotes. Now the World Bank has supplemented the snapshot evidence with more comprehensive measures.

Take-off to tomorrow, and to yesterday

The bank has drawn up indices based on the usual array of numbers: computers and mobile phones per head, patents and scientific papers published; imports of high-tech and capital goods. In addition, it uses things such as the number of hours of electricity per day and airline take-offs to capture the absorption of 19th- and 20th-century technologies. It tops this off with measures of educational standards and financial structure, which show whether technology companies can get qualified workers and enough capital. The results, laid out in January 2008 in the bank's annual *Global Economic Prospects* report, measure technological progress in its broadest sense: as the spread of ideas, techniques and new forms of business organisation.

Technology so defined is fundamental to economic advance. Without it, growth would be limited to the contributions of increases in the size of the labour force and the capital stock. With it, labour and capital can be used and combined far more effectively. So it is good news that the bank finds that the use of modern technology in emerging economies is coming on in leaps and bounds.

Between the early 1990s and the early 2000s, the index that summarises the indicators rose by 160% in poor countries (with incomes per person of less than about $900 a year at 2008 exchange rates) and by 100% in middle-income ones ($900–11,000). The index went up by only 77% in industrialised countries (with average incomes above $11,000), where technology was more advanced to start with. Poor and middle-income nations, the bank concludes, are catching up with the West.

The main channels through which technology is diffused in emerging economies are foreign trade (buying equipment and new ideas directly); foreign investment (having foreign firms bring them to you); and emigrants in the West, who keep families and firms in their countries of origin abreast of new ideas. All are going great guns.

To me, to you, to me, to you

Start with trade. Between 1999 and 2008 the ratio of poor countries' imports of high-tech products to their GDPs rose by more than 50%. The ratio in middle-income countries increased by over 70%. Capital goods (mainly industrial machinery) often embody new technology, and imports of these increased faster in middle-income countries than in rich ones.

The gain in high-tech exports was more striking still: emerging economies' share of global trade in such goods rose by 140% between the mid-1990s and the mid-2000s. Some of the world's fastest-growing multinationals have sprung from such countries. These include Brazil's Petrobras, owner of some of the world's best deep-sea oil-drilling technology, and Mittal, a company of Indian origin that is now the world's largest steelmaker.

Relative to GDP, inflows of foreign direct investment to developing economies have increased sevenfold since the 1980s. In some countries, such as Hungary and Brazil, foreign firms account for half or more of all R&D spending by companies. This has had dramatic demonstration effects. Local French-language call centres in Morocco and Tunisia got going only after French operators began outsourcing to the Maghreb. A quarter of Czech managers said they learned about new technologies by watching foreign companies in the Czech Republic.

Emigrants are arguably the most important source of new ideas and capital. Granted, emigration can be costly: computer engineers, scientists and doctors, trained at public expense at home, go to work abroad. But money and skills flow back. Nearly half the $40

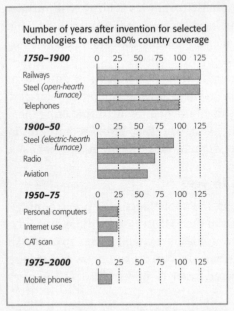

Number of years after invention for selected
technologies to reach 80% country coverage

1750–1900   0   25   50   75   100   125

Railways
Steel *(open-hearth furnace)*
Telephones

1900–50   0   25   50   75   100   125

Steel *(electric-hearth furnace)*
Radio
Aviation

1950–75   0   25   50   75   100   125

Personal computers
Internet use
CAT scan

1975–2000   0   25   50   75   100   125

Mobile phones

Source: World Bank

FIG 2.5 High-tech leapfrog

billion-worth of foreign direct investment in China in 2000 came from Chinese abroad. Remittances have doubled in the past ten years and now account for roughly 2% of developing countries' GDPs – more than foreign aid. An émigré banker returned to set up Bangladesh's Grameenphone banking network in 2007; by early 2008 it had 15m customers. Bata, a Czech shoemaker, has been saved twice by foreign connections. Facing bankruptcy in the early 1900s, Tomas Bata went to America to learn about mass production. He came back and established branches from India to Poland. After the second world war his son fled to Canada to escape the communists. He returned in 1989 and used late-20th-century know-how to expand in eastern Europe and open factories in China and India.

The upshot is that technology is spreading to emerging markets faster than it has ever done anywhere. The World Bank looked at how much time elapsed between the invention of something and its widespread adoption (defined as when 80% of countries that use a technology first report it; see Figure 2.5). For 19th-century technologies the gap was long: 120 years for trains and open-hearth steel furnaces, 100 years for the telephone. For aviation and radio, invented in the early 20th century, the lag was 60 years. But for the PC and CAT scans the gap was around 20 years and for mobile phones just 16. In most countries, most technologies are available in some degree.

But the degree varies widely. In almost all industrialised countries,

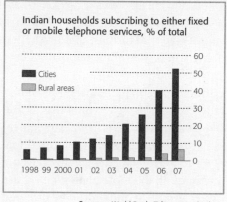

Indian households subscribing to either fixed or mobile telephone services, % of total

- Cities
- Rural areas

1998 99 2000 01 02 03 04 05 06 07

Sources: World Bank; Telecommunications and Regulatory Authority of India

FIG 2.6 Well-connected?

once a technology is adopted it goes on to achieve mass-market scale, reaching 25% of the market for that particular device. Usually it hits 50%. In the World Bank's (admittedly incomplete) database, there are 28 examples of a new technology reaching 5% of the market in a rich country; of those, 23 went on to achieve over 50%. In other words, if something gets a foothold in a rich country, it usually spreads widely.

In emerging markets this is not necessarily so. The bank has 67 examples of a technology reaching 5% of the market in developing countries – but only six went on to capture half the national market. Where it did catch on, it usually spread as quickly as in the West. But the more striking finding is that the spread was so rare. Developing countries have been good at getting access to technology – and much less good at putting it to widespread use.

As a result, technology use in developing countries is highly concentrated. Almost three-quarters of China's high-tech trade comes from just four regions on the coast. More than two-thirds of the stock of foreign investment in Russia in 2000 was in Moscow and its surroundings. Whereas half of India's city-dwellers have telephones, little more than one-twentieth of people in the countryside do.

Not only is there a technology gap between emerging economies and the West, and another within emerging economies: there are also surprising differences between apparently comparable emerging economies. For example, China imports and exports far more high-tech goods than India does and its exports are as technologically advanced as a country three times as rich. India and Bangladesh are neighbours with comparable levels of GDP per head. But electricity losses in India are about 30% of output; in Bangladesh, they are below 10%. And although Africa as a whole has low levels of mobile-phone use, in six countries (Botswana, Gabon, Mauritius, the Seychelles, Sierra Leone and South Africa) more than 30% of the population uses them.

The question is how much this unevenness matters. It is tempting to say, not much. What really counts, say techno-optimists, is that technology should get a toehold. Once it does, its grip will strengthen. So although only 6% of India's rural poor have phones, urban folk were at the same stage in 1998 – and look what happened (see Figure 2.6). Optimism about diffusion seems all the more plausible because of leapfrogging. Technologies such as mobile phones can be dropped into developing countries without the slog of building expensive infrastructure (such as land lines) and can circumvent the failings of old 19th- and 20th-technology. Poor countries will leapfrog into the next generation.

Fast or forget it

But this view – essentially, that technological diffusion is a problem that will take care of itself – may be too sanguine. The evidence from successful emerging markets is that if they absorb a new technology they usually do so fairly quickly. The corollary is that if a technology is not diffused promptly, it may at best be diffused only slowly and incompletely.

Judging by the World Bank's index, that is what seems to be happening in some places. As a general rule, technological achievement rises fastest in poor and middle-income countries and then levels off as these countries approach Western living standards (see Figure 2.7). But now compare Latin America and Europe. Eastern Europe is following the path taken by America and western Europe a few years before. But in Latin America the slope flattens at lower levels than elsewhere.

The region has less installed bandwidth and fewer broadband subscribers than poorer East Asia, and not many more internet users or PCs. High-tech exports account for less than 7% of the total in Argentina and Colombia, against one-third in East Asia. In Chile and Brazil less than 2% of the business workforce is in ICT. This relative

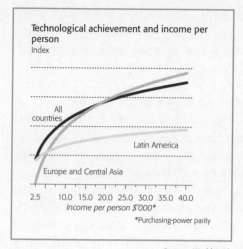

Technological achievement and income per person
Index

All countries

Latin America

Europe and Central Asia

2.5   10.0 15.0 20.0 25.0 30.0 35.0 40.0
Income per person $'000
*Purchasing-power parity

Source: World Bank

FIG 2.7 Latin lag

technophobia probably reflects years of inward-looking economic policies, import substitution and disappointing education systems. Here, slow technological dispersal may not be just the result of a time lag. It may be evidence of more fundamental problems.

Broadly, two sets of obstacles stand in the way of technological progress in emerging economies. The first is their technological inheritance. Most advances are based on the labours of previous generations: you need electricity to run computers and reliable communications for modern health care, for instance. So countries that failed to adopt old technologies are at a disadvantage when it comes to new ones. Mobile phones, which require no wires, are a prominent exception.

The adoption of older technologies varies widely among countries at apparently similar stages of development. Soviet central planners loved to build electricity lines everywhere; the result is that ex-communist countries enjoy near-universal access to electricity (an extremely rare example of a beneficial legacy from communism). Latin American countries had no such background and as a result consume only about half as much electricity per person as eastern Europe and central Asia.

This partly explains the patchiness in countries' technological achievements overall. Call centres in Kenya, for example, pay more than ten times as much per unit of bandwidth as do rivals in India, because India's fibre-optic cable system is far better and cheaper. So sometimes you cannot leapfrog. As countries get richer, older technology constraints do not always fall away. It depends in part on how governments organise basic infrastructure like transport and communications.

The other set of problems has to do with the intangible things that affect a country's capacity to absorb technology: education; R&D; financial systems; the quality of government. In general, developing countries' educational levels have soared in the past decade or so. Middle-income countries have achieved universal primary-school enrolment and poor countries have increased the number of children completing primary school dramatically. Even so, illiteracy still bedevils some middle-income countries and many poor ones.

A similar pattern can be seen with R&D. Emerging economies spend less on R&D than rich ones: rich countries spend 2.3% of GDP on R&D, East Asians 1.4%, and Latin America 0.6%. Also important, though, is who spends the money; and this also varies considerably. East Asia's pattern is similar to the West's: companies spend most of the money and do most of the research. In eastern Europe and Latin America, by contrast, the government is the largest source of finance, and in Latin America universities do the largest share of the work. Sometimes government-supported research is fine: it triggered South Korea's technology boom in the 1980s. But in general, companies tend to be the most efficient and effective promoters of technology (mobile phones are a case in point).

And in rich countries, high-tech-firms get money from banks, stockmarkets and venture capitalists in ways that emerging-market entrepreneurs can only dream of. Here, and in government policy towards technology firms – meaning everything from trade openness to product standards – there has been little catch-up with the West. In Kenya, flower-growing counts as a technology-improving activity because it requires fertilisers, irrigation, greenhouses and just-in-time delivery. The damage wrought by political chaos is a reminder that technology is far more fragile in poor countries than in the West.

Yet it would be wrong to be gloomy about the technological outlook of emerging economies. The channels of technology transfer have widened enormously over the past ten years. Technological literacy has risen, especially among the young. But all this has helped emerging economies mainly in the first stage: absorption. The second stage – diffusion – has so far proved much more testing.

Clarification

The data underlying the World Bank's analysis of the speed of technological diffusion did not come from the bank itself but from the Cross-Country Historical Adoption of Technology (CHAT) database, created by Diego Comin of Harvard Business School and Bart Hobijn of the Federal Reserve Bank of New York.

Order in the jungle

The rule of law has become a big idea in economics. But it has had its difficulties

"AM I THE ONLY ECONOMIST guilty of using the term [rule of law] without having a good fix on what it really means?" asks Dani Rodrik of Harvard University. "Well, maybe the first one to confess to it."

The rule of law is usually thought of as a political or legal matter. The world's newest country, Kosovo, says its priority is to improve the rule of law in order to reduce corruption and build up the state. But in the past ten years the rule of law has become important in economics too. Indeed, it has become the motherhood and apple pie of development economics – which makes Mr Rodrik's confession the more striking. The rule of law is held to be not only good in itself, because it embodies and encourages a just society, but also a cause of other good things, notably growth. "No other single political ideal has ever achieved global endorsement," says Brian Tamanaha, a legal scholar at St John's University, New York.

But as an economic concept the rule of law has had a turbulent history. It emerged almost abruptly during the 1990s from the dual collapses of Asian currencies and former Soviet economies. For a short time, it seemed to provide the answer to problems of development from Azerbaijan to Zimbabwe, until some well-directed criticism dimmed its star. Since then it has re-established itself as a central concept in understanding how countries grow rich – but not as the panacea it once looked like.

Economists became fascinated by the rule of law after the crumbling of the "Washington consensus". This consensus, which was economic orthodoxy in the 1980s, held that the best way for countries to grow was to "get the policies right" – on, for example, budgets and exchange rates. But the Asian crisis of 1997–98 shook economists' confidence that they knew which policies were, in fact, right. This drove them to re-examine what had gone wrong. The answer, they concluded, was the institutional setting of policymaking, especially the rule of law. If the rules of the game were a mess, they reasoned, no amount of tinkering with macroeconomic policy would produce the desired results.

This conclusion was strengthened by events in the former Soviet empire. Many post-communist countries got their policies roughly right fairly quickly. But it soon became clear this was not enough. "I was a traditional trade and labour economist until 1992," says Daniel Kaufmann, former head of the World Bank Institute's Global Governance group. "When I went to Ukraine, my outlook changed. Problems with governance and the rule of law were undermining all our efforts."

Pretty quickly, "governance" – political accountability and the quality of bureaucracy as well as the rule of law – became all the rage. Economists got busy calculating what it was, how well countries were doing it and what a difference it made. Mr Kaufmann and his colleague Aart Kraay worked out the "300% dividend": in the long run, a country's income per head rises by roughly 300% if it improves its governance by one standard deviation. One standard deviation is roughly the gap between India's and Chile's rule-of-law scores, measured by the bank. As it happens, Chile is about 300% richer than India in purchasing-power terms. The same holds for South Africa and Spain, Morocco and Portugal, Botswana and Ireland. Economists have repeatedly found that the better the rule of law, the richer the nation. (Figure 2.8 shows the results of three studies, put on a comparable basis by Mr Kaufmann.) Every rich country with the arguable exceptions of Italy and Greece scores well on rule-of-law measures; most poor countries do not.

Mr Rodrik reviewed the contributions to growth of governance ("institutions", he called it), geography and openness to trade. He concluded, to use the title of an article he published in 2002, that "Institutions Rule". Writing from the perspective of a political scientist, Francis Fukuyama of Johns Hopkins University concurred: "I believe that the institutionalists have won this argument hands down."

Partly because of this, and also because the rule of law is desirable for its own sake, governments and aid agencies began splurging money on rule-of-law reforms, such as training judges, reforming prisons and setting up prosecutors' offices. Such reforms had begun

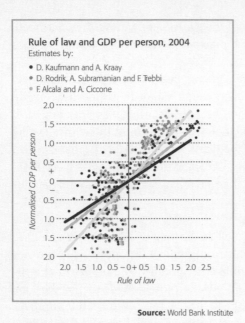

Rule of law and GDP per person, 2004
Estimates by:

• D. Kaufmann and A. Kraay
• D. Rodrik, A. Subramanian and F. Trebbi
• F. Alcala and A. Ciccone

Normalised GDP per person

Rule of law

Source: World Bank Institute

FIG 2.8 Clearly linked, m'lud

in Latin America in the mid-1980s. Now they became universal.

The European Union insists that all its members satisfy standards for the rule of law. It requires applicants to commit themselves to legal reforms to meet those standards and dispatches armies of lawyers to advise them how to bring their legal systems up to scratch. America's Millennium Challenge Corporation, set up in 2004 to improve the effectiveness of American official aid, confines its largesse to countries that have committed themselves to minimum rule-of-law standards (one of three basic requirements). Western donors have poured billions into rule-of-law projects over the past 20 years. The World Bank is now running such projects (narrowly defined) worth almost $450m; on a wider definition, almost half the bank's total lending of $24 billion in 2006 had some rule-of-law component (for example, advice on conflict resolution in village-development projects, or on bankruptcy law in privatisation programmes). In roughly a decade the rule of law has gone from a specialist political and legal topic into a staple of economic thinking and the subject of a vast aid-giving effort.

So it came as an unwelcome surprise when, in 2003, one of the world's acknowledged experts on governance wondered aloud whether the emperor had any clothes. Thomas Carothers of the Carnegie Endowment for International Peace, a think-tank in Washington, DC, wrote a paper politely entitled "Promoting the Rule of Law Abroad: The Problem of Knowledge". According to Mr Carothers, the problem was, as William Goldman said of Hollywood, that nobody knows anything.

Mr Carothers argued that the intrinsic difficulty of defining the rule of law, combined with the problems of knowing how specific laws work in practice, meant that "the rapidly growing field of rule-of-law assistance is operating from a disturbingly thin base of knowledge at every level." Many of the difficulties are inherent, he said. But not all: aid organisations always look forward to the next project, rather than back to the lessons of experience; lawyers who carry out the work are not much interested in development; university professors are not gripped by applied policy research. As a result, according to one rule-of-law promoter, "deep down, we don't really know what we are doing."

The shock of Mr Carothers's argument was salutary. In response, there has been a flurry of rule-of-law studies. A new body of work has appeared, which could be called the economics of the rule of law. It shows the rule of law can indeed be improved. It has made clearer what economists and others mean when they talk about the rule of law. It has laid down some guidelines about reforms, helping show what works when, say, training judges or policemen. What it has not yet shown beyond doubt is that the rule of law is a precondition for economic growth everywhere. In the process, the subject of law as an economic matter has begun to grow up. It has passed from vigorous childhood into more troubled adolescence.

Unruly law

In "The Rule of Law and Development", Michael Trebilcock of the University of Toronto and Ron Daniels of the University of Pennsylvania tackle the question of what economists mean by the rule of law. A report by a new research group, the Hague Institute for the Internationalisation of Law, does the same thing. Both publications argue that people routinely use two quite different definitions, which they call "thick" and "thin".

Thick definitions treat the rule of law as the core of a just society. In this version, the concept is inextricably linked to liberty and democracy. Its adherents say a country can be spoken of as being ruled by law only if the state's power is constrained and if basic freedoms, such as those of speech and association, are guaranteed. The "declaration of Delhi" drawn up by the International Commission of Jurists in that city in 1959 followed this line in saying that the rule of law "should be employed to safeguard and advance the civil and political rights of the individual" and create "conditions under which his legitimate aspirations and dignity may be realised." Among other proponents of a thick definition are Friedrich Hayek, an Austrian economist, and Cass Sunstein of the University of Chicago. In their view, the rule of law includes elements of political morality.

Thin definitions are more formal. The important things, on this account, are not democracy and morality but property rights and the efficient administration of justice. Laws must provide stability. They do not necessarily have to be moral or promote human rights. America's southern states in the Jim Crow era were governed by the rule of law on thin definitions, but not on thick.

The existence of competing definitions of something may seem fatally to undermine its usefulness. If you argue that the rule of law is vital to growth, which version do you mean – the one that defends human rights or the one that guarantees property rights? But economists love competition. Their differing definitions of the rule of law reflect competing explanations of what drives economic growth.

One account of growth – associated with Douglass North of Washington University in St Louis, Missouri – is "institutional". It focuses on the importance of property rights, transaction costs and economic organisation. On this view, stable, predictable laws encourage investment and growth. Thin definitions of the rule of law fit this well. The other – associated with Amartya Sen of Harvard – says that if you expand people's "capabilities" (Mr Sen's term), they will do things that help countries grow rich. Freeing people to take advantage of their capabilities usually means lifting the oppressive burden of the state and guaranteeing certain basic rights – a much thicker concept.

The distinction between thick and thin versions of the rule of law overlaps another distinction between legal traditions. Starting in 1997, a group of economists led by Andrei Shleifer of Harvard and Robert Vishny of Chicago started to compare the economic performance of common-law countries (such as America and Britain) with that of civil-law ones (France, Germany and Scandinavia). They argued that common-law countries have more secure property rights, better protection of shareholders and creditors, more diversified share ownership, and tougher disclosure and liability laws – to the benefit, they claimed, of stockmarket performance.

Like the initial claims for the rule of law, those on behalf of the common law were subject to harsh criticism at about the same time, mostly from continental economists. Some claimed the differences between common and civil law were not as sharp as they seemed, and were proxies for differences of politics, history and culture. Others pointed out that a country's legal origins do not seem to explain much about how it is faring economically or in terms of the rule of law. North and South Korea have the same legal origins.

But just as rule-of-law scholars have responded to criticism with more research, so have the legal-origins crowd. In a stream of papers they have found strong evidence that civil-law countries encourage government ownership of the media and banks, a higher burden of entry into business, more labour-market regulation and greater formalism of court procedures – to their detriment, they claim.

Perhaps such arguments can never be resolved. As Rainer Grote of the Max Planck Institute for Comparative Public Law and International Law in Heidelberg says, the rule of law "belongs to the category of open-ended concepts which are subject to permanent debate." This part of the new economics of the rule of law clarifies its role, but no more. Other findings, though, are more constructive.

Scales of justice

There have been huge improvements in monitoring and measuring the rule of law, even though people cannot agree exactly what it is. "Fifteen years ago, we didn't talk about this stuff," says Steve Radelet of the Centre for Global Development, a Washington think-tank. "Ten years ago, there was no data." Now, the Worldwide Governance Indicators project – "one of the best kept secrets at the World Bank", believes Gordon Johnson, a grand old man of aid-giving – is the state of the art. It gathers data on more than 60 indicators (the extent of crime, the quality of police, judicial independence and so on) to create rule-of-law and governance measures for virtually every country in the world. Aggregating like this (and being honest about the margin of error), says Mr Kaufmann, is far from perfect, but is a decent approximation.

These measures confirm what is clear anyway: some countries have been able to improve their legal framework even in a short time. In 2000 Mikhail Saakashvili, then Georgia's minister of justice, sacked two-thirds of his country's judges for failing to pass an exam. Four years later as president, he fired all the country's traffic police. Georgia's World Bank rule-of-law score rose from nine out of 100 in 2002 (in the bottom 10%) to 33 at the end of 2006 – low, but better. Central European and Baltic countries are doing better still: the radical legal changes required by membership of the EU improved their economies as well as their judicial systems.

In general, the measures suggest, bold reforms work better than gradual ones. Latin America modernised its penal codes and made trials more transparent. Chile, for instance, established a new public-prosecution system beginning in 2003. But many of its officials lack experience and have met resistance from the police. Russia implemented some judicial reforms in the 1990s and raised spending on the courts in 2000 – to no avail: its rule-of-law scores fell in five of the years between 2000 and 2007.

The difference between central Europe and Latin America may be one of political backing. Messrs Trebilcock and Daniels divide countries into three: those where politicians, legal professionals and the public all support reform (central Europe after the fall of communism, South Africa after apartheid); those where politicians support reform, but lawyers and police do not (Chile and Guatemala); and those where lawyers want change, but not politicians (Pakistan). Only in the first group, the professors say, does rule-of-law reform get far.

Consistent with that rather gloomy finding, some new research finds only a weak link between the rule of law and economic growth. The connection with wealth is well established (see Figure 2.8) but that is different: it has been forged over decades, even centuries. The link with shorter-term growth is harder to see. China appears to be a standing contradiction to the argument that the rule of law is needed for growth. It is growing fast and is the world's largest recipient of foreign investment, yet has lots of corruption and nothing that most Westerners would recognise as a rule-of-law tradition. (It does, though, guarantee some property rights and its government is good at formulating and implementing policies.)

On the other hand, there is surely a connection between the legal reforms carried out in central Europe and the Baltics and their fast growth rates, or between Spain's post-Franco legal opening and its long boom. And there are proxy indicators connecting legal reform with growth in other areas. The value of rural land in Brazil, Indonesia, the Philippines and Thailand increased sharply when people were given title deeds, because owners were more willing to invest. One independent study for the World Bank a decade ago found a surprising link between projects the bank financed and civil liberties: projects in countries with strong civil liberties had far higher rates of return than those in countries with weak traditions of liberty.

But such links do not tell you anything about causation. Perhaps growth helps the rule of law, not vice versa. Perhaps countries can afford the luxury of the rule of law only after they have grown rich. The persistence of "frontier justice" into the 1930s in America gives a colour of plausibility to that idea.

Yet it is not Mr Kaufmann's view. He argues that rule-of-law improvements tend to help growth; that few countries have sustained gains in growth without improving their rule of law; and that places that have grown without such improvement have subsequently lurched backwards (Argentina used to be one of the ten richest countries in the world). The real puzzle is to explain the exceptions: why crony capitalism has flourished in parts of fast-growing Asia or Kremlin banditry in Russia. The answer, he says, is that, without a rule of law, well-connected crooks can grab an unfair share of the spoils of growth, especially if these include windfall gains from oil and raw materials.

The existence of crony capitalism and "state capture" by robber barons is, of course, an argument for trying to strengthen the rule of law where you can, since it suggests growth will not necessarily create law automatically. There are other arguments, too: the rule of law is desirable for its own sake – to improve human rights or to increase citizens' chances of justice against predatory governments. As John Locke wrote in 1690, "wherever law ends, tyranny begins." Plainly, in some countries, such as Myanmar and Zimbabwe, legal abuses and over-mighty regimes are direct obstacles to growth. Reforms would help – if they could be implemented.

But as a generalisation, the efforts of the past few years have thrown up mixed messages. They suggest the rule of law can be improved sharply; that rule-of-law reform is at root a political not a technical undertaking; and that it is linked to growth, if weakly in the short term. But they do not really bear out the assertion that the rule of law is an underlying prerequisite for growth. Rather, the more economists find out about the rule of law, the more desirable it seems – and the more problematic as a universal economic guide.

Sources

"Growth without Governance", by Daniel Kaufmann and Aart Kray.

"Governance Matters IV", by Daniel Kaufmann, Aart Kray and Massimo Mastruzzi.

"Civil Liberties, Democracy, and the Performance of Government Projects", by Daniel Kaufmann, J. Isham and L.H. Pritchett.

"Institutions Rule", by Dani Rodrik, Arvind Subramanian and Francesco Trebbi.

"Promoting the Rule of Law Abroad: The Problem of Knowledge", by Thomas Carothers.

"Rule of Law Reform and Development", by Michael Trebilcock and Ron Daniels.

"Institutions, Institutional Change and Economic Performance", by Douglass North.

"Development as Freedom", by Amartya Sen.

"Law and Finance", by Andrei Shleifer, Robert Vishny *et al.*

The faith that moves Mammon

Only rarely does the glue that binds the financial system come unstuck

THE NEAR-COLLAPSE of the banking system has shown just how deep some central parts of economic life are buried. Who, for instance, bothered much about the static interbank market before it seized up in August 2007? The supply of credit is bound up with something even more subterranean: trust. The very word comes from *credere*, to trust in Latin. When institutions, such as banks, that are supposed to embody trust are shown to be brittle, it leads to concerns about the fragility of the entire economy.

Much in modern economies is taken on trust. Even the most basic goods depend on complex links between suppliers strewn across the globe. The glue that binds the whole system together is trust – trust that suppliers will deliver the right goods on time; trust that the payments will duly pass down the supply chain. That raises a question: what makes people who might not even lend to their neighbours happy to lend their life savings to unknown borrowers whom they will never meet? Put it like that, and the surprise is not that there are sometimes periodic panics, but that there are so few of them.

In his 2004 book "The Company of Strangers" Paul Seabright, a professor at the Toulouse School of Economics, explored the roots of such seemingly reckless trust. He identified two helpful human traits. One is the capacity to weigh up the costs and benefits of trusting others. Allied to this is an instinct to return favours in kind, and to seek revenge when trust is betrayed. When workers are treated generously, they work hard; when customers are swindled, they raise a fuss. Reciprocal ties become strongest between people who meet and trade frequently. But reciprocity thrives elsewhere too, because it is embedded in habits of thinking and rules of behaviour. Tourists often leave tips in restaurants to conform to a social norm, though they may never eat there again.

These informal mechanisms are buttressed by state institutions such as regulators, bankruptcy procedures and the courts. These are used to settle only a small minority of disputes. The state is acting as a backstop for informal monitoring: in stable societies, transactions between strangers are mostly self-policing. A reputation for honest dealing is valuable for firms and employees alike. Suppliers gamble the rewards from future commerce for a short-term gain when they bilk their customers.

The comfort of strangers

When it works well, the banking system underpins trust and allows strangers to deal with each other safely. Banks enable savers to reduce risks by pooling their resources. Deposits offer safer returns than those from making a loan to any one borrower – even a trustworthy one who is known to the lender. Trust in banks depends on an illusion that funds are readily accessible, when most are tied up in long-term loans. It is an illusion that depositors play along with because they know that, absent a panic, not many of them will ever need to withdraw cash at the same time.

Yet banks are complex and opaque firms, which makes it hard for depositors to police their activities. Even regulators and informed investors struggle. A rumour, even a false one, is enough to trigger a run. Trust in institutions is so ingrained an instinct that, before the crisis, there was little concern about the safety of banks. Now, however, there is a noticeable surge in cash in circulation (because of banknote withdrawals) and a greater awareness of the limits of deposit-insurance schemes.

In these responses there are still signs of a durable trust in institutions, albeit ones backed by governments. When panicky investors sell stocks or liquidate their bank deposits, they renounce claims on real assets – factories, office buildings, homes – for pieces of paper with no intrinsic worth. Although the banking illusion has been unsteady, the illusion behind fiat money seems to have a tenacious hold.

Since banks are pillars of trust, the various bail-out schemes will have an impact beyond the securing of credit lines. Small businesses rely on informal credit to survive. If one firm fears that another cannot get an overdraft because its bank is in trouble, it may demand that bills are paid sooner or even settled in advance. That loss of trust could sink many small but otherwise sound firms. Indeed Mr Seabright thinks that business cycles may be driven as much by the waxing and waning of trust in related firms as by "confidence" – firms' hopes and fears about future demand for their products.

Although trust in banks can be salvaged by state backstops, faith in the financial system may be harder to repair. For many, the crisis is the result of a shift from traditional "relationship banking", where borrowers are well known to lenders, to a new system of arms-length finance, where investors buy bundles of anonymous loans packaged in a security. A study published in the IMF's October 2008 *World Economic Outlook* found that downturns are bigger in countries with arms-length finance, which dries up quickly in bad times. But the new finance merely mirrors (and even lags behind) a more general trend in modern economies towards arms-length commercial ties. The solution may not be a retreat to old-style banking, but better mechanisms to foster trust in the new finance.

For his part, Mr Seabright concludes that the main reason people place their trust in others is because it is less risky than the alternative. He senses a "nostalgia for self-sufficiency" induced by anxieties about globalisation. But this, he says, overlooks that "self-sufficiency is fantastically risky". Isolated people are often more vulnerable because they lack access to basic medical care and – when their harvests fail – to food. Integration with others massively reduces risk. Trust in strangers may be at odds with some of our instincts, but it is a price worth paying for a richer life.

Trade's bounty

A 2005 study estimates America's gains from past and future global integration

SOME OF THOSE who are sceptical about globalisation concede that rich countries, at least, gain from it. But many Americans seem unconvinced. "Offshoring", the use of poor-country labour to drive down costs, has worried many voters in recent American elections. Congress has taken a protectionist turn in recent years. George Bush, who fancied himself a free-trader, backed egregious protection of America's farmers and steelmakers. A 2005 paper,[1] by Scott Bradford, Paul Grieco and Gary Hufbauer, of the Institute for International Economics in Washington, DC, helped to set them all straight. It surveys the evidence and puts a dollar figure on America's past and prospective gains from trade.

That is no easy task, because trade can affect an economy in many ways. There is the traditional route of comparative advantage: by specialising in ways that exploit differences in productivity and resources, countries can use trade to consume more than they could in commercial isolation. Economies of scale are also important: by gaining access to bigger markets, firms can spread fixed costs over more output. Trade also helps to diffuse the best production technologies around the world. Imports benefit consumers by providing a wider and cheaper variety of goods and by inducing competition that spurs productivity.

Not surprisingly, the authors are unable to distinguish the effects of pro-trade policies – notably, the eight completed global trade rounds since the second world war – from those of the mostly serendipitous improvements in, say, transport and telecoms that have also made trade easier. They draw on several approaches to estimate the total effect, because any single study is bound to be imprecise.

One method is to look at macroeconomic models of the effects of trade over time. The OECD has studied the impact of trade "exposure" on incomes per person in several countries. It concludes that trade accounted for 20% of the gain in America's GDP per person between 1950 and 2003.

Other techniques are more microeconomic, and try to add up the benefits to consumers and the gains to firms. A study cited by the authors suggests that, by bringing greater product variety, trade has boosted consumers' purchasing power by 2.8% of GDP, or $300 billion a year. On the corporate side, competition from abroad has induced changes in the mix of capital and labour and the incorporation of new technologies that raise productivity. Such "sorting and sifting" is reckoned to yield an additional 5.8% of GDP. Combine the benefits of greater product variety and the gains from sorting and sifting, and the total impact of trade is to raise the level of GDP by 8.6%.

A third approach is to consider a counterfactual: what if the wave of global trade liberalisation that began after the second world war had never taken place? One study estimates that a return to 1930s-style protectionism today would reduce America's GDP by 2.4%. If other countries retaliated with higher barriers of their own, GDP would fall by 2.1% more. Once again, consumers' lost product variety would have to be considered too. On this method, the total value of trade to America is put at 7.3% of GDP.

Taking the average of the estimates, the authors conclude that the American economy is roughly $1 trillion a year better off thanks to "global integration". That means about $9,000 of extra income for each American household.

Since there has been so much liberalisation already, you might think there was little to gain from going further. The average American import tariff, after all, has fallen from 40% to 4% since the second world war: surely there is not much more to squeeze out? In fact, say the authors, the opposite is true: there is still plenty to be had.

Eyes on the prize

First, tariff measures are not the only measure of trade openness. Trade in many services, from finance to health care, remains highly restricted. Freeing services could yield even greater gains than continued liberalisation in manufactures and farm products. Second, although American tariffs have fallen, those in poor countries remain high. A third, more speculative, potential gain comes from the "commercial certainty" of liberalisation agreements. When firms can count on free trade, they can commit themselves to investments that raise incomes further.

Mr Bradford, Mr Grieco and Mr Hufbauer use the same techniques to glimpse the effects of future liberalisation. Clearly, there are huge margins of error, but the gains look big: anywhere from $450 billion to $1.3 trillion annually, if America concluded free-trade deals with all its trading partners. The authors think that this "final march" to freer trade could safely be expected to generate gains equivalent to about half of those already achieved, or around $4,500 per American household per year.

There are caveats. The authors do not analyse how the gains from trade have been or will be shared among rich and poor households. Nor do they estimate the number of households that are net losers from trade. But they think the total economic costs of trade-related job losses if America eliminated all trade barriers would amount at most to $54 billion, far less than the economic gains.

Crucially, this is a one-time cost. The benefits of trade, by contrast, accrue year after year as long as free-trade policies are in place. Because the benefits from trade are vastly bigger than the costs, the losers could in theory easily be compensated. America has already taken some steps towards turning this theory into practice. It can and should go much further.

Note

1 "The Payoff to America from Global Integration", in Fred Bergsten (ed.), *The United States and the World Economy: Foreign Economic Policy for the Next Decade*, Institute for International Economics, January 2005.

Opening the floodgates

Imports can be as useful to developing countries as exports are

PAUL KRUGMAN, who won the 2008 Nobel prize in economics for his work on trade, wrote in 1993: "What a country really gains from trade is the ability to import things it wants. Exports are not an objective in and of themselves; the need to export is a burden that a country must bear because its import suppliers are crass enough to demand payment."

This view does not dominate the public debate. Most are thrilled by the idea of export growth, but cower at the prospect of more imports. Such prejudice certainly prevailed in India in 1991, when the IMF foisted tariff cuts on the economy as one of the conditions attached to a $2.5 billion bail-out package. Pessimists fretted that a flood of imports would destroy Indian industry.

For a group of American economists,[1] however, that sudden trade liberalisation has provided an unusually clear lens through which to study the way that commerce affects the economy. This is precisely because it was externally imposed. That the government had to hew to the IMF's diktats and slash tariffs across the board gave industries little scope to jockey for exemptions. This made the researchers confident that tariff cuts, and not differences in industries' ability to lobby the government, were responsible for changes in India's trade patterns after liberalisation.

As part of those reforms, India slashed tariffs on imports from an average of 90% in 1991 to 30% in 1997. Not surprisingly, imports doubled in value over this period. But the effects on Indian manufacturing were not what the prophets of doom had predicted: output grew by over 50% in that time. And by looking carefully at what was imported and what it was used to make, the researchers found that cheaper and more accessible imports gave a big boost to India's domestic industrial growth in the 1990s.

This was because the tariff cuts meant more than Indian consumers being able to satisfy their cravings for imported chocolate (though they did that, too). It gave Indian manufacturers access to a variety of intermediate and capital goods which had earlier been too expensive. The rise in imports of intermediate goods was much higher, at 227%, than the 90% growth in consumer-goods imports in the 13 years to 2000.

Theory suggests several ways in which greater access to imports can improve domestic manufacturing. First, cheaper imports may allow firms to produce existing goods using the same inputs as before, but at a lower cost. They could also open up new ways of producing existing goods, and even allow entirely new goods to be made. All this seemed to hold in India. For example, its prolific film industry had continued to make some black-and-white films into the 1970s, in part because of the difficulty of importing enough supplies of colour film. But proving whether the theory applies in practice requires more detailed data, not just about how much firms produced but what they produced, and how all this changed over time.

Most attempts at addressing these questions have foundered because such information is not available. But with India, the researchers were helped, perversely enough, by highly restrictive industrial policies that the country had introduced in the 1950s. These included rules that required companies to report to the authorities every little tweak to their product mix – a burden for firms, but a gold mine for researchers. Happily, the economists found that the data backed up the theory: lower import tariffs did lead to an expansion in product variety through access to new inputs. They found that about 66% of the growth in India's imports of intermediate goods after liberalisation came from goods the country had simply not bought when its trade regime was more restrictive. These new inputs caused the price of intermediate goods to fall by 4.7% per year after 1989. And detailed data linking inputs to final goods showed that the imports led to an explosion in the variety of products made by Indian manufacturers; the average firm made 1.4 products before liberalisation, but by 2003, this had increased to 2.3. The increases in variety were largest for industries where the input tariffs were cut most, and these industries also saw increased spending on research and development. Overall, the new products that Indian companies introduced were responsible for 25% of the growth in the country's manufacturing output between 1991 and 1997.

Slash and churn

But one aspect of India's experience after trade liberalisation did not conform to what the researchers had expected. Normally, as new products are introduced, some older ones stop being made. This "churn" in the market is part of what makes people uncomfortable about lower trade barriers, because it may cause difficult adjustments for some workers or companies. But the Indian variant of creative destruction seemed unusually benign. The researchers found that firms rarely dropped products. One reason for this may be the diversity of India's economy: there is always a segment lower down the economic pecking order which is happy to buy products that richer consumers scoff at.

This may be unique to countries like India where many levels of development coexist. But Penny Goldberg, one of the authors, thinks that the methods used in the studies on India can be applied to many other countries where trade has been similarly liberalised and which have good data on firms, such as Colombia and Indonesia. She notes that one of her co-authors, Amit Khandelwal, visited a Coca-Cola bottling plant in China, and noticed that all the machinery was either Japanese or German. China, of course, is known as a big exporter. But it may never have achieved this success without access to a range of imports.

Note

1   Penny Goldberg, Amit Khandelwal, Nina Pavcnik and Petia Topalova, "Multi-product firms and Product Turnover in the Developing World: Evidence from India", *Review of Economics and Statistics*, November 2010. Other papers available at www.princeton.edu/~pennykg/

Development piecemeal

Small policy changes, not upheaval, may be the trigger of economic growth

OVER THE PAST 20 years or so, economists have developed a long list of now-familiar remedies for developing countries hoping to grow their way to prosperity. This "Washington Consensus" includes the removal of trade protection and the introduction of deregulation, as well as fiscal and monetary discipline. And these are just for starters. The trouble is that many governments find it almost impossible to stick to these prescriptions. Meanwhile, other economists have suggested that development depends not on specific policies but on "institutional" factors, such as a respect for property rights, which constrain the powers of the state. This can sound like a counsel of despair, because such institutions and customs can take many years, even centuries, to become established.

However, two new studies suggest that there is no need to be so gloomy. They argue that institutional overhaul and broad economic reforms are not necessary to spur economic growth. In fact, quantitative evidence that they do so is surprisingly difficult to find. Smaller policy changes may serve just as well, and pave the way for later reforms of institutions.

In one of these papers,[1] Edward Glaeser, a Harvard economist, and three co-authors question several prominent studies that treat institutions as a wellspring of development. Mr Glaeser and his colleagues point out a problem with theories stressing the importance of institutional reform: it is fiendishly hard to find a quantitative measure for institutional quality that can be plugged into a statistical model explaining economic growth. They show that the measures typically used in such studies – such as "risk of expropriation" or "government effectiveness", which are often based on investor surveys – merely reflect the result of governments' behaviour, not of reasonably permanent and durable institutional features, such as the protection of property rights and contracts. Indeed, in some countries, such as Argentina, the standard indices of "institutions" fluctuate wildly with the electoral cycle. Sometimes a dictator chooses to secure property rights without enshrining it in the rules, as in South Korea until the 1980s; sometimes he does not. The authors find that "there is no relationship between growth and constitutional measures of institutions."

This is not to say that guaranteed rules of the game are unimportant in sustaining growth, as opposed to sparking it. However, countries tend to escape poverty in the first place through good policies. Only then do they go on to improve their institutions, the authors argue. Andrei Shleifer, one of the researchers, points to China. The policies introduced by Deng Xiaoping from 1978 led to economic growth and the emergence of a vibrant middle class, which in turn demanded formal guarantees, such as 2004's constitutional amendment defining property rights as "inviolable". The point is that institutional reforms came after the policies that fostered growth; they did not precede it.

Reform something, anything

So what does cause growth to take off? Another study[2] finds that the spark can be a surprisingly small change in policy. The researchers, at Harvard's Kennedy School of Government, looked at 83 instances between 1957 and 1992 in which annual GDP growth increased by at least two percentage points and the higher growth was sustained for at least eight years.

These bursts of growth were not normally preceded by a big shift in policy, or by full-blown economic and political reforms – such as liberalisation or a move towards democracy. This is something the authors are at a loss to explain. Financial liberalisation does help stimulate growth for a while. More investment and exports and a competitive real exchange rate can also give a temporary boost. And positive external shocks (such as a rise in the price of an exported commodity) tend to hasten growth that quickly fizzles out.

What struck the authors was the humble nature of the initial triggers of growth. These usually consist of nothing more than relaxing specific constraints on private activity. In South Korea in 1964, devaluation and an increase in interest rates overseen by the dictatorship

of General Park Chung Hee brought the returns to private investment closer into line with those to the economy as a whole. In 1983,
General Augusto Pinochet pulled the same trick in Chile. In China in
1978, the ruling party introduced market-oriented incentives. In India
in 1980, Indira Gandhi removed shackles from enterprises and began
sending pro-business signals, a decade before more formal reforms
(although there is a hot debate about which set of policies mattered
most). Policymakers, say the authors, have merely to identify the relevant constraints. "Instigating growth is a lot easier in practice than
the standard Washington recipe, with its long list of institutional and
governance reforms, would lead us to believe," writes Dani Rodrik,
one of the authors, in a separate article.[3]

However, grander reforms do seem to be correlated with take-
offs in growth that are sustained over a longer period, of 15 years or
more. This suggests that big reforms are not needed to start growth,
but they are a great help in keeping it going. And at the outset an
awful lot still comes down to luck. "There was nothing inevitable
about Deng [Xiaoping]," Mr Shleifer says. "It just so happened that
they [the Chinese] picked a dictator who decided to give some protection to property rights." Hopefully China has now moved too far in
the direction of a market economy for some new leader abruptly to
change his mind.

Notes

1   Edward Glaeser, Rafael La Porta, Florencio Lopez-de-Silanes and Andrei
    Shleifer, "Do institutions cause growth?", NBER Working Paper No. 10568.
2   Ricardo Hausmann, Lant Pritchett and Dani Rodrik, "Growth
    accelerations", NBER Working Paper No. 10566.
3   "Getting institutions right", www.cesifo.de/%7EDocCIDL/dicereport204-
    forum2.pdf CESifo DICE Report, Summer 2004.

Finance: trick or treat?

During recent decades, financial transactions have grown much faster than global output. What role does the financial system play in a modern economy?

THEODORE ROOSEVELT, an American president, once claimed that there was no moral difference between gambling on cards or horses and gambling on the stockmarket. Jacques Chirac, when president of France, denounced currency speculators as "the AIDS of the world economy". Bankers are widely condemned either as greedy usurers or as incompetent fools. At best, the financial system is seen as a wasteful sideshow that relies on churning money earned in "real" businesses and adds no economic value. At worst, it is portrayed as an irrational casino, in which 22-year-old traders are able to bankrupt economies. Might we be better off without all the financiers?

A stockmarket crash or a run of bank failures can clearly do serious economic harm. The worst recessions in history, including the Great Depression in the 1930s and, more recently, Japan's stagnation during the 1990s and East Asia's slump in 1997–98, all followed financial crises. Yet, for all its failings, the financial system provides services that are vital for long-term economic growth.

Finance has existed in some form since the dawn of recorded history. Credit was used in agriculture in Mesopotamia in 3000BC. Banks existed in Egypt in 200BC. Even derivatives are not new: futures contracts were traded on the Amsterdam exchange in the 17th century. There is nothing inherently new about borrowing, lending and investing.

Even so, in *Hamlet*, Polonius advised his son "neither a borrower nor a lender be". If everybody followed that advice the financial system would not exist. Most people, however, need to borrow or save at some time in their life – from taking out a student loan or home mortgage to paying into a savings account or a pension fund. Even share ownership is no longer the preserve of a rich few. America entered the 21st century with half of all households owning shares

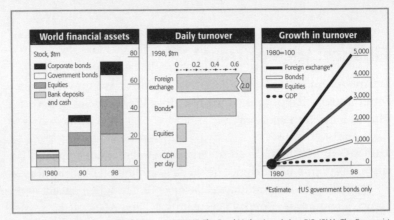

Sources: IFC; Salomon Smith Barney; MSCI; IMF; The Bond Market Association; BIS; ISMA; *The Economist*

FIG 2.9 The financial flood

directly or through mutual funds, compared with 25% in the mid-1980s and only 5% in the 1950s.

In the 1980s and 1990s there was, indeed, something of a financial revolution. Advances in computing and telecoms, financial innovation and liberalisation of capital controls combined to reduce the costs of financial transactions. There was a corresponding explosion in the volume of transactions. The global stock of financial assets (shares, bonds, bank deposits and cash) increased more than twice as fast as the GDP of rich economies, from $12 trillion in 1980 to almost $80 trillion in 1999. The volume of trading in financial securities increased even faster (see Figure 2.9). Note that the markets for bonds and foreign exchange have far higher turnover (ie, are more "liquid") than does the equity market.

The go-betweens

Financial firms come in many shapes and sizes, but they all serve the same purpose: to channel funds from those who wish to save to those who need to borrow. In many ways, finance is like any other market, matching demand and supply – in this case of loanable or investable funds. However, financial markets are special in one crucial way: they link the present and the future, allowing savers to convert current income into future spending, and borrowers to do the reverse. By acting as a channel through which savings can finance investment, the financial system helps to spur growth.

In doing this, financial institutions can be divided into two broad types. First, savers provide money indirectly to borrowers through intermediaries, such as banks, savings-and-loan associations (building societies), mutual funds and pension funds. Banks, for instance, take deposits from savers, which they use to make loans to borrowers. Mutual funds sell "units" to the public and invest the proceeds in different securities.

The second type of institution is one where savers provide money to firms or governments directly through financial markets. These include the stockmarket, the bond market (government and corporate) and the money market for short-term securities, such as commercial paper. Alongside these markets stand other markets such as those for foreign exchange; and for various instruments derived from standard securities, such as futures, swaps and options (collectively known as "derivatives"), all meant to help the primary markets to work more efficiently.

In a classic analysis of the financial system,[1] Robert Merton and Zvi Bodie, two American economists, identify several important functions that financial intermediaries and markets perform:

- **Clearing and settling payments.** Cheque accounts, credit cards and wire transfers provide means of payment for the exchange of goods and services, and financial assets. The total value of financial payments in America jumped from around five times GDP in the mid-1960s to around 80 times in 1997 (see Figure 2.10). Wire-transfer systems such as FedWire and CHIPs (the Clearing House Interbank Payments System) account for about 85% of all payments by value; cheques and credit cards account for only 13%. But by volume, however, cheques and credit cards account for 98% of transactions.
- **Pooling of savings.** If the owner of a factory had to rely entirely on his own savings, he would be unable to make large capital investments. Big firms such as GM or IBM could not exist.

US payments volume
Ratio to GDP

Sources: R.Merton and Z.Bodie; BIS

FIG 2.10 Money-go-round

Instead, the financial system gives entrepreneurs access to the savings of millions of households. The pooling of savings makes financial assets much more liquid. If you invest all your savings in a neighbour's factory, it is difficult to get your money back quickly if you need it. Financial markets and intermediaries allow people to hold assets in more liquid form, such as shares or bank deposits. By pooling the funds of small savers, mutual funds also reduce transaction costs (eg, brokers' fees) through economies of scale. There has been an increasing concentration of assets in the hands of mutual funds, pension funds and insurance companies. By 1999, institutional investors managed more than two-fifths of American households' financial assets, twice as much as in 1980.

Savers do not like to relinquish control of their savings for long periods, so increased liquidity makes it easier for firms to finance long-term investment. Sir John Hicks, a British economist, argued that the increased liquidity of capital markets and not technological innovation was the critical new ingredient that ignited growth in 18th-century England. Most of the early manufactured products had been invented earlier, but large-scale capital investment was impossible without liquid capital markets. Without a financial revolution, the industrial revolution might never have taken place.

■ **Transfers across time and space.** Financial intermediaries and markets allow individuals to reallocate consumption over their lifetimes. For instance, the young may borrow to buy a house, and the middle-aged may save for their retirement. Likewise a newly emerging economy often requires large amounts of capital to support growth, but more mature economies will tend to have surplus income. An efficient financial system ensures that savings can flow to the most productive industry or economy.

■ **Pooling of risk.** It is risky for an individual to invest all his savings in a single firm, because it could go bust. Financial intermediaries such as mutual funds allow individuals to reduce their risks by diversifying their investment portfolios. By pooling the risks of millions, insurance companies are able to sell protection against future loss – whether through fire, burglary or death. Derivatives can also help firms to manage their risks. For example, a risk-averse firm might use derivatives to hedge against a possible rise in interest rates by shifting the risk to an investor more willing to take it.

■ **Reduce information costs.** The financial system communicates information about borrowers' creditworthiness. Prices of securities provide signals that assist managers in making investment decisions and households in making savings decisions, helping to ensure that funds are efficiently allocated. Banks and capital markets help to reduce "information asymmetries" caused because a borrower tends to know more about his prospects than a lender. An individual finds it costly to obtain information on a borrower's creditworthiness. If a financial intermediary does it on behalf of thousands of such small savers, search costs are reduced. This is not to say that markets are perfect at processing information. They can often be subject to herd behaviour that drives asset prices out of line with fundamentals.

Follow the money

Several empirical studies have confirmed that there is a strong link between financial development and economic growth. Countries with well-developed banking systems and capital markets tend to enjoy faster growth than those without. A study[2] by two economists, Ross Levine and Sara Zervos, examines 47 economies over the period from 1976 to 1993. They find that stockmarket liquidity (the value

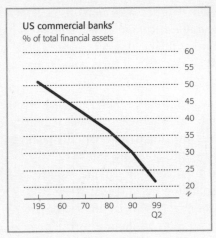

US commercial banks'
% of total financial assets

60
55
50
45
40
35
30
25
20

195   60   70   80   90   99
                            Q2

Source: Federal Reserve

FIG 2.11 Shrinking share

of shares traded relative to stockmarket capitalisation) and the size of the banking sector (measured by lending to the private sector as a percentage of GDP) are good predictors of future rates of growth – even after controlling for other factors such as the initial level of income, education and political stability.

In rich economies the assets of financial intermediaries and the size of stock and bond markets all tend to be bigger in relation to GDP than in poor ones. In emerging economies, the banking system is often quick to develop, but capital markets take longer because they need a financial infrastructure that provides, among other things, adequate accounting standards, a legal system that enforces contracts and protects property rights, and bankruptcy provisions.

Alan Greenspan, when chairman of America's Federal Reserve, stressed the importance of a diversified financial system, which, he argued, helps to cushion an economy in times of stress. For example, when America's banks got into trouble in 1990 as a result of the property bust, capital markets provided an alternative source of finance. And in autumn 1998, when capital-market liquidity dried up, America's banks took up some of the slack.

In contrast, Japan, more heavily dependent on bank lending and with poorly developed corporate-debt markets, has suffered a prolonged credit crunch. East Asia is another example of how countries with narrow capital markets and few alternatives to banks can suffer deep recessions. During the boom times, nobody worried about Asia's dependence on bank lending. "The lack of a spare tyre", said Mr Greenspan, "is no concern if you do not get a flat." Japan and, later, East Asia, found out they were missing one too late.

Notes

1 "A Conceptual Framework for Analysing the Financial Environment", in *The Global Financial System: a Functional Perspective*, Harvard Business School Press, 1995.
2 "Stockmarket, Banks and Economic Growth", *American Economic Review*, June 1998.

Capital bonanzas

Does Wall Street's meltdown show financial globalisation itself is part of the problem?

"THANK GOD," said one Latin American finance minister in 2008. "At least this time it isn't our fault."

The meltdown of America's financial system may look very different from the emerging-market crises that overwhelmed Thailand in 1997 or Russia in 1998. This time there has been no currency collapse, no government default. Then, there were no collateralised-debt obligations or credit-default swaps.

Yet the minister was justified in seeing parallels between America's crisis and the emerging-market episodes. In all of them vast current-account deficits were financed by huge capital inflows. The afflicted countries saw housing speculation, asset bubbles and cheap loans followed by a credit crunch and the seizing up of the financial system. And Wall Street's meltdown raises the same questions as the crises of a decade ago: what will the direct effects on emerging markets be? If the world's richest economies are vulnerable to global financial turmoil, should developing countries not seek to insulate themselves from it?

Two papers[1] cast light on these questions. They conclude that, although financial globalisation has big costs, these can be minimised and potential gains increased by better policy. Financial globalisation itself, they imply, ought to be seen not so much as a bad thing, but as too much of a good one.

Beware markets bearing gifts

Most emerging markets see their ability to attract foreign money as proof of good management. From this point of view, it should be a blessing that private capital flows to developing countries rose, according to the World Bank, to $1 trillion in 2007, the highest ever. Yet if the study by Carmen and Vincent Reinhart is anything to go by, this should be little cause for celebration.

Taking the experience of 181 countries since 1980, the authors reckon that middle- and low-income countries had a roughly 20% chance of suffering a banking crisis and a 30% chance of a currency crisis, external-debt default or inflation spike (to more than 20% a year) if they experienced what the authors call a "capital-flow bonanza" in the three years beforehand. (They define such a bonanza as an unusual shift of the current account into the red, using that as a proxy for capital inflows since the capital and current accounts mirror each other.) These seem unenviable odds.

The authors point out that countries might have suffered disasters anyway, without being showered with money. That turns out to be true – but their chances were quite a bit lower: between 14% and 24% for countries that did not attract so many dollars. In other words, a foreign inflow, as well as financing good things such as public infrastructure and corporate investment, is also associated with debt defaults, inflation and currency crises.

The authors focus on the level of capital flows, rather than their composition. Presumably, countries that attract more foreign direct investment suffer less than those that have a greater amount of footloose portfolio investment or short-term bank lending. But overall, most countries that suck in foreign money show the classic signs of an economic bubble. Using a subset of 66 countries for which there are more detailed figures, the authors show that share prices rose by more than 10% in real terms in the two years before what they call a bonanza, then fell relentlessly for four years, ending below where they started. House prices went up by more than that – 15% in real terms over four years during a bonanza – before falling back.

So why would countries seek out foreign money at all, if its impact is so malign? The answer is that it is not so much the amount of investment that is the trouble; it is its volatility, and especially its tendency to dry up. That makes today's climate worrying. Mansoor Dailami, the World Bank's manager of international finance, said in 2008 that private inflows to emerging markets might fall from $1 trillion to only $800 billion-850 billion during the year. That would be particularly troublesome because of another difference between this crisis and the Asian one: in 1997–98, more debt was sovereign. Now, much of it is corporate, taken out by Indian, Chinese and other emerging-market companies. That implies a global credit tightening could have as big an impact on emerging markets as slowing import demand in the rich world.

Critics of financial globalisation argue that these problems are so great that emerging markets ought to be insulating themselves through capital controls. Many have been doing so. Yet even setting aside doubts about how far this is desirable (it is hard to believe growth in India or Brazil would have reached today's levels without foreign capital), the studies raise questions about whether capital controls are really the right response.

The second study points out that "sudden stops" of capital inflows tend to be an inverted U-shape: the poorest countries are the least vulnerable to global financial shocks; middle-income countries are the most; but, as you get richer and more integrated into global finance, your vulnerability tends to fall again – and that remains true despite the crisis in America. So it might still make sense for countries like India and Brazil to carry on liberalising. Moreover, as the Reinharts show, a big part of the problem is that capital flows are endemically boom-bust: money floods in and out. They argue that fiscal policy should be used to smooth out such cycles: governments should reduce deficits or run surpluses during bonanzas – the opposite of what they usually do. This implies something of a paradox. Capital flows are supposed to be a reward for good economic behaviour. But as Dani Rodrik, a Harvard professor, says, "these policy conclusions turn capital inflows into an imperative for even deeper reform."

Note

1 Carmen Reinhart and Vincent Reinhart, "Capital Flow Bonanzas", National Bureau of Economic Research (NBER) Working Paper No. 14321. Guillermo Calvo, Alejandro Izquierdo and Luis-Fernando Mejía, "Systemic Sudden Stops", NBER Working Paper No. 14026.

The material on pages 26–90 was first published in *The Economist* in September 2008 (pages 26–9 and 88–90), November 2008 (pages 30–2), February 2008 (pages 33–5 and 51–9), September 2005 (pages 36–42), June 2008 (pages 43–6), November 2009 (pages 47–50), March 2008 (pages 60–8), October 2008 (pages 69–71), December 2004 (pages 72–4), May 2009 (pages 75–7), August 2004 (pages 78–80) and October 1999 (pages 81–7).

3 Macroeconomic management: fiscal and monetary policy

Monopoly power over money

Central banks have a huge influence over the financial system. How do they conduct monetary policy?

DURING THE COLD WAR, Russian leaders' every word was scrutinised by an army of Kremlinologists. Now, that honour is accorded to the world's central bankers, whose pronouncements are pored over by throngs of well-paid financial analysts.

For all central banks' importance, they remain tiny participants in huge financial markets. So how do they affect prices, ie, interest rates, in those markets? Consider America. Its fixed-income market (government and private) was worth some $13.6 trillion in 1999. Every day hundreds of billions of dollars of these securities change hands, and it is not unusual for a single private firm to buy or sell more than $1 billion in one go. The Fed itself buys or sells only between $1 billion and $5 billion of these securities each year: a mere drop in the ocean of a $14 trillion market. Yet somehow it affects the level and structure of prices and yields.

The reason the Fed can set interest rates is that it has a monopoly on supplying bank reserves. Banks are required to hold a fraction of the money deposited with them in a reserve account at the Fed (see Figure 3.1). They usually hold more, for precautionary reasons. The interest rate at which banks' demand for reserves matches the Fed's supply is known as the federal funds rate; this is also the rate at which banks lend reserves to each other overnight. The Fed controls it by changing the supply of reserves through sales and purchases

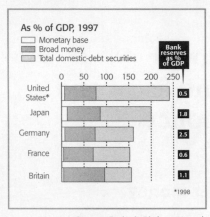

As % of GDP, 1997

☐ Monetary base
▨ Broad money
☐ Total domestic-debt securities

Sources: Benjamin Friedman, Harvard

FIG 3.1 Powerful reserves

of government securities, known as open-market operations.

When the Fed wants to raise the federal funds rate, it sells government securities. It receives payment by reducing the account of the buyer's bank, which reduces the volume of reserves in the banking system. This is illustrated in Figure 3.2 by a shift in the supply curve for reserves from S to S2. Because banks' demand for reserves exceeds supply, the federal funds rate is bid up (from f to f2) until excess demand is eliminated. And when the Fed wants to lower the rate, it buys securities, which increases banks' reserves and bids down interest rates. The supply curve shifts from S to S1, and the rate falls from f to f1.

The Fed can also influence the federal funds rate indirectly, by changing the discount rate (d in Figure 3.2), the rate at which it will lend reserves to banks, or altering banks' reserve requirements, the fraction of their deposits that they are required to hold as reserves. Raising the discount rate makes it less attractive for banks to borrow reserves. This reduces the volume of reserves, which pushes up the federal funds rate. Increasing reserve requirements boosts banks' demand for reserves, which also bids up the federal funds rate. But the Fed usually prefers to control the rate through open-market operations, which have a more stable and predictable impact on the money market.

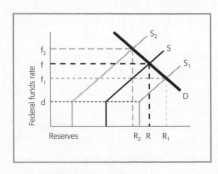

FIG 3.2 Money market

The long and short of it

Changes in the federal funds rate ripple through financial markets and the economy. They have knock-on effects on the interest rates at which banks lend to households and firms, and hence the amount of credit in the economy. And they influence long-term market interest rates too.

Take the yield on a five-year government bond. It is simply the weighted average of expected short-term interest rates over the next five years, plus a risk and a liquidity premium. A rise in short-term interest rates typically has two effects on long-term rates. It raises the five-year weighted average slightly. And it also affects expectations of future short-term interest rates.

If, for example, investors believe the Fed is raising rates pre-emptively to prevent inflation rising, then expected future interest rates may fall, and so would five-year yields. However, if the rate increase is seen as a belated recognition by the Fed that inflation is likely to rise, five-year rates may rise in anticipation of further rate increases to come.

The graphical relationship between interest rates on securities of different maturities is known as the yield curve. Yield curves typically slope upwards, as Germany's does in Figure 3.3, because investors demand a risk premium on bonds of longer maturities to compensate for the extra uncertainty associated with lending for a longer period. But when monetary policy is tightened and short-term interest rates are increased, it is possible sometimes for the yield curve to become inverted, as Britain's is in the chart, sloping downwards for all but the shortest maturities.

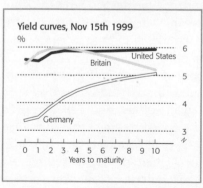

Source: Salomon Smith Barney

FIG 3.3 Di erent slopes

The monetary-policy maze

The simple rules by which central banks lived have crumbled. A messier, more political future awaits

IN THE WORLD that existed before the financial crisis, central bankers were triumphant. They had defeated inflation and tamed the business cycle. And they had developed a powerful intellectual consensus on how to do their job, summarised by David Blanchflower, a former member of the Bank of England's monetary policy committee, as "one tool, one target". The tool was the short-term interest rate, the target was price stability.

This minimalist formula fitted the laissez-faire temper of the times. A growing array of financial markets could price risk and allocate credit efficiently. Central bankers had merely to calibrate their interest-rate tools and all other markets would automatically adjust. Central banks still cared about financial stability and full employment, but could argue these were best served by stabilising prices – without, if you please, interference from politicians.

The financial crisis has upended all that. The business cycle was supposedly subdued, yet the world is in the deepest recession since the 1930s. Deflation has become a more dangerous enemy than inflation; with interest rates in many countries at or close to zero, central banks have had to reach for other tools.

More fundamentally, the collapse of stable relationships in financial markets has forced central banks to make judgments they once left to the private sector. From lenders of last resort, they became lenders of first resort when banks stopped trusting each other. They are, increasingly, arbiters of which types of borrowers get credit. With the reputation of market discipline in tatters, central bankers will get vast new supervisory powers. All this is dragging central banks back towards political turf from which they had been distancing themselves for years.

Central bankers still believe that once the crisis has passed they will return to their pre-2007 roles as apolitical technocrats pulling

Changes in central-bank operations since 2007

	Lending operations				Outright purchases				Bail-outs,
	More counter-parties	More liberal collateral	Longer term	Foreign exchange swaps	Foreign exchange	Equities	Private debt	Gov't debt	capital injections
Australia		✔	✔	✔					
Britain		✔	✔	✔			✔	✔	✔
Canada	✔	✔	✔	✔			possible	possible	
Euro area		✔	✔	✔			possible	possible	
Japan		✔	✔			✔	✔	✔	possible
Sweden	✔	✔	✔	✔					
Switzerland		✔	✔		✔				✔
United States	✔	✔	✔	✔			✔	✔	✔

Source: Central banks

FIG 3.4 Broader-minded banking

a single lever and eyeing a single variable. It may be a vain hope. "When you question the basic premise which you have worked under for the last 15 to 20 years, which is that markets are rational and efficient, there is a case for a different approach to both monetary policy and regulation," says Thomas Mayer, chief European economist of Deutsche Bank.

Start with the most immediate question: what tools will central banks use to steer the economy in the near future? Before the crisis almost all leading central banks operated through the short-term (usually overnight) money-market rate. By itself, that rate mattered much less to economic activity than, say, those on 12-month corporate loans or 30-year mortgages. But the links between these and official rates were stable enough to allow the central banks to influence overall financial conditions and hence the entire economy.

Those links came under strain before the crisis, as a global saving glut caused a decoupling of long- and short-term rates. During the crisis they disintegrated as lenders worried that loans could not be sold on or would not be repaid. Central banks responded by expanding their lending operations through a mixture of more types of credit and collateral, longer terms and more counterparties (see Figure 3.4).

The Federal Reserve began lending to investment banks. The European Central Bank (ECB) guaranteed unlimited funds for up to six months instead of one week. Some have gone much further. The Bank of Japan has bought equities and the Swiss National Bank has intervened in the currency markets.

Central bankers assume they will wind down these measures when the crisis ends. The Fed, for example, is required by law to end some when the need is no longer urgent. It charges a penalty for some programmes so that borrowers will return to private markets once these have healed. An exit strategy is necessary to "end up with a market-based economy that is more balanced and more resilient," Donald Kohn, the Fed's vice-chairman, has said. Mervyn King, governor of the Bank of England, has said the exit strategy will be dictated by the outlook for inflation and that central banks should not support markets that cannot survive on their own.

In need of new targets

But withdrawal may be harder than it sounds. A 2008 study by IMF staff asked, "What will 'normal' look like?" It argued: "There is no expectation that markets will return to their pre-crisis mode of operation soon, if ever. Market spreads taking account of credit and liquidity risk had arguably become too compressed pre-August 2007, and are now wider than they should be long-term. But it is not clear what the appropriate level should be."

After the Bank of Japan became the primary supplier of overnight funds to banks earlier this decade, the interbank market atrophied. It remains a fraction of its former size. European banks today are now heavily dependent on the Fed for dollars (supplied via swap lines with local central banks) and on the ECB for six-month euro funds.

A tepid recovery will make central banks reluctant to withdraw support from critical markets, especially if business or politicians protest. In 1942 the Fed agreed to hold down long-term interest rates to help the Treasury finance the war; it did not extract itself from the commitment until 1951. When the time comes to sell its large holdings of mortgage debt, it may face resistance from America's housing lobby.

Central banks may not just have to rethink their tools. They may also have to rethink their goals. Governments and central banks had come to agree that they should focus only on achieving low and stable inflation. The Fed by law must emphasise employment and inflation equally, but in practice it, too, targets inflation. This consensus was forged in central banks' research departments and universities, and its adoption paralleled a rise by academics to the top ranks of central banks: among the leading lights are not only Ben Bernanke, chairman of the Fed, and Mr King but also Lucas Papademos, vice-president of the ECB, and Lars Svensson, a deputy governor of Sweden's Riksbank.

Macroeconomics in general has come under fire for depending too much on assumptions of efficient markets and its inability to incorporate the spasms of emotion that create economic manias and panics. "As a monetary policymaker I have found the 'cutting edge' of current macroeconomic research totally inadequate in helping to resolve the problems we currently face," said Mr Blanchflower, a labour economist, in a speech he gave on March 24th 2009.

The exclusive focus on low and stable inflation is being questioned for the same reason. The recession began against a backdrop of price stability – as did America's Depression and Japan's lost decade. "Inflation targeting alone will not suffice," Mr Blanchflower said. "This approach failed to prevent the build-up of imbalances that presaged the crisis and was insufficient in dealing with failing banks and financial-market stress as the crisis developed. There is now a consensus that new tools are required to regulate the financial sector and prevent such crises in the future."

Mr Bernanke and his predecessor, Alan Greenspan, argued before the crisis that bubbles are hard to identify before they burst. Pricking them is even harder without wrecking the economy. Central banks should act only if bubbles threaten price stability; otherwise, they should wait and clean up after they burst. The shallow recession that followed the tech-stock boom of the late 1990s seemed to vindicate them.

Recent experience does not help their argument. William White, who retired in 2008 as chief economist of the Bank for International Settlements, argues that because central banks were focused on price

Consumer-price inflation rates, %

O Forecast, 2010   ▉ Target level or range

Japan
Switzerland
United States
Sweden
Canada
Euro area
Britain
Australia

*Not a formal target   †Below 2
‡Below but close to 2

Sources: IMF; Central banks

FIG 3.5 Undershooting

stability in the medium term, they allowed bubbles to form. The bursting of these raises the risk of deflation in the long run.

Inflation in many countries was negative in 2009 mainly because of cheaper fuel. But even in 2010, as that effect faded, inflation was expected to stay below the 2% most central banks define as price stability. In a forecast, published on April 22nd 2009, the IMF said prices would fall in America, Japan and Switzerland (see Figure 3.5).

To be sure, many central banks are more sanguine, noting that inflation expectations are, in the jargon, well-anchored. Many in the market fear that once the crisis passes central banks will be too slow to raise rates and wind down their credit programmes, unleashing inflation. But persistently falling prices would constrain central banks' ability to boost growth, because they would be unable to push interest rates below inflation – ie, make them negative in real terms. Using the Taylor rule, a popular rule of thumb, economists at Deutsche Bank suggest that given today's degree of economic slack and inflation rates, short-term rates should be negative in America, Britain and the euro area. Instead, they are at or near zero (see Figure 3.6). Were deflation to deepen, real interest rates would rise, further hampering economic activity.

Eric Rosengren, president of the Federal Reserve Bank of Boston, noted recently that the Fed has hit, or all but hit, the zero limit twice this decade. That is more often than earlier simulations had indicated – and it suggests higher inflation targets should be considered. Another proposal is that central banks aim at a path for the price level rather than the inflation rate. Suppose that this path rose by 2% each year. Then after deflation of 1% in year one, the central bank would aim for

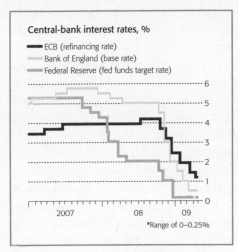

Central-bank interest rates, %

━━ ECB (refinancing rate)
▬▬ Bank of England (base rate)
▬▬ Federal Reserve (fed funds target rate)

2007   08   09
*Range of 0–0.25%

Source: Thomson Datastream

FIG 3.6 The limit of normality

inflation of more than 2% in later years (inflation of 5% in year two, say) to bring prices back up to the target. Greg Mankiw, a Harvard University economist, goes further, suggesting that inflation simply be given lower priority. "There are worse things than inflation," he says. "We have them today."

Altering or abandoning inflation targets would make a big dent in the credibility that central banks took decades to establish and is therefore highly unlikely. And although benign neglect of bubbles no longer appears an option, central bankers are not ready to advocate pre-emptive popping, because the problem of identifying them early enough remains unsolved. Better, they argue, to use regulation to identify and defuse dangerous accumulations of risk in the financial system.

The term for this is "macroprudential" supervision. In 2008 Mr Bernanke laid out how this would differ from the normal supervision of individual banks. He said a single firm may have an acceptable exposure to a particular type of risk that would be unacceptable if replicated across many firms. Similarly, a supervisor might press a particular bank to lend less during a slump whereas a "macroprudential supervisor would recognise that, for the system as a whole," that could make matters worse.

The embrace of macroprudential supervision represents a reversal of another pre-2007 trend – for central banks to shed supervisory duties and concentrate on monetary policy. Academics argued that supervision was a distraction from the pursuit of price stability and created potential conflicts: a central bank might run an inflationary policy to cushion a failing banking system, or prop up an insolvent bank to cushion the economy. Central banks in Australia and Britain gave up some or all of their supervisory roles. The ECB was created with none.

The run on Northern Rock, a British bank, and problems at state-owned German banks were blamed in part on inadequate involvement by the central bank in supervision. In 2009 the Bank of England received a more formal role in overseeing banks. A commission headed by Jacques de Larosière, a former head of both the Bank of France and the IMF, has recommended that the ECB chair a new European Systemic Risk Council made up of its member central banks and supervisors, but that it remain out of firm-specific supervision. The Fed until recently was the leading candidate to fill the American Treasury's proposed job of "systemic risk regulator", empowered to examine any corner of the financial system and act against emerging risks.

Yet macroprudential supervision smacks of a fad that will not live up to its billing. It faces the same difficulty as conventional monetary policy does in spotting and popping bubbles. Moreover, there has been no correlation between a central bank's supervisory responsibilities and its ability to prevent or deal with the crisis. The Fed is America's most powerful and best informed financial regulator but the trouble began under its nose. Neither Australia's central bank nor Canada's has any supervisory duties, yet the financial systems of both countries have been virtually unscathed. This record has less to do with who supervises the financial system than with local laws and behaviour. Subprime mortgages peaked at about 1% of the total in Australia and 2.5% in Canada, compared with more than 14% in the United States.

New combatants in the political arena

Rightly or wrongly, central banks will emerge from the crisis with a bigger role in the markets and in supervision. This will challenge another element of the pre-2007 consensus: that central banks be as far removed from politics as possible. Formal independence insulated the central bank from politicians' desire to play fast and loose with inflation. And part of the appeal of "one tool, one target" was that it made monetary policy explicitly a technical rather than political affair.

The divide between central banking and politics looks much less clean today. Unconventional policies often require a central bank to make loans that may not be repaid in full. Because taxpayers will bear any losses, finance ministries need some say. Credit allocation and tighter regulation make some firms winners and others losers, and so require more public accountability. With interest rates at zero, the Fed and the Bank of England are buying government debt to boost the quantity of credit and the money supply. But governments could come to rely on such purchases to finance budget deficits. The potential for political conflict extends abroad too. Having cut its rates to zero, the Swiss National Bank has bought foreign currency to drive down the Swiss franc. Some labelled this competitive devaluation.

Managing such conflicts is a delicate job. The Fed and the Treasury attempted to assuage concerns by releasing a joint statement affirming the Fed's sole responsibility for price stability. Mr King broke a longstanding silence on fiscal policy to warn the British government against adding to a fast-growing national debt.

Such tensions are unlikely seriously to dent the institutional protections built around central banks in recent decades. In 2008 Japanese opposition parties blocked the appointments of two candidates to head the Bank of Japan on the ground they were insufficiently independent of the government. There are exceptions: Iceland's government amended the law so that it could fire David Oddsson, the head of its central bank. But Mr Oddsson had presided, first as prime minister and then as central-bank governor, over the policies that led to the country's crisis.

Central bankers' jobs matter even more than they did before 2007. At the same time, they have been drawing more criticism and political scrutiny. Public disapproval ratings have risen notably for Mr Bernanke, the Bank of England and the ECB. They are having to defend their policies to the public as well as to the markets. Mr Bernanke agreed to a profile by "60 Minutes", a news programme, in which he strolled down the streets of his hometown. Mr King sat for an interview with the BBC to explain quantitative easing. The six members of the ECB's executive board gave 200 interviews in 2008.

After the Riksbank slashed its interest-rate target to 0.5% on April 21st 2009, its governor, Stefan Ingves, took questions from the public in an online chat session. Asked what he liked most about his job, the former economics professor said that what he used to study in theory he now gets to put into practice. He added: "It's fun to go to work every day." You may wonder how many of his peers would agree with him.

The state's take

Governments differ dramatically in how they tax – and how much they raise

THANKS TO THE COLLATERAL DAMAGE from the financial crisis, government deficits have surged across the rich world. Once the recovery is entrenched this fiscal deterioration will need to be tackled. Although spending cuts could, and should, be the preferred route to prudence, taxes are all too likely to be part of the mix – at least judging from the experience of those countries that have already acted. Spain raised its value-added tax rate (VAT) from 16% to 18%. Ireland raised its top income tax rate from 41% to 46%. In both Britain and America current law promises higher future tax rates on wealthier folk.

The economic consequences of raising taxes will depend not just on the scale of the tax increase, but also on how the revenue is raised. The less efficient the type of taxation, the greater the burden on the economy. There is already striking variation in the size of the state and the structure of taxation, both among advanced economies, and between them and their emerging counterparts. Comparing countries' tax takes can offer useful clues to the most efficient ways to raise funds in future.

Figure 3.7 compares government revenue and its sources for some of the world's biggest rich and emerging economies. The state looms largest in France, where almost 50% of GDP flowed through the government's coffers in 2007. In China, in contrast, government revenue accounts for less than 20% of GDP. Broadly speaking, total government revenues (including both central and local) are a bigger share of the economy in continental Europe than in Anglo-Saxon economies, and are higher in richer economies than in poorer ones without generous social safety-nets. But not all emerging economies have a low tax burden. At almost 35% of GDP, Brazil's government revenue is bigger relative to the size of its economy than America's.

Taxes of varying kinds form the bulk of governments' revenues. But non-tax receipts – such as profits from state-owned enterprises

– are often significant sources of cash, especially for commodity exporters. Russia's overall government revenue, which includes oil proceeds, is almost 50% of GDP. Its tax take is closer to 30%.

These broad ratios suggest that there is less room to increase taxes in Europe than elsewhere. But they mask big differences in how governments raise their funds. Anglo-Saxon economies tend to rely most on income taxes (on wages, profits and capital gains). In Australia 60% of tax revenue is raised from such levies. In America it is almost 50%. Most governments gain the bulk of their income-tax revenue from individuals, though in both Japan and South Korea almost half the total is extracted from firms. Contrary to popular perception, European countries rely much less on corporate taxes than America does.

European countries reap a bigger share of revenue from payroll taxes and other social contributions, as well as from indirect taxes on spending. France and Germany gain more than 40% of their tax take from social contributions and around a quarter from expenditure taxes, particularly VAT. America, the only industrial country without a VAT, gets only a sixth of its government revenue from expenditure taxes, most of that through sales taxes at the state and local level. Brazil's tax structure roughly mirrors that of European countries, while China and India raise more money from indirect taxes than any other big economies. Over 60% of China's central government tax revenue comes from expenditure taxes.

How best to inflict pain

Which of these combinations is best for economic growth? In theory, expenditure taxes are better than income taxes, since they do not punish saving. Flat tax-rates on a broad base are less distortive than high marginal rates on a narrow base. By the same token, taxes on things that cannot be moved easily, such as property, are less distortive than taxes on mobile economic agents, particularly firms. Among expenditure taxes, a flat tax-rate on final goods is less distortive than a panoply of excise taxes since it affects spending decisions less. (That said, sometimes, such as with carbon taxes, the goal is to influence decisions.)

An analysis of the relationship between tax structure and growth in 21 rich countries between 1970 and 2004 by Jens Arnold of the

Government taxation, 2007

	Advanced economies									BRICs			
	Australia	Britain	Canada	France	Germany	Italy	Japan*	South Korea	United States	Brazil	China*	India	Russia
Total revenue†, % GDP	35.9	41.8	41.4	49.6	43.8	46.4	34.5	33.6	33.7	34.8	18.1	22.3	47.7
Total tax, % GDP	29.5	37.7	34.8	44.7	40.4	43.0	28.2	28.7	28.0	32.3	16.4	18.9	33.2
Total tax, $bn§	268.5	1,055.6	496.7	1,161.2	1,344.6	910.5	1,230.2	301.1	3,941.7	430.7	435.9	207.8	429.7
Structure, % of total tax													
Income and capital**	59.2	37.8	49.9	23.4	30.9	34.2	35.4	37.6‡	48.3	32.3‡	28.4‡	47.7‡	26.0
people	*37.5*	*28.7*	*36.2*	*16.7*	*23.5*	*26.7*	*18.5*	*19.6‡*	*37.5*	*na*	*7.4‡*	*17.1‡*	*na*
companies	*21.2*	*9.1*	*12.4*	*6.6*	*3.4*	*7.5*	*17.0*	*17.9‡*	*10.8*	*na*	*21.0‡*	*30.7‡*	*na*
Employment	4.5	nil	1.9	2.7	nil	nil	nil	nil‡	nil	6.0‡	nil‡	nil‡	9.5
Property	9.1	12.0	9.7	10.2	2.1	1.9	9.1	4.4‡	10.9	0.1‡	0.9‡	0.1‡	nil
Goods and services**	25.4	28.1	22.4	24.1	26.2	28.7	18.6	30.3‡	15.6	25.3‡	64.9‡	34.1‡	24.2
consumption	*13.2*	*17.0*	*13.7*	*15.7*	*17.0*	*14.1*	*9.2*	*20.7‡*	*7.6*	*na*	*49.0‡*	*0.2‡*	*na*
excise	*7.4*	*8.5*	*4.4*	*4.5*	*6.5*	*4.8*	*7.4*	*9.6‡*	*3.5*	*na*	*15.3‡*	*23.8‡*	*na*
Other	1.8	nil	1.0	nil	nil	4.4	nil	9.4‡	0.7	11.5‡	5.8‡	18.0‡	22.0
Social contributions	nil	22.0	15.0	40.2	40.8	30.8	36.6	18.3‡	24.5	24.9‡	nil‡	0.2‡	18.3

*2006 data   †Taxation plus other government income   §At market prices   **Sub-categories are not exhaustive   ‡Central government only

Sources: CEIC; IMF; OECD; National statistics offices

FIG 3.7 On top of the world

OECD bears out these theoretical insights. He found property taxes were the least damaging to growth, followed by consumption taxes. Income taxes were the least growth-friendly, especially those levied on firms. The study suggests that shifting tax revenues from income to consumption and property taxes could have a significant impact on GDP per head.

Most tax systems have become more growth-friendly in recent decades. The top rate of marginal income tax in OECD economies, for instance, has fallen from an average of almost 70% in 1981 to just over 40%, with the biggest declines in Japan and America. Still, America's tax system stands out as one of the least efficient. The heavy reliance on income taxation is compounded by the narrowness of the tax base, thanks to oodles of complexity-inducing deductions. Though Europeans still rely too much on job-deterring social contributions, they have been able to extract higher revenues overall thanks to greater use of more efficient taxes, especially VAT.

Expenditure taxes are not always well designed, however, particularly in federal countries. Brazil has long been trying to reform its VAT, which is levied in a fragmented manner at the state rather than national level. India, too, is trying to reform its potpourri of expenditure taxes. China's heavy reliance on consumption taxes may not be optimal in an economy that saves too much and spends too little.

Nor is tax policy only about efficiency. Politicians also care about fairness and political appeal. Property taxes may be non-distorting, but they are deeply unpopular with voters. Tax progressivity is often at odds with efficiency. A VAT, for instance, falls disproportionately on poorer people who spend a higher share of their income than richer folk. Thanks to its reliance on income taxes, America – by some measures – has the most progressive tax system in the OECD. Different countries will always strike different compromises between efficiency, fairness and simplicity. But as their debt burdens rise, the world's big rich economies would do well to focus most on efficiency.

Tax from scratch

A new report lays out a blueprint for the ideal tax system

"DEATH, TAXES AND CHILDBIRTH! There's never any convenient time for any of them," wrote Margaret Mitchell in "Gone With the Wind". There may also be no convenient time for radical tax reform. But the global recession, which reduced tax receipts even as it forced governments to spend unprecedented amounts to prop up their economies, has left government budgets across the rich world in tatters. Many countries will have to make some changes to their tax systems as a result. A group of economists, headed by Sir James Mirrlees, a Nobel-prize-winning founder of the modern theory of optimal taxation, urged governments to do more than tinker at the margins.

The economists acknowledge that taxation always imposes economic costs, both because money is needed to collect taxes and because it distorts people's consumption and work choices. But in a review of Britain's tax system from the Institute for Fiscal Studies, a think-tank, which was released on November 10th 2010, they argue that most governments could find a way to raise the amount of money they need from the tax system while imposing much lower costs than they currently do.

The economists propose a tax system with three main features. It would be progressive (that is, it would place a larger burden on richer people); it would not discriminate between income earned in different ways; and it would be simple. Such ideals are not new, of course, but Sir James and his colleagues contrast them with Britain's current system, which they describe as being marked by "a jumble of tax rates, a lack of a coherent vision of the tax base, and arbitrary discrimination across different types of economic activities". Other rich-world countries also fall short.

Most income-tax systems are already progressive, and who could disagree with a simpler system? The challenge lies in reconciling these principles. In practice progressivity has tended to imply more than one rate of tax, for instance, which is necessarily less simple than a flat tax rate. The Mirrlees review has some useful ideas on how to square the circle: indeed, perhaps its biggest message is that thinking holistically about the tax system helps resolve some of these conflicts. It is the system as a whole that needs to be progressive, not every single tax.

For example, Britain and Ireland justify not charging value-added tax (VAT) on a number of "essential" products like children's clothing on the ground that doing so would hurt the poor, who spend more of their income on these goods. But such a system distorts people's choices. Moving to a single rate of VAT without exemptions would eliminate this distortion but it would also be regressive. No matter, argue the economists: far better to have undistorted consumption choices and to fulfil the government's redistributive aims more efficiently through the income-tax system. The report reckons that the British government could get rid of most reduced- and zero-rate VAT, compensate those whose welfare was hurt and still have £3 billion ($4.8 billion) left over. As Richard Blundell of University College, London, points out, one of the more redistributive societies on earth, Denmark, does pretty much what the panel recommends.

The Mirrlees review also has some interesting thoughts on progressivity itself. This is usually taken to mean that people who earn more should pay a larger share of their income as tax. But the economists argue that people whose income is temporarily low – perhaps because they have taken time out to study – often borrow and therefore consume more than their immediate income would allow. Basing taxes partly on expenditure rather than just income would therefore go some way towards the ideal of progressivity over a person's lifetime. How that might be implemented is a different question entirely.

The economists also worry that many tax systems, including Britain's, do not provide enough incentives for people to work. Here they recommend a departure from simplicity, urging governments to use the tax system to target incentives to those who will be most responsive. This might involve making tax rates conditional on certain demographic features such as age. Mothers of school-age children, for instance, could be urged back into the workforce by changing the way child tax credits are structured, making them more generous when the child is younger than five and less generous afterwards.

The authors reckon that this change could increase employment in Britain by 52,000, or 0.2%. Similarly, using the tax system to give those nearing retirement age a bigger incentive to keep working could increase employment by 157,000 and add £2 billion to British national income.

The report also argues that the costs of generating income should not be taxed. This has some interesting implications. Since forgoing consumption in order to save money can be thought of as the "cost" of future income, the report suggests that the normal, or risk-free, return on saving should not be taxed, but that returns above this amount should be taxed exactly like other income. More generally, the report says tax systems should not differentiate between income earned in different ways – between working for someone else, say, and self-employment.

But will it happen?

The economists are well aware of the enormous political difficulty such reforms would face. But they argue that elements of the optimal tax system already exist in some countries. The report advocates a corporate-tax deduction equal to a fraction of a firm's outstanding equity, which is designed to remove the bias towards debt finance when interest is deductible. James Poterba of the Massachusetts Institute of Technology, a member of the group, points out that this concept has been implemented in several countries, including Brazil, Austria and Croatia. Even if few governments are likely to undertake wide-ranging reform of the type the group advocates, having an idea of what a better tax system might look like is no bad thing.

Much ado about multipliers

Why do economists disagree so much on whether fiscal stimulus works?

IT IS THE biggest peacetime fiscal expansion in history. Across the globe countries have countered the recession by cutting taxes and by boosting government spending. The G20 group of large and emerging economies introduced stimulus packages worth an average of 2% of GDP in 2009 and 1.6% of GDP in 2010. Co-ordinated action on this scale might suggest a consensus about the effects of fiscal stimulus. But economists are in fact deeply divided about how well, or indeed whether, such stimulus works.

The debate hinges on the scale of the "fiscal multiplier". This measure, first formalised in 1931 by Richard Kahn, a student of John Maynard Keynes, captures how effectively tax cuts or increases in government spending stimulate output. A multiplier of one means that a $1 billion increase in government spending will increase a country's GDP by $1 billion.

The size of the multiplier is bound to vary according to economic conditions. For an economy operating at full capacity, the fiscal multiplier should be zero. Since there are no spare resources, any increase in government demand would just replace spending elsewhere. But in a recession, when workers and factories lie idle, a fiscal boost can increase overall demand. And if the initial stimulus triggers a cascade of expenditure among consumers and businesses, the multiplier can be well above one.

The multiplier is also likely to vary according to the type of fiscal action. Government spending on building a bridge may have a bigger multiplier than a tax cut if consumers save a portion of their tax windfall. A tax cut targeted at poorer people may have a bigger impact on spending than one for the affluent, since poorer folk tend to spend a higher share of their income.

Crucially, the overall size of the fiscal multiplier also depends on how people react to higher government borrowing. If the government's actions bolster confidence and revive animal spirits, the multiplier could rise as demand goes up and private investment is "crowded in". But if interest rates climb in response to government borrowing then some private investment that would otherwise have occurred could get "crowded out". And if consumers expect higher future taxes in order to finance new government borrowing, they could spend less today. All that would reduce the fiscal multiplier, potentially to below zero.

Different assumptions about the impact of higher government borrowing on interest rates and private spending explain wild variations in the estimates of multipliers from today's stimulus spending. Economists in the Obama administration, who assume that the federal funds rate stays constant for a four-year period, expect a multiplier of 1.6 for government purchases and 1.0 for tax cuts from America's fiscal stimulus. An alternative assessment by John Cogan, Tobias Cwik, John Taylor and Volker Wieland uses models in which interest rates and taxes rise more quickly in response to higher public borrowing. Their multipliers are much smaller. They think America's stimulus will boost GDP by only one-sixth as much as the Obama team expects.

When forward-looking models disagree so dramatically, careful analysis of previous fiscal stimuli ought to help settle the debate. Unfortunately, it is extremely tricky to isolate the impact of changes in fiscal policy. One approach is to use microeconomic case studies to examine consumer behaviour in response to specific tax rebates and cuts. These studies, largely based on tax changes in America, find that permanent cuts have a bigger impact on consumer spending than temporary ones and that consumers who find it hard to borrow, such as those close to their credit-card limit, tend to spend more of their tax windfall. But case studies do not measure the overall impact of tax cuts or spending increases on output.

An alternative approach is to try to tease out the statistical impact of changes in government spending or tax cuts on GDP. The difficulty here is to isolate the effects of fiscal-stimulus measures from the rises in social-security spending and falls in tax revenues that naturally accompany recessions. This empirical approach has narrowed the range of estimates in some areas. It has also yielded interesting cross-country comparisons. Multipliers are bigger in closed economies than open ones (because less of the stimulus leaks abroad via imports). They have traditionally been bigger in rich countries than emerging ones (where investors tend to take fright more quickly, pushing interest rates up). But overall economists find as big a range of multipliers from empirical estimates as they do from theoretical models.

These times are different

To add to the confusion, the post-war experiences from which statistical analyses are drawn differ in vital respects from the current situation. Most of the evidence on multipliers for government spending is based on military outlays, but today's stimulus packages are heavily focused on infrastructure. Interest rates in many rich countries are now close to zero, which may increase the potency of, as well as the need for, fiscal stimulus. Because of the financial crisis relatively more people face borrowing constraints, which would increase the effectiveness of a tax cut. At the same time, highly indebted consumers may now be keen to cut their borrowing, leading to a lower multiplier. And investors today have more reason to be worried about rich countries' fiscal positions than those of emerging markets.

Add all this together and the truth is that economists are flying blind. They can make relative judgments with some confidence. Temporary tax cuts pack less punch than permanent ones, for instance. Fiscal multipliers will probably be lower in heavily indebted economies than in prudent ones. But policymakers looking for precise estimates are deluding themselves.

Note

A list of relevant papers is available at Economist.com/multipliers

The material on pages 91–112 was first published in The Economist in November 1999 (pages 91–3), April 2009 (pages 94–102), November 2009 (pages 103–6), October 2010 (pages 107–9) and September 2009 (pages 110–12).

4　Microeconomics: the economics of everything

A biased market

Skewed news reporting is taken as a sign of a dysfunctional media. In fact, it may be a sign of healthy competition

BARACK OBAMA told a writer for the *New York Times Magazine* that he was convinced he might be two or three percentage points better off in the polls for the 2008 American presidential election if Fox News, a right-leaning television station, did not exist. Sarah Palin, the Republican nominee for vice-president, made hay railing against the bias of the "liberal media". Allegations of partial news reporting are common in American politics. But few stop to ask what leads to differences in the way the news is reported.

Bias can be thought of as a supply-side phenomenon that arises from ideology. Owners' or employees' political views will determine how a newspaper or channel slants its coverage of a piece of news. But this does not square with the assumption that readers and viewers value accuracy. If so, then competition should hurt media outlets that systematically distort the news (in any direction). The brouhaha about bias in America, as free a media market as any, suggests something else is going on.

The key to understanding why bias flourishes in a competitive market may lie in thinking more clearly about what readers actually want. Sendhil Mullainathan and Andrei Shleifer, two Harvard economists, argued in an influential paper[1] that it may be naive to think that people care about accuracy alone. Instead, they modelled the consequences of assuming that newspaper readers also like to have their beliefs confirmed by what they read. As long as readers have different beliefs, the Mullainathan-Shleifer model suggests that competition, far from driving biased reporting out of the market, would encourage newspapers to cater to the biases of different segments of the reading public. A later paper[2] by Matthew Gentzkow and Jesse Shapiro, two economists at the University of Chicago's business school, set out to test this proposition.

To do so, they first needed a way to measure the political slant of American news coverage. Their solution was rather imaginative. The researchers ran computer programs that analysed debates in Congress and identified phrases that were disproportionately used by Republicans or Democrats. The list of frequent Democratic phrases, for example, included "estate tax". While talking about the same issue, Republicans tended to use the phrase "death tax". (This is not just coincidence. Mr Gentzkow and Mr Shapiro quote an anonymous Republican staffer as saying that the party machine trained members to say "death tax", because "'estate tax' sounds like it hits only the wealthy but 'death tax' sounds like it hits everyone".) Having identified partisan phrases, the academics then analysed the news coverage of more than 400 American newspapers to see how often they cropped up in reporting. This gave them a precise measure of "slant", showing the extent to which the news coverage in these papers tended to use politically charged phrases.

Mr Gentzkow and Mr Shapiro then needed to assess the political beliefs of different newspapers' readerships, which they did using data on the share of votes in each newspaper's market that went to President Bush in the 2004 presidential elections, and information on how likely people in different parts of that market were to contribute to entities allied to either Democrats or Republicans. The researchers were now able to look at the relationships between circulation, slant, and people's political views.

First, they measured whether a newspaper's circulation responded to the match between its slant and its readers' views. Not surprisingly, they found that more "Republican" newspapers had relatively higher circulations in more "Republican" zip codes. But their calculations of the degree to which circulation responded to political beliefs also allowed them to do something more interesting: to calculate what degree of slant would be most profitable for each newspaper in their sample to adopt, given the political make-up of the market it covered.

They compared this profit-maximising slant to their measure of the actual slant of each newspaper's coverage.

They found a striking congruence between the two. Newspapers tended, on average, to locate themselves neither to the right nor to the left of the level of slant that Mr Gentzkow and Mr Shapiro reckon would maximise their profits. And for good commercial reasons: their model showed that even a minor deviation from this "ideal" level of slant would hurt profits through a sizeable loss of circulation.

Have I got skews for you

Showing that newspapers have a political slant that is economically rational does not necessarily answer the question of whether owner-ship or demand determines bias. Here, the academics are helped by the fact that large media companies may own several newspapers, often in markets that are politically very different. This allowed them to test whether the slants of newspapers with the same owner were more strongly correlated than those of two newspapers picked at random. They found that this was not so: owners exerted a negligible influence on slant. Readers' political views explained about a fifth of measured slant, while ownership explained virtually none.

None of this is particularly helpful to seekers of the unvarnished truth. These conscientious sorts still have to find the time to read lots of newspapers to get an unbiased picture of the world. But by serving demand from a variety of political niches, competition does allow for different points of view to be represented. After all, just as Mrs Palin does not spend her time condemning Fox News, Mr Obama is unlikely to have too many complaints about the *New York Times*.

Notes

1 "The Market for News", *American Economic Review*, September 2005.
2 "What Drives Media Slant? Evidence from U.S. Daily Newspapers", May 2007. http://faculty.chicagogsb.edu/matthew.gentzkow/biasmeas081507.pdf

Commons sense

Why it still pays to study medieval English landholding and Sahelian nomadism

IN 1968 GARRETT HARDIN, a professor of biology, published an article in the journal *Science* that was to have a profound impact on the social sciences, including economics. In it, he explained "The Tragedy of the Commons". "Picture a pasture open to all," he wrote. A herdsman grazing his animals on the land will have an incentive "to add another animal to his herd. And another; and another ... But this is the conclusion reached by each and every rational herdsman sharing a commons. Therein is the tragedy." Each herdsman captures all the benefit from an extra animal but the cost of overgrazing is borne by all.

Hardin's example was not new. It was first mentioned by a mathematician, William Foster Lloyd, in 1833; the idea goes back to Aristotle. But it struck a chord. The idea seemed plausible in itself and was borne out by history. Britain had had a system of common land before the 18th century; its enclosure (privatisation by landowners) made possible the agricultural revolution.

Hardin's analysis suggested two things. First, that the commons are somehow backward, characteristic of tribes living in rainforests, or of pastoral nomads in African drylands. Second, that tragedy is inevitable. From the point of view of efficiency, the commons should probably be replaced by systems of public or personal ownership. An unsolvable problem of the past might not seem like fertile ground for debate. But 40 years after Hardin's article, the problem of the commons is still pressing.

It is not simply that three-quarters of those living on less than $2 a day still depend in some way on commonly held resources. The concept of the commons is also spreading to new areas. Their essential feature is that they share one characteristic with private property and one with public goods. Like public goods, they are not "excludable": the common resource is too extensive to keep people out very easily. But they are also "subtractable" (or "rivalrous"), like private property: if one person uses them, another's access is diminished. (With a classic public good, such as street lighting, one person's usage does not affect anyone else.) Many things other than rainforests or drylands share these attributes.

Indeed an entire industry seems to have sprung up to identify "new commons" (such as the internet) or to claim as commons things not always seen that way. Silence, for example, should arguably be seen as a commons, because if one person interrupts it, there is less of it for others to enjoy. At the biennial meeting of the International Association for the Study of the Commons in July 2008, Charlotte Hess of Syracuse University extended the concept of the commons from traditional natural resources to things such as medicine, knowledge and what are usually seen as global public goods, like the oceans and Antarctica.[1]

The other implication of Hardin's analysis – that the commons are doomed – came under attack early on. When economists began to look at how systems of commonly managed resources actually worked, they found to their surprise that they often worked quite well. Swiss Alpine pastures; Japanese forests; irrigation systems in Spain and the Philippines. All these were examples of commons that lasted for decades. Some irrigation networks held in common were more efficiently run than the public and private systems that worked alongside them. Though there were failures, too, it seemed as if good management could stave off the tragedy. Before he died, Hardin admitted he should have called his article "The Tragedy of the Unmanaged Commons".

In "Governing the Commons", which was published in 1990, Elinor Ostrom of Indiana University described the rules needed to keep a commons going. She showed that there are almost always elaborate conventions over who can use resources and when. What you take out of a commons has to be proportional to what you put in. Usage has to be compatible with the commons' underlying health (ie, you cannot just keep grazing your animals regardless). Everyone has to have some say in the rules. And people usually pay more attention to monitoring abuses and to conflict resolution than to sanctions and punishment.

The comedy of the commons

Defining the commons is also vital. In systems run by a few families, people are very precise about which bit of forest or seashore they manage. In systems too large for a single group, there are layers of decision-making: the nomads of the Sahel, for example, used to have overlapping informal authorities up and down the Niger river. Tragedy often occurs when governments come along in hobnailed boots and trample over these informal systems, as happened in the Sahel during a dreadful drought in the 1970s.

The big unanswered question is how far the things that economists have learnt about traditional commons apply to the "new commons". In the case of global warming, the commons is the whole earth. It is not easy to see how rules that encourage shared responsibility can be made to stick. Yet this has happened in other international examples. Mrs Ostrom suggests the so-called "miracle of the Rhine" – the clean-up of Europe's busiest waterway – should be seen as an example of successful commons management because it was not until local pressure groups, city and regional governments and non-governmental organisations got involved that polluters were willing to recognise the costs they were imposing on others, and cut emissions. An inter-governmental body (the International Commission for the Protection of the Rhine) did not have the same effect.

The economics of the new commons is still in its infancy. It is too soon to be confident about its hypotheses. But it may yet prove a useful way of thinking about problems, such as managing the internet, intellectual property or international pollution, on which policy-makers need all the help they can get.

Note

More information is available at http://dlc.dlib.indiana.edu/dic/

Selling sex

Economists let some light in on the shady market for paid sex

IT IS ALL TOO EASY to become a lost soul in New Orleans. The annual meeting of the American Economic Association in January 2008 was part of a huge gathering of social scientists sprawled across the city. Each venue itself was a warren of meeting rooms. Take a wrong turning and a delegate seeking an earnest symposium on minimum wages might innocently end up in the conference session devoted to the market for paid sex.

The star attraction there was Steven Levitt, an economics professor at the University of Chicago and co-author of "Freakonomics", a best-selling book. Mr Levitt presented preliminary findings[1] from a study conducted with Sudhir Venkatesh, a sociologist at Columbia University. Their research on the economics of street prostitution combines official arrest records with data on 2,200 "tricks" (transactions), collected by Mr Venkatesh in co-operation with sex workers in three Chicago districts.

The results are fascinating. Almost half of the city's arrests for prostitution take place in just 0.3% of its street corners. The industry is concentrated in so few locations because prostitutes and their clients need to be able to find each other. Earnings are high compared with other jobs. Sex workers receive $25–30 per hour, roughly four times what they could expect outside prostitution. Yet this wage premium seems paltry considering the stigma and inherent risks. Sex without a condom is the norm, so the possibility of contracting a sexually transmitted infection (STI) is high. Mr Levitt reckons that sex workers can expect to be violently assaulted once a month. The risk of legal action is low. Prostitutes are more likely to have sex with a police officer than to be arrested by one.

Pricing strategies are much like any other business. Fees vary with the service provided and prostitutes maximise returns by segmenting the market. Clients are charged according to their perceived ability to pay, with white customers paying more than black ones.

When negotiating prices, prostitutes will usually make an offer to black clients, but will solicit a bid from a white client. There are some anomalies. Although prices increase with the riskiness of an act, the premium charged for forgoing a condom is much smaller than found in other studies. And attractive prostitutes were unable to command higher fees.

By chance, the authors were able to study the effects of a demand shock. As people gathered for the July 4th festivities around Washington Park (one of the neighbourhoods studied), business picked up by around 60%, though prices rose by just 30%. The market was able to absorb this rise in demand partly because of flexible supply. Regular prostitutes worked more hours and those from other locations were drawn in. So were other recruits – women who were not regular prostitutes but were prepared to work for the higher wages temporarily on offer.

One controversial finding is that prostitutes do better with pimps – they work fewer hours and are less likely to be arrested by the police or preyed on by gang members. The paper's discussant at the conference, Evelyn Korn of Germany's University of Marburg, said that her favourite result from the study was that pimps pay "efficiency wages". In other words, pimps pay above the minimum rate required by sex workers in order to attract, retain and motivate the best staff. Mr Levitt said that a few prostitutes asked the researchers to introduce them to pimps.

A separate paper[2] on sex workers in Ecuador echoed some of these findings. As in Chicago, the paid-sex market in Ecuador is tiered, with licensed brothel workers earning more per hour than unlicensed street prostitutes. These gradations might reflect different tastes: brothel workers tend to be younger, more attractive and better educated. They are also slightly less likely to have an STI. Condom use is the norm: 61% of street prostitutes surveyed used a condom in the previous three transactions. In Chicago, condoms were used in only a quarter of tricks.

What about the johns?

These studies contribute to our understanding of the suppliers of paid sex, but tell us little about their customers. The session's organiser, Taggert Brooks of the University of Wisconsin, attempted to fill this gap in knowledge. He shed light on the sex industry's demand side in his analysis[3] of men who attend strip clubs. He argued that habitués of strip clubs featuring nude or semi-nude dancers are in search of "near-sex" – an experience of intimacy rather than sexual release. They are aware that paid sex is on offer elsewhere, should they desire it.

Strip-club patrons are more likely to be college-educated (cue some uneasy seat shifting from conference delegates), to have had an STI, and to have altered their sexual behaviour because of AIDS, than non-patrons are. They are typically unmarried, relatively young (against the stereotype of old married men) and are characterised as "high-sensation seekers".

Although all speakers at the session were careful not to draw very strong conclusions from preliminary findings, a few broad themes nevertheless emerged. In many respects, the paid-sex industry is much like any other business. Pricing strategies are familiar from other settings. Despite evidence of a myopic attitude towards risk, there have been plenty of examples of that in the finance industry too. Illegality and lack of regulation are likely to heighten public-health risks. The Ecuador study concluded that rigorous policing of street prostitution might limit the spread of STIs by directing sex workers into the safer environs of licensed brothels. For an audience facing an evening away from home in the Big Easy, there was much to ponder.

Notes

1 "An Empirical Analysis of Street-Level Prostitution".
2 Paul Gertler (University of California, Berkley) and Manisha Shah (University of Melbourne), "Sex Work and Infection: What's Law Enforcement Got to Do with it?"
3 "In Da Club: An Econometric Analysis of Strip Club Patrons".

The unkindest cuts

Discounting that promotes competition is hard to distinguish from predatory pricing

TWO DECADES BEFORE he won the Nobel prize for economics in 1991, Ronald Coase wrote an essay decrying the poor state of research in industrial organisation, the discipline in which he established his reputation. The field, he complained, was devoted to the study of monopoly and antitrust policy. That, he said, made for bad scholarship: an economist faced with a business practice that he cannot fathom, according to Mr Coase, "looks for a monopoly explanation".

A lot has changed in the years since that lament. The broader research effort for which Mr Coase called has fostered a richer understanding of how firms respond to customers and rivals. Monopoly explanations now compete with theories that see the same behaviour as helpful to consumers. That has made it harder to sort malign from benign business practices. The recent antitrust finding against Intel, a maker of computer chips, is a case in point. After a long investigation, ending in a bulky 524-page verdict, the European Union in May 2009 fined Intel €1.06 billion ($1.44 billion) for illegally using its muscle to price AMD, a rival chipmaker, out of the market. Intel rejects the charge of predatory pricing and has appealed. Its lawyers have a block of theory on which to build a defence.

Allegations of predatory pricing have a long history. The Sherman Antitrust Act of 1890, the foundation of America's competition policy, was partly a response to complaints by small firms that larger rivals wanted to drive them out of business. Trustbusters need to be wary of such claims. Low prices are one of the fruits of competition: penalising business giants for price cuts would be perverse. But in rare circumstances, a big firm with cash in reserve may cut prices below costs in order to starve smaller rivals of revenue. The profits sacrificed in the short term can be recouped by higher prices once competitors are out of the way.

Establishing that a firm is guilty of predation is difficult. If rivals stumble or fail, that may be down to their own inefficiency or poor products, and not because they were preyed upon. Proving that a firm is pricing below its costs is tricky in practice. Even where a reliable price-cost or profit-sacrifice test is feasible, failing it need not imply sinister intent. There are often pro-competitive reasons to forgo short-term profits. Firms with a new product, or a new version of an existing one, may wish to pick a lossmaking price to defray the cost to consumers of switching, or because they expect their own costs to fall as they perfect the production process (video-game consoles are a classic example). Losses would then be a licit investment in future profits.

Predation is even trickier to uncover when goods are sold together. A firm that enjoys fat profits on one good may "bundle" it with another on which margins are lower. If the discount on the bundle is hefty enough, other firms may struggle to offer as enticing a deal. In 2001 the EU blocked a proposed tie-up between GE and Honeywell for fear that the merged firm might use bundled discounts to squeeze rival suppliers. In 2007 a committee of antitrust experts appointed by the American government proposed a test for whether bundling is predatory. First, assume the discount applies solely to the low-margin good. So if each good sells for $10 separately and $16 as a bundle, allocate the $4 discount to the more "competitive" product. Next, apply a price-cost test: if the product costs over $6 to make, the bundle is predatory.

That check seems neat but sound business practices may still fall foul of it. It may be cheaper for a firm to sell the two goods together, because of cost savings on distribution. Firms also often use bundling as a way of charging high-demand users more. Thin margins on sales of printers, for example, can be made up by bundling in more profitable toners. This kind of "metering" is an efficient way of recovering fixed costs such as research.

Another ambiguous tactic is to offer rebates to customers that reach certain sales targets. Bulk buyers generally pay lower unit prices to reflect suppliers' economies of scale. Rebates can also help align incentives. Suppliers want retailers to promote their products, offer in-store information and keep plentiful stocks. The trouble is, retailers bear all the costs of such sales efforts but reap only some of the benefits. Rebates provide incentives for retailers to drive sales, as profits are bigger once the target is met.

The price of loyalty

The EU reckons that Intel's use of such rebates was nefarious. It is in the nature of rebates that, just above the target threshold, the price of each additional purchase can be negative. If, say, a firm charges $1 for each sale of up to nine units, and a unit price of 80 cents (a rebate of 20%) for sales of ten items or more, the price of the tenth sale is minus $1, since nine units cost $9 and ten units cost only $8. A dominant firm like Intel can rely on a certain market share (an "assured base", in the jargon). It could in theory set a rebate threshold above that mark, where smaller rivals may hope to mount an effective challenge but cannot match the negative marginal prices on offer to buyers.

Intel's conduct was certainly worth investigating. Its rebates kicked in if customers gave the firm between 80% and 100% of their business. The schemes looked like a response to a competitive threat from AMD. Yet the EU's trustbusters cannot feel too sure of themselves. Intel's rival is still alive and kicking: AMD has not been excluded from the market (though its investment plans may have been thwarted and potential entrants deterred). Moreover, such a complex case, with a bulky ruling which is still not in the public domain, does not offer much guidance on what sort of rebate schemes might be deemed predatory.

Trustbusters have moved away from the practice that so concerned Mr Coase in the early 1970s – of being too quick to condemn big firms on the basis of crude judgments. But they are unlikely to find a robust and simple rule to put in place of the old presumption that firms with market power are always suspect.

Two sides to every story

Capping credit-card levies on retailers and other merchants could hurt consumers

WHEN FINANCE is not being blamed for wrecking the economy, it is being attacked for profiteering. In October 2009 the 7-Eleven chain of convenience stores in America presented a petition with more than 1.6m signatures to Congress, calling for a reduction of the fees levied by payment-card firms and their member banks each time a purchase is made using plastic. The financial reform bill passed in America in 2010 will allow regulators to cap these "swipe fees", known in the industry as merchant-interchange fees. In America these are 1.5–2% of the price of an average purchase, which is high by rich-world standards. Retailers grumble that the charges inflate their costs, which they are forced to pass on to consumers – even those who choose to pay by cash.

Similar complaints have already prompted regulatory action elsewhere. Visa and MasterCard, the payment-card giants, are fighting an attempt by the European Union to limit swipe fees to 0.3% of a transaction's value whenever a credit card issued in one EU country is used in another. (Until 2007 the EU's competition authorities had been pacified by Visa's pledge to bring average interchange fees down to 0.7%.) In Australia, where regulators set charges in relation to the payment system's running costs, the average swipe fee has fallen to around 0.4%.

The case for tight regulation seems strong, at first glance. In rich countries, where paying by plastic is now commonplace, the firms that run card-payment systems look like other utilities, which have long been subject to price caps. Visa and MasterCard are associations run on behalf of their member banks. Competition officials are usually wary of such shared ventures but accept that it is more efficient for rival banks to band together in one network in order to process payments and settle accounts. A common fee structure stops members from abusing the rule that retailers must take all cards issued with the association's brand. It also obviates the need for countless bilateral deals between thousands of banks. Even so, regulators still fret that banks might use their combined heft to overcharge.

They need to tread carefully. Judging how much credit-card firms ought to charge for their services is trickier even than setting the right price for water or energy supplies. That is because the payment-card system is a "two-sided" market. What sets this type of enterprise apart is that it caters for two distinct groups of customers and each sort benefits the more custom there is from the other sort. Consumers will sign up for a credit-card brand if it is widely accepted as a means of payment. Merchants will more willingly accept a card if lots of consumers use it.

Building up a two-sided market, and balancing the needs of each side, require pricing strategies that would make little sense in more traditional, one-sided industries. Charges may have little relation to costs and often lean to one side of the market. For instance, outfits that act as matchmakers for lonely hearts (dating clubs, singles bars, and so on) often levy higher charges on men than on women. They judge that single men will be keener to join clubs that are visited by lots of women. Computer operating systems make more money from users than from software developers. Most media outfits rely on a mix of charges to both sides of the market that is tilted towards advertisers. Broadcast networks and some local newspapers provide their wares free and charge advertisers for access to consumers. Others are now opting for a one-sided business model, without advertisers, where consumers pay directly for news and programmes.

Skewed pricing is one solution to the central challenge of two-sided industries: how to lure one set of clients with the promise of custom from the other. In its early days, the Diners Club card took a hefty 7% cut of the tab from restaurants that accepted it. They did so because the eateries were given privileged access to the wealthy New Yorkers who had been given the card free. With one side on board, Diners Club found it easier to charge the other. As a rule, the side that bears more of the cost of bringing both sides together is the one that is least reluctant to pay – the side that Jean-Charles Rochet of Toulouse University, an expert in two-sided markets, describes as "caught". But because finding the right mix of charges is so crucial to a successful two-sided business, regulating prices could upset a delicate balance. It is hard for firms to know what the "right" prices are in two-sided markets. Cut charges on one side and it will raise them on the other, chasing customers away and making the business shrink.

Not going Dutch

Trustbusters are nevertheless suspicious of a credit-card business model where one side covers all of the running costs. That looks sinister on two counts. First, in mature markets merchants may have little choice but to take the main credit cards. If so, it may allow the big brands to overcharge, pushing merchants' profits down and consumer prices up. Second, to the extent that card issuers use some of their excess profits from interchange fees to compete for cardholders – through lower fees, loyalty schemes and other benefits – a hefty swipe fee could distort the payments markets by favouring credit cards over other forms of settlement, such as debit cards, cheques or cash.

Even so, that does not add up to a compelling case for regulation, since it is hard to see how consumers could be made better off. The tentative evidence from Australia is that caps on interchange fees for retailers have not been offset by any gain in the form of lower consumer prices. If interchange fees merely shift economic rents from merchants to card firms, then that is not a concern for competition policy (especially if some of the rents end up washing back to cardholders). It is true that interchange fees facilitate credit-card usage, which can encourage indebtedness with all its attendant problems. That makes them a tempting target for crisis-burned regulators. But if consumer debt is the problem, tinkering with swipe fees is the wrong way to tackle it.

Looking good by doing good

Rewarding people for their generosity may be counterproductive

A LARGE PLAQUE in the foyer of Boston's Institute for Contemporary Art (ICA), a museum housed in a dramatic glass and metal building on the harbour's edge, identifies its most generous patrons. Visitors who stop to look will notice that some donors – including two who gave the ICA over $2.5m – have chosen not to reveal their names. Such reticence is unusual: less than 1% of private gifts to charity are anonymous. Most people (including the vast majority of the ICA's patrons) want their good deeds to be talked about. In "Richistan", a book on America's new rich, Robert Frank writes of the several society publications in Florida's Palm Beach which exist largely to publicise the charity of its well-heeled residents (at least before Bernard Madoff's alleged Ponzi scheme left some of them with little left to give).

As it turns out, the distinction between private and public generosity is helpful in understanding what motivates people to give money to charities or donate blood, acts which are costly to the doer and primarily benefit others. Such actions are widespread, and growing. The $306 billion that Americans gave to charity in 2007 was more than triple the amount donated in 1965. And though a big chunk of this comes from plutocrats like Bill Gates and Warren Buffett, whose philanthropy has attracted much attention, modest earners also give generously of their time and money. A 2001 survey found that 89% of American households gave to charity, and that 44% of adults volunteered the equivalent of 9m full-time jobs. Tax breaks explain some of the kindness of strangers. But by no means all.

Economists, who tend to think self-interest governs most actions of man, are intrigued, and have identified several reasons to explain good deeds of this kind. Tax breaks are, of course, one of the main ones, but donors are also sometimes paid directly for their pains, and the mere thought of a thank-you letter can be enough to persuade others to cough up. Some even act out of sheer altruism. But most interesting is another explanation, which is that people do good in part because it makes them look good to those whose opinions they care about. Economists call this "image motivation".

Dan Ariely of Duke University, Anat Bracha of Tel Aviv University, and Stephan Meier of Columbia University sought, through experiments, to test the importance of image motivation, as well as to gain insights into how different motivating factors interact. Their results, which they report in a 2009 paper,[1] suggest that image motivation matters a lot, at least in the laboratory. Even more intriguingly, they find evidence that monetary incentives can actually reduce charitable giving when people are driven in part by a desire to look good in others' eyes.

The crucial thing about charity as a means of image building is, of course, that it can work only if others know about it and think positively of the charity in question. So, the academics argue, people should give more when their actions are public.

To test this, they conducted an experiment where the number of times participants clicked an awkward combination of computer keys determined how much money was donated on their behalf to the American Red Cross. Since 92% of participants thought highly of the Red Cross, giving to it could reasonably be assumed to make people look good to their peers. People were randomly assigned to either a private group, where only the participant knew the amount of the donation, or a public group, where the participant had to stand up at the end of the session and share this information with the group. Consistent with the hypothesis that image mattered, participants exerted much greater effort in the public case: the average number of clicks, at 900, was nearly double the average of 517 clicks in the private case.

However, the academics wanted to go a step further. In this, they were influenced by the theoretical model of two economists, Roland Benabou, of Princeton University, and Jean Tirole, of Toulouse University's Institut d'Economie Industrielle, who formalised the idea that if people do good to look good, introducing monetary or other rewards into the mix might complicate matters. An observer who sees someone getting paid for donating blood, for example, would find it hard to differentiate between the donor's intrinsic "goodness" and his greed.

Blood money

The idea that monetary incentives could be counterproductive has been around at least since 1970, when Richard Titmuss, a British social scientist, hypothesised that paying people to donate blood would reduce the amount of blood that they gave. But Mr Ariely and his colleagues demonstrate a mechanism through which such confounding effects could operate. They presumed that the addition of a monetary incentive should have much less of an impact in public (where it muddles the image signal of an action) than in private (where the image is not important). By adding a monetary reward for participants to their experiment, the academics were able to confirm their hypothesis. In private, being paid to click increased effort from 548 clicks to 740, but in public, there was next to no effect.

The trio also raise the possibility that cleverly designed rewards could actually draw out more generosity by exploiting image motivation. Suppose, for example, that rewards were used to encourage people to support a certain cause with a minimum donation. If that cause then publicised those who were generous well beyond the minimum required of them, it would show that they were not just "in it for the money". Behavioural economics may yet provide charities with some creative new fund-raising techniques.

Note

1 "Doing Good or Doing Well? Image Motivation and Monetary Incentives in Behaving Prosocially", *American Economic Review*, March 2009.

New-year irresolution

How to combat the natural tendency to procrastinate

EACH NEW YEAR'S DAY lots of people make plans to do more exercise or give up smoking. But by January 2nd many of them have not moved from the sofa or are lighting another cigarette. Such triumphs of optimism over experience are common enough. But like other examples of repeated procrastination, they are hard to explain using standard economic models.

These models recognise that people prefer to put off unpleasant things until the future rather than do them today. Asked on January 1st to pick a date for that first session in the gym, say, you may well choose to start in two weeks' time rather than tomorrow. But the standard models also assume that your choices about future actions are "time-consistent" – they do not depend on when you are asked to make the choice. By January 14th, in other words, you should still be committed to going to the gym the next day. In the real world, however, you may well choose to delay your start-date again.

In a 1999 paper on the economics of procrastination, Ted O'Donoghue and Matthew Rabin pointed out that people are often unrealistically optimistic about their own future likelihood of doing things – such as exercise or saving – that involve costs at the time they are done, but whose benefits lie even further ahead. Mr O'Donoghue and Mr Rabin showed that this sort of behaviour can be explained if people are time-inconsistent. "Present-biased" preferences mean that people will always tend to put off unpleasant things until tomorrow, even if the immediate cost involved is tiny. As long as they are unsure of the precise extent of this bias, they believe (incorrectly) that they will in fact "do it tomorrow". But since they feel this way at each point in time, tomorrow never quite comes. Such a model can therefore explain endless procrastination.

It can also suggest ways to change behaviour. A recent NBER paper by Esther Duflo, Michael Kremer and Jonathan Robinson argues that a tendency to procrastinate may explain why so few African farmers use fertiliser, despite knowing that it raises yields and profits. In trials on the farms of maize farmers in western Kenya, the three economists found that using half a teaspoon of fertiliser per plant increased seasonal profits by an average of 36% per acre, even if farmers made no other changes to their farming techniques. Doing so after it was clear that the seeds had sprouted eliminated most of the risk of paying for fertiliser in a year of poor weather. Only 9% of the farmers believed fertiliser would not increase their profits. Yet only 29% had used any in either of the two preceding seasons.

When asked why, almost four-fifths of farmers said that they did not have enough money to buy fertiliser for the land they farmed. Yet fertiliser was readily available in multiples of a kilogram, so even poor farmers earned enough to buy fertiliser for at least a fraction of their fields. Better intentions made little difference: virtually all farmers said they planned to use fertiliser the following season, but only 37% actually did so.

The reason for this gap between intent and action, the economists argue, is that many farmers are present-biased and procrastinate repeatedly. Right after the harvest, when farmers are cash-rich, most can afford to buy fertiliser. But going to town to buy it imposes a small cost: a half-hour walk, say, or a bus ticket. So farmers postpone the purchase, believing they will make it later. But they overestimate their ability to put aside enough money to do that, ensuring that their plans to buy fertiliser meet much the same fate as a typical new-year resolution.

A model of such preferences generates several interesting predictions. It suggests that a tiny discount – enough to make up for the small costs associated with buying fertiliser – should induce present-biased farmers to make the purchase. The model also suggests that a given discount would be more effective if offered immediately after the harvest rather than just before the next planting period, by which time it would be useful only for those farmers who had no problems with saving money.

Solving St Augustine

The economists devised a scheme in which farmers paid the full market price for fertiliser, but had it delivered to their homes by a non-governmental organisation at no additional cost. A subset received this "discount" at harvest time, while another group were also offered free delivery, but only when planting time was imminent. Still others were offered a 50% subsidy on the market price, an approach commonly taken by governments to encourage fertiliser use. As the model of time-inconsistent preferences predicted, the offer of free delivery early in the season pushed up usage of fertiliser by 11 percentage points over a control group who were not offered anything. The same discount late in the season, however, had a statistically insignificant effect. A 50% subsidy later in the season, a much costlier policy than free delivery, pushed up usage by about as much as the early discount.

Interestingly, nearly half of a group of farmers who were offered a choice picked early rather than late free delivery. Early delivery means advance payment, with any interest that might have been earned in the interim being forgone. Many farmers, it seemed, were well aware of their own tendency to procrastinate and were looking for a way to force themselves to buy fertiliser.

Such devices can help other procrastinators, too. In recent field trials in the Philippines some smokers who wanted to quit were offered a "commitment contract". Those who signed up put money into a zero-interest bank account. If they passed a test certifying that they were nicotine-free six months later, they got their money back. If not, it went to charity. The contract increased the likelihood of quitting by over 30% over a control group. Those new-year resolutions need not turn to ash.

Note

The papers referred to in this article are:

Ted O'Donoghue and Matthew Rabin, "Doing it Now or Later", *American Economic Review*, March 1999.

Esther Duflo, Michael Kremer and Jonathan Robinson, "Nudging Farmers to Use Fertilizer: Theory and Experimental Evidence from Kenya", NBER Working Paper, No. 15131, July 2009.

Xavier Gine, Dean Karlan and Jonathan Zinman, "Put Your Money Where Your Butt Is: A Commitment Contract for Smoking Cessation", World Bank Policy Research Working Paper 4985, July 2009.

Common-room quarterbacks

Stadiums make the best laboratories

PASS, OR SLIP THE FOOTBALL to the running back? Fastball or curveball? Place the penalty kick to the goalkeeper's left, or to his right? To those who play sport for a living, the choice can mean glory or ignominy; to fans, ecstasy or agony.

To economists, it is a test of the "minimax" theory of how two-person, zero-sum games should be played. A player should mix up his choices in such a way that the chance of success is the same: the probability of scoring a goal, say, should be the same whether he kicks to the left or the right. And his choice should not depend on what he did last time.

Do people who play games for a living behave as the theory predicts? Not according to a 2009 paper[1] by Kenneth Kovash, of Mozilla, the organisation behind the Firefox web browser, and Steven ("Freakonomics") Levitt, of the University of Chicago, who crunched the evidence from 3.1m pitches in Major League Baseball and 128,000 plays in the National Football League (NFL).

In baseball, fastballs were the most common type of pitch, making up 65% of the sample. However, batters enjoyed significantly more success against them, on average, than against other types. That implies pitchers sent down too many. Worse still for the theory, having thrown a fastball, a pitcher was less likely to throw another next time. Cutting down on fastballs and removing the correlation between pitches, the authors suggest, might be worth a couple of games a season – enough to help a team squeeze into the playoffs in a tight year.

Mr Kovash and Mr Levitt find similar flaws in the NFL. Teams tended to pass the ball too little and to run it too often, and were less likely to pass if they had passed on the previous play. Over a 16-game season, these choices might cost a team the equivalent of half a win.

Past evidence from sport has tended to back the minimax theory. Ignacio Palacios-Huerta, of the London School of Economics, found in a 2003 paper that professional soccer players were remarkably adept game theorists when taking and saving penalty kicks. Mr Kovash and Mr Levitt suggest that their vast data set allows a sterner test of the theory. It may also be that pitchers and quarterbacks have a harder task than penalty-takers and are likelier to make mistakes. That one, however, is an argument for the pub.

Note

1 "Professionals Do Not Play Minimax: Evidence From Major League Baseball and the National Football League", NBER Working Paper No. 15347, September 2009.

The material on pages 113–35 was first published in *The Economist* in November 2008 (pages 113–5), August 2008 (pages 116–18), January 2008 (pages 119–21), August 2009 (pages 122–4), October 2009 (pages 125–7 and 134–5), January 2009 (pages 128–30) and January 2010 (pages 131–3).

PART 2

The global economy

The first decade of the 21st century began with a short, shallow recession in America and culminated in the global recession of 2008–09, the deepest since the Great Depression. The story of the world economy in this eventful decade is the subject of the articles in this section. The global recession is, inevitably, central to this story. But the articles here try to put it in a broader context. They look back at the period before the slump to get to grips with its underlying causes, and ahead to the challenges that it has left in its wake.

The years before the recession were marked by the growing economic importance of the emerging world, whose combined output at purchasing power parity outstripped that of the rich countries for the first time in 2005. But as Chapter 5 points out, it was also a time of increasing macroeconomic imbalances, with emerging giants like China saving a huge fraction of their national income even as America and several other rich countries ran large and growing current-account deficits. Cheap money from the emerging world also kept interest rates in rich countries at record lows, fuelling a housing bubble of enormous proportions in America (and also some other parts of the rich world, such as Ireland and Spain). Many worried about the sustainability of this pattern of growth.

In the event, the "hard landing" some had warned about came not because foreigners suddenly lost their appetite for the greenback, but because American house prices plummeted as "the biggest housing bubble in history" deflated. As house prices fell, the losses on the complicated debt instruments built on the mortgages that financed them brought the financial system close to collapse, which was averted only by massive government intervention. The turmoil spread through the financial system and eventually resulted in the global economic crisis. The articles in Chapter 6 chronicle what happened as the recession spread, leaving in its wake repossessed houses, plummeting trade flows and many millions of jobless people.

Not surprisingly, the sometimes unconventional choices that policymakers made as they struggled to deal with the bust led to a great deal of debate about economic policy. Questions about the efficacy of discretionary fiscal policy and the limits of monetary policy came to the fore. Could governments spend their way out of recession? How effective was such pump-priming? How should monetary policy be conducted when interest rates could not be cut any further? Chapter 7 describes these debates and the economic evidence available to policymakers as they made very difficult decisions.

By late 2010, most countries had emerged from recession and the world economy was growing again. But growth remained sluggish in many rich countries, even as big emerging ones were racing ahead. Rich countries debated how best to put public finances back on an even keel without endangering economic growth in a contentious discussion about the relative merits of austerity and stimulus. Chapter 8 lays out the scope of the problem of sub-par growth, and the options available to rich-world policymakers as they try to deal with it.

Meanwhile, renewed discord about exchange-rate policy and current-account balances provided a timely reminder that the problem of imbalances had not been addressed. Whether the world economy eventually returns to a more sustainable pattern of growth depends on the answer to several questions such as whether China can reduce its savings rate and whether America can increases its own. How might all this happen? The last four articles discuss the task confronting four big economies with persistent deficits and surpluses – Germany, Japan, America and China – assessing the prospects for change in each case.

5 Before the storm: the forces at work

The new titans

China, India and other developing countries are set to give the world economy its biggest boost in the whole of history, says Pam Woodall. What will that mean for today's rich countries?

IN 2005 THE COMBINED OUTPUT of emerging economies reached an important milestone: it accounted for more than half of total world GDP (measured at purchasing-power parity). This means that the rich countries no longer dominate the global economy. The developing countries also have a far greater influence on the performance of the rich economies than is generally realised. Emerging economies are driving global growth and having a big impact on developed countries' inflation, interest rates, wages and profits. As these newcomers become more integrated into the global economy and their incomes catch up with the rich countries, they will provide the biggest boost to the world economy since the industrial revolution.

Indeed, it is likely to be the biggest stimulus in history, because the industrial revolution fully involved only one-third of the world's population. By contrast, this new revolution covers most of the globe, so the economic gains – as well as the adjustment pains – will be far bigger. As developing countries and the former Soviet block have embraced market-friendly economic reforms and opened their borders to trade and investment, more countries are industrialising and participating in the global economy than ever before. These economic newcomers are affecting the developed world in many ways. As it happens, their influence helps to explain a whole host of puzzling economic developments, such as the record share of profits in national income, sluggish growth in real wages, high oil prices alongside low inflation, low

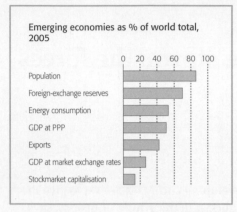

Emerging economies as % of world total, 2005

Population
Foreign-exchange reserves
Energy consumption
GDP at PPP
Exports
GDP at market exchange rates
Stockmarket capitalisation

Sources: IMF; MSCI; BP

FIG 5.1 Why they matter

global interest rates and America's vast current-account deficit.

Emerging countries are looming larger in the world economy by a wide range of measures (see Figure 5.1). Their share of world exports has jumped to 43%, from 20% in 1970. They consume over half of the world's energy and accounted for four-fifths of the growth in oil demand between 2001 and 2005. They also hold 70% of the world's foreign-exchange reserves.

Of course there is more than one respectable way of doing the sums. So although measured at purchasing-power parity (which takes account of lower prices in poorer countries) the emerging economies now make up over half of world GDP, at market exchange rates their share is still less than 30%. But even at market exchange rates, they accounted for well over half of the increase in global output in 2005. And this is not just about China and India: those two together made up less than one-quarter of the total increase in emerging economies' GDP in 2005.

There is also more than one definition of emerging countries, depending on who does the defining. Perhaps some of these countries should be called re-emerging economies, because they are regaining their former eminence. Until the late 19th century, China and India were the world's two biggest economies. Before the steam engine and the power loom gave Britain its industrial lead, today's emerging economies dominated world output. Estimates by Angus Maddison, an economic historian, suggest that in the 18 centuries up to 1820 these economies produced, on average, 80% of world GDP (see Figure 5.2). But they were left behind by Europe's technological revolution and the first wave of globalisation. By 1950 their share had fallen to 40%.

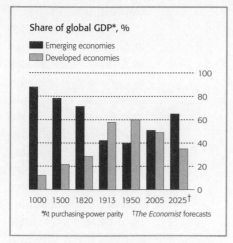

Share of global GDP*, %

■ Emerging economies
▣ Developed economies

1000 1500 1820 1913 1950 2005 2025†

*At purchasing-power parity   †*The Economist* forecasts

Sources: OECD, Angus Maddison; IMF

FIG 5.2 Re-emerging

Now they are on the rebound. Between 2001 and 2005 their annual growth averaged almost 7%, its fastest pace in recorded history and well above the 2.3% growth in rich economies. The IMF forecast that between 2006 and 2010 emerging economies would grow at an average of 6.8% a year, whereas the developed economies will notch up only 2.7%.[1] If both groups continued in this way, in 20 years' time emerging economies would account for two-thirds of global output (at purchasing-power parity). Extrapolation is always risky, but there seems every chance that the relative weight of the new pretenders will rise.

Faster growth spreading more widely across the globe makes a huge difference to global growth rates. Since 2000, world GDP per head has grown by an average of 3.2% a year, thanks to the acceleration in emerging economies. That would beat the 2.9% annual growth during the golden age of 1950–73, when Europe and Japan were rebuilding their economies after the war; and it would certainly exceed growth during the Industrial Revolution. That growth, too, was driven by technological change and by an explosion in trade and capital flows, but by today's standards it was a glacial affair. Between 1870 and 1913 world GDP per head increased by an average of only 1.3% a year. This means that the first decade of the 21st century could see the fastest growth in average world income in the whole of history.

Financial wobbles in summer 2006 acted as a reminder that emerging economies are more volatile than rich-country ones; yet their long-run prospects look excellent, so long as they continue to move

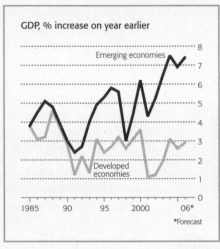

GDP, % increase on year earlier

Emerging economies

Developed economies

1985   90   95   2000   06*

*Forecast

Source: IMF

FIG 5.3 Speeding ahead

towards free and open markets, sound fiscal and monetary policies and better education. Because they start with much less capital per worker than developed economies, they have huge scope for boosting productivity by importing Western machinery and know-how. Catching up is easier than being a leader. When America and Britain were industrialising in the 19th century, they took 50 years to double their real incomes per head; today China is achieving the same feat in nine years.

What's new

Emerging economies as a group have been growing faster than developed economies for several decades. So why are they now making so much more of a difference to the old rich world? The first reason is that the gap in growth rates between the old and the new world has widened (see Figure 5.3). But more important, emerging economies have become more integrated into the global system of production, with trade and capital flows accelerating relative to GDP between 1996 and 2005.

China joined the World Trade Organisation only in 2001. It is having a bigger global impact than other emerging economies because of its vast size and its unusual openness to trade and investment with the rest of the world. The sum of China's total exports and imports amounts to around 70% of its GDP, against only 25–30% in India or America. By 2007, China accounted for nearly 10% of world trade, up from 4% in 2000.

What is also new is that the internet has made it possible radically to reorganise production across borders. Thanks to information technology, many once non-tradable services, such as accounting, can be provided from afar, exposing more sectors in the developed world to competition from India and elsewhere.

Faster growth that lifts the living standards of hundreds of millions of people in poor countries should be a cause for celebration. Instead, many bosses, workers and politicians in the rich world are quaking in their boots as output and jobs shift to low-wage economies in Asia or eastern Europe. Yet on balance, rich countries should gain from poorer ones getting richer. The success of the emerging economies will boost both global demand and supply.

Rising exports give developing countries more money to spend on imports from richer ones. And although their average incomes are still low, their middle classes are expanding fast, creating a vast new market. Over the decade 2006–15, almost a billion new consumers will enter the global marketplace as household incomes rise above the threshold at which people generally begin to spend on non-essential goods. Emerging economies have already become important markets for rich-world firms: over half of the combined exports of America, the euro area and Japan go to these poorer economies. The rich economies' trade with developing countries is growing twice as fast as their trade with one another.

The future boost to demand will be large. But more important in the long term will be the stimulus to the world economy from what economists call a "positive supply shock". As China, India and the former Soviet Union have embraced market capitalism, the global labour force has, in effect, doubled. The world's potential output is also being lifted by rapid productivity gains in developing countries as they try to catch up with the West.

This increased vitality in emerging economies is raising global growth, not substituting for output elsewhere. The newcomers boost real incomes in the rich world by supplying cheaper goods, such as microwave ovens and computers, by allowing multinational firms to reap bigger economies of scale, and by spurring productivity growth through increased competition. They will thus help to lift growth in world GDP just when the rich world's greying populations would otherwise cause it to slow. Developed countries will do better from being part of this fast-growing world than from trying to cling on to a bigger share of a slow-growing one.

Stronger growth in emerging economies will make developed countries as a whole better off, but not everybody will be a winner. The integration of China and other developing countries into the world trading system is causing the biggest shift in relative prices and incomes (of labour, capital, commodities, goods and assets) for at least a century, and this, in turn, is leading to a big redistribution of income. For example, whereas prices of the labour-intensive goods that China and others export are falling, prices of the goods they import, notably oil, are rising.

In particular, the new ascendancy of the emerging economies has changed the relative returns to labour and capital. Because these economies' global integration has made labour more abundant, workers in developed countries have lost some of their bargaining power, which has put downward pressure on real wages. Workers' share of national income in those countries has fallen to its lowest level for decades, whereas the share of profits has surged. It seems that Western workers are not getting their full share of the fruits of globalisation. This is true not just for the lowest-skilled ones but increasingly also for more highly qualified ones in, say, accountancy and computer programming.

If wages continue to disappoint, there could be a backlash from workers and demands for protection from low-cost competition. But countries that try to protect jobs and wages through import barriers or restrictions on offshoring will only hasten their relative decline. The challenge for governments in advanced economies is to find ways to spread the benefits of globalisation more fairly without reducing the size of those gains.

The high share of profits and low share of wages in national income are not the only numbers that have strayed a long way from their historical average. An alarming number of economic variables are currently way out of line with what conventional economic models would predict. America's current-account deficit is at a record high, yet the dollar has remained relatively strong. Global interest rates are still historically low, despite strong growth and heavy government borrowing. Oil prices have tripled since 2002, yet global growth remains robust and inflation, though rising, is still relatively low. House prices, however, have been soaring in many countries.

Puzzling it out

All of these puzzles can be explained by the growing impact of emerging economies. For instance, low bond yields and the dollar's refusal to plunge are partly due to the way these countries have been piling up foreign reserves. Likewise, higher oil prices have mostly been caused by strong demand from developing countries rather than by an interruption of supply, so they have done less harm to global growth than in the past. And their impact on inflation has been offset by falling prices of goods exported by emerging economies. This has also made it easier for central banks to achieve their inflation goals with much lower interest rates than in the past.

All this will require some radical new thinking about economic policy. Governments may need to harness the tax and benefit system to compensate some workers who lose from globalisation.

Monetary policy also needs to be revamped. Central bankers like to take the credit for the defeat of inflation, but emerging economies have given them a big helping hand, both by pushing down the prices of many goods and by restraining wages in developed countries. This has allowed central banks to hold interest rates at historically low levels. But they have misunderstood the monetary-policy implications of a positive supply shock. By keeping interest rates too low, they have allowed a build-up of excess liquidity which has flowed into the prices of assets such as homes, rather than into traditional inflation. They have encouraged too much borrowing and too little saving. In America the overall result has been to widen the current-account deficit.

The central banks' mistake has been compounded by the emerging economies' refusal to allow their exchange rates to rise, piling up foreign-exchange reserves instead. Bizarrely, by financing America's deficit, poor countries are subsidising the world's richest consumers. The opening up of emerging economies has thus not only provided a supply of cheap labour to the world, it has also offered an increased supply of cheap capital. But the developing countries will not be prepared to go on financing America's massive current-account deficit for much longer.

At some point, therefore, America's cost of capital could rise sharply. There is a risk that the American economy will face a sharp financial shock and a recession, or an extended period of sluggish growth. This will slow growth in the rest of the world economy. But America is less important as a locomotive for global growth than it used to be, thanks to the greater vigour of emerging economies. America's total imports from the rest of the world in 2005 amounted to only 4% of world GDP. The greater risk to the world economy is that a recession and falling house prices would add to Americans' existing concerns about stagnant real wages, creating more support for protectionism.[2] That would be bad both for the old rich countries and the new emerging stars.

But regardless of how the developed world responds to the emerging giants, their economic power will go on growing. The rich world has yet to feel the full heat from this new revolution.

Notes

1   These forecasts were made before the global recession dented growth rates in the emerging world and sent the rich world into a deep recession. Nevertheless, the broad prediction – namely, that the emerging world would grow much faster than the rich world – remained valid.

2   This did indeed happen, in the form of the global recession of 2008–09, which is discussed in the next section.

The frugal giant

China's enormous saving surplus may rise further before it falls

IN THE HAIDAN DISTRICT of western Beijing stands the world's biggest shopping mall. Six storeys high, with 230 escalators and over 6m square feet (558,000 square metres) of retail space, it is a temple to consumption. Over 1,000 shops sell everything from clocks to cats; the "Fantawild Hitech Family Funplex" offers entertainment; an ice-rink beckons.

Only one thing is missing: customers. On a weekday morning in early July 2005, the place was virtually empty, and such visitors as there were seemed to be window-shopping rather than buying. Like the rest of the world, the "Golden Resources Shopping Mall" is still waiting for a big Chinese consumption boom.

Thanks to rocketing economic growth, the Chinese are spending a lot more than they used to. There are now 59 washing machines per 100 households, up from one in 1985. The number of Chinese travelling abroad rose by 43% in 2004, to 29m. But Chinese saving is growing even more rapidly. Since 2000, the country's overall saving rate – already the world's highest by far – has risen sharply, to nearly 50% of GDP (see Figure 5.4). Even though China is investing at the staggering rate of 46% of GDP, it is still running a net saving surplus, and that surplus is still growing. It rose from 1.9% of GDP in 2000 to 4.2% in 2004, and shows no signs of stopping.

Noting that imports have recently been subdued, many China-watchers expected the country's current-account surplus to rise to 7% or even 8% of GDP in 2005. China may still be poor, but it has become one of the world's biggest exporters of capital. And its impact on the allocation of global capital is even bigger than its current-account surplus suggests. This is because it recycles a lot of savings from other countries and redirects those funds towards America. China is a big recipient of foreign investment ($55 billion of net FDI in 2004), and even more speculative capital has flowed in as investors have been betting on a rise in China's currency, the yuan.

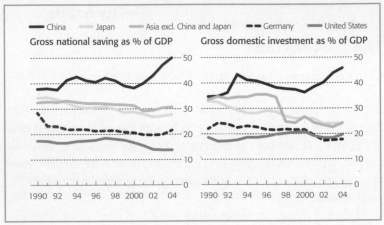

Source: IMF

FIG 5.4 In a league of its own

Rather than allow these capital inflows to strengthen the currency, China's central bank has chosen to pile up foreign-currency reserves, many of which are invested in American Treasury bonds. Thanks to its own saving surplus and its recycling of savings, China had $711 billion-worth of reserves at mid-2005.

On July 21st 2005, the central bank announced that the yuan would no longer be pegged to the dollar but managed against a basket of currencies instead. After an initial 2% rise against the dollar, the yuan barely moved, but the change is potentially important all the same. China's new currency regime could affect both its saving surplus in general and its appetite for American assets in particular.

China's capacity for thrift has long perplexed economists. A 2000 study by Aart Kraay, an economist at the World Bank, found that between 1978 and 1995 China's national saving rate was, on average, more than ten percentage points of GDP higher than the country's economic characteristics would suggest. It has since risen further. What is going on?

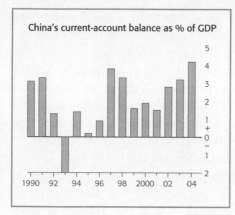

China's current-account balance as % of GDP

1990 92 94 96 98 2000 02 04

Source: IMF

FIG 5.5 Piling up

Thrifty habits

Household saving is the easiest to make sense of. First, Chinese households have not changed their consumption patterns fast enough to keep up with the huge rise in their incomes. The boost to saving from higher incomes has been further strengthened by a rise in income inequality: a large part of China's growing income has been going to the relatively small share of the population living in coastal areas. Richer people save more than poorer ones.

Demography, too, has played a big role, as the share of workers in the population has risen. Moreover, the one-child policy has made it harder for people to rely on their children as a source of support in old age, further encouraging thrift. Franco Modigliani and Shi Larry Cao argue in a study published in 2004 (posthumously, in Mr Modigliani's case) that these factors together explain virtually all of the rise in Chinese household saving between the mid-1970s and the 1990s.

A further incentive to saving is the weakness of social safety nets. Under the old economic regime many Chinese workers could count on health and pension benefits from state enterprises (the "iron rice bowl"). No longer. The state sector has shrunk dramatically as a share of the economy, and even those workers still employed by state-owned firms have seen their benefits dwindle.

Pension coverage is low: only about 120m people pay into formal pension schemes, fewer than half the estimated 265m urban workers. Worse, pensions are organised largely at the municipal level, and are not easily portable. A migrant worker in Shanghai who plans to retire to his home village cannot assume that he will get his pension there. In rural areas, pensions are almost non-existent.

Health care is also getting more expensive. China's government spends little on public health services and has been shifting costs on to consumers. Enter the lobby of a Chinese hospital, and you might think you are in a bank. A huge electronic noticeboard flashes up the price of treatments – 200 yuan for a cardiogram, 101 yuan for an abortion in one Beijing hospital. A row of tellers lines the wall. You pay cash up front. A serious operation can easily cost a year's salary. With state firms reducing their health coverage and private insurance in its infancy, that is another reason for saving.

Education, too, requires deep pockets, even with fewer children. Again, the state spends little on this, around 2.3% of GDP, much less than in Thailand, Malaysia or India. In a 2005 survey of people's reasons for saving, education came top.

The relative lack of credit is another factor. Although the mortgage market is growing rapidly, thanks to the government's policy of selling off state housing, consumer credit is still in its infancy. Its growth is hampered by the lack of credit-rating agencies and by the ropy banking system. Like the Japanese in the 1960s, the Chinese need to save a lot because they find it hard to borrow.

And save a lot they do. Chinese household saving, at around 25% of disposable income, is astonishingly high by international standards. But although households account for a large part of China's exalted national saving rate, they were not responsible for the sharp rise in national thrift since 2000. After falling steeply in the late 1990s, China's household saving rate has been more or less steady since 2000 (see Figure 5.6). The recent rise in national saving was led by the government and the corporate sector. Louis Kuijs of the World Bank has examined sectoral saving patterns in China and points out that both these sectors are far more frugal than many observers realise.

The fiscal accounts show the government's revenue to be about 20% of GDP and expenditure slightly higher, resulting in a deficit of about 2% of GDP. But Mr Kuijs argues that these numbers mask a lot of government saving and investing. The government spends only about 13% of GDP on goods, services and wages. The remainder – almost 10% of GDP – is, in effect, government saving, which is then invested, largely through direct capital transfers for infrastructure projects or to support state firms.

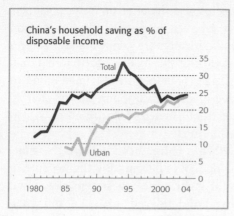

China's household saving as % of disposable income

Source: World Bank

FIG 5.6 Needs must

Chinese firms, both state-owned and private, are also big savers. Corporate profits soared after 2000, thanks to rapid growth, low interest rates, rising productivity and cuts in employee benefits. Both private and state-owned firms are flush with cash, so their saving has risen sharply. China's firms are now bigger savers than its households.

But unlike their peers in the rest of the world, they are investing their surpluses. With no need to pay dividends (state firms do not have to make any transfers to central government) and little shareholder pressure to ensure that their investment is cost-effective, Chinese firms went on a capital-spending binge, concentrated in industries such as aluminium, steel, car production and cement.

That splurge may well prove unsustainable. Profit growth has slowed sharply over the past year because of excess capacity in the most over-invested sectors, such as cement and steel. Grace Ng of JPMorgan, a bank, points out that whereas in early 2004 overall profits in industrial firms were expanding at the rate of 40% a year, by May 2005 the growth rate had slowed to 16%.

Slower profit growth means less corporate saving, but investment seems to be slowing even faster, at least in the most over-invested sectors. The rate of growth of China's imports of capital goods, for instance, is now less than a third of what it was in 2004. But Chinese firms are still selling the fruit of past investment on world markets. As a result, the country's external surpluses are rising. According to Arthur Kroeber, editor of the *China Economic Quarterly*, the investment slowdown will result in "at least a couple of years of blockbuster trade surpluses".

How far a cyclical slowdown in investment translates into a rise in China's national saving surplus also depends on how consumers react. If firms create fewer jobs, or even lay people off, consumption could catch a cold – which would mean more saving and even bigger external surpluses. Nicholas Lardy, of the Institute for International Economics in Washington, DC, points out that the last time China had an investment bust, in the mid-1990s, consumption slowed sharply and the current account shifted from a deficit of around 2% of GDP in 1993 to a surplus of around 4% in 1997.

So far, consumption growth has barely been affected this time. Retail sales, for instance, show no sign of flagging. But China's current account was already in surplus when the investment slowdown started, and is rising faster than it did a decade ago, so if and when the effects feed through to consumption, the change in the current account could be much bigger than last time. A saving surplus of 10% of GDP, or even more, is not unthinkable.

Whatever the scale of the current cyclical investment slowdown, the pace of China's investment is likely to fall over the medium term. At an aggregate level, China's investment rates seem inefficiently high. Japan and South Korea, for instance, achieved similar rates of growth in the 1960s and 1980s, respectively, with investment levels that were ten percentage points lower than China's. Although investment efficiency has been improving, particularly in the growing private sector, many state firms – which account for much of the over-investment – still earn negative returns on capital. That will change as market reforms continue. As Chinese banks, for instance, face foreign competition, they will care more about whom they lend to. Shareholders will become more active and demand higher returns on capital. The introduction of dividend policies would shift more corporate profit to households.

Will consumers wake up?

Better corporate governance will also reduce corporate saving. What happens to China's national saving surplus will depend on whether China's households will save less and spend more, thus becoming the engine of the domestic economy.

The example of Japan is sobering. Although Japanese households now save much less than they used to, their country never really made the shift from export-led to consumer-led growth. It has been running current-account surpluses for four decades. China, however, is different in important ways. Its economy is already much more open than Japan's ever was. Exports and imports add up to the equivalent of 70% of China's GDP, compared with only 20% in Japan. And if July's exchange-rate adjustment turns out to be the beginning of a gradual appreciation, China seems to be shifting away from an undervalued currency far more quickly than Japan did.

Over time, a stronger currency will encourage a reorientation of China's economy towards the domestic consumer, but this is likely to take several years. Although American policymakers may be clamouring for a rapid rise in the yuan, there is no sign in Beijing that the government plans anything of the sort. China's leaders are concerned about unemployment in urban areas as the export sector is squeezed by a stronger yuan, and they worry about unrest in rural areas as farmers have to compete with cheaper imported grain.

A government that depends on rapid economic growth to legitimise itself will not want to risk instability with a sudden rise in the currency, so a much stronger yuan seems an unlikely route to a quick reduction in China's saving surpluses. Reforms to encourage consumer credit and reduce uncertainty about pensions and health-care costs are a better bet. Some such reforms are already under way. China's central bank, for instance, intended to set up credit bureaus in seven provinces in 2005 [this happened in early 2006] to help boost the development of consumer finance, and pilot schemes to improve the pension system are in progress in several provinces. Top Communist Party leaders talk a lot about shifting the emphasis of government spending from investment to social safety nets, and they promised free nine-year education for children in rural areas. But the government's overall fiscal position actually tightened in 2005.

Redirecting an economy as big as China's towards domestic consumption takes time. China's saving surpluses will not last forever, but nor will they disappear overnight. And trying to move too fast can be disastrous, as the mess in Asia's other emerging markets shows.

Forever free

Can America go on borrowing abroad indefinitely?

"IF SOMETHING IS UNSUSTAINABLE, it will stop." This phrase, coined long ago by Herb Stein, an economic adviser to Richard Nixon, has become a staple of the debate on America's current-account deficit. Officials at the Federal Reserve began to fret about America's "unsustainable" imbalances in 1997, when the deficit was less than 3% of GDP. There was much hand-wringing in 2003 when the deficit passed 5% of GDP, a widely accepted indicator of things going seriously awry. In 2005 the deficit stood at more than $700 billion, well over 6% of GDP, and was set to rise further.[1] The world is still going round. Is it time to stop worrying about the sustainability of America's foreign borrowing?

High time, argues a growing band of optimists, most of them American. They offer a variety of reasons. First, they believe that the current-account imbalance is a sign of American strength not weakness: it is caused by foreigners rushing in to share in the proceeds of the country's highly productive and efficient economy. Second, they dismiss the current-account deficit as insignificant in relation to America's total wealth. Who cares about borrowing an annual $700 billion from abroad when American households are worth more than $30 trillion?

Some of these arguments are plainly wrong-headed. If foreigners were keen to share in the gains of American productivity, they would be investing in American shares and factories. That is what happened in the late 1990s. But since 2000, growth in net foreign investment in American shares as well as foreign direct investment in America has slowed sharply. The growing surplus of saving abroad is mainly flowing into American bonds, especially government bonds. Foreigners are lending America money to consume.

The comparison with household wealth is misleading. Most of the recent rise in America's household wealth has come from house prices, and if there is indeed a bubble in the housing market, some

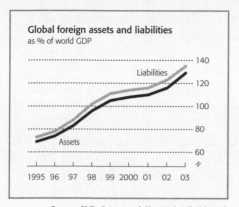

Source: Philip R. Lane and Gian Maria Milesi-Ferretti,
The External Wealth of Nations database

FIG 5.7 Moving in step

of this wealth will turn out to be illusory.[2] Even if the gains are real, they cannot easily be turned into income with which to service America's external debt. Eventually, America will need to export more than it imports to pay its external creditors.

Still, the growth in global capital flows does call for some rethinking about America's current-account deficits. Both foreign assets and foreign liabilities have mushroomed as people across the globe have invested in each other's economies on an unprecedented scale. Gian Maria Milesi-Ferretti of the IMF and Philip Lane of Trinity College, Dublin, have built the world's best database of foreign assets and liabilities in over 120 countries, accounting for more than 99% of world GDP. They found that the stock of all foreign assets owned by these countries was worth the equivalent of 130% of world GDP at the end of 2003, double its level in 1995. The figures for foreign liabilities move roughly in parallel with the ones for assets (see Figure 5.7).

A bigger pool

This rise in cross-border portfolios has had several effects. First, it means that net saving surpluses or deficits are now the balance of much larger gross flows. Given that the pool of internationally mobile capital is much bigger than it used to be, individual countries might be able to run larger imbalances for longer than they used to. According to Messrs Milesi-Ferretti and Lane, America's foreign liabilities as a share of foreigners' overall holdings of foreign assets have fallen in recent years, thanks mainly to a drop in the dollar. In 1999, America accounted for 34% of the rest of the world's foreign-asset holdings. By

2003, that share had fallen to 27%. This does not seem excessive: it is below America's share of the global economy.

Second, the greater volume of cross-border investment means that market fluctuations in the value of a country's gross assets and liabilities can have a bigger effect than new debt. Even if a country is borrowing 6% of GDP a year, the new borrowing can be dwarfed by changes in the value of its stock of cross-border assets and liabilities.

That is exactly what has happened in America. At the end of 2003, America's net external debt position – the difference between the value of America's foreign assets and its foreign liabilities – was $2.4 trillion, or the equivalent of 22% of GDP. In 2004, America ran a current-account deficit of almost 6% of GDP, suggesting that the debt stock at the end of the year should have risen to 28% of GDP. In fact, it rose by only $170 billion, or less than 2% of GDP, because valuation gains in America's overall portfolio of foreign assets and liabilities offset much of the current-account deficit.

Why did American investments abroad perform so much better than foreign investments in America? The main reason is the dollar. It is the world's reserve currency, and America – unlike many other debtors – can issue bonds in its own currency. Virtually all America's foreign liabilities are denominated in dollars, whereas around 70% of its foreign assets are in foreign currencies.

Most of America's foreign assets are in Europe, so when the dollar falls against the euro and sterling, as it did in 2004, America's balance-sheet strengthens as the value of its debt falls and the dollar value of its assets rises. According to Pierre-Olivier Gourinchas, an economist at Berkeley, and Helene Rey, of Princeton, this

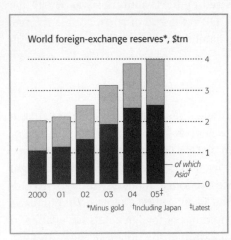

World foreign-exchange reserves*, $trn

of which Asia†

2000 01 02 03 04 05‡

*Minus gold †Including Japan ‡Latest

Source: IMF

FIG 5.8 Too much of a good thing

valuation effect is worth about 5% of GDP for every 10% drop in the dollar. That suggests the shift in America's current-account balance needed to stabilise the country's debt profile may be smaller than many people seem to think.

There is a catch, however. At some point, foreign lenders should be demanding higher interest rates to make up for the risk of the dollar falling. According to Messrs Milesi-Ferretti and Lane, foreigners suffered negative returns on their investments between 2001 and 2004. Why did they not balk? One reason is the thrift shift. Thanks to a highly unusual constellation of circumstances, surplus saving in the world outside America has risen in recent years.

Trust central bankers?

But that is not all. A second reason for unusually low interest rates is that a large chunk of those surplus savings has been under the control of central banks, particularly in Asia. Thus far, these banks have cared less about risk-adjusted returns than about stopping their currencies from rising. The sustainability of America's deficit and the risk of a hard landing depends on whether they will continue to do so.

Central banks have been amassing foreign-exchange reserves on a huge scale. The world's central banks have increased their foreign-exchange reserves by some $2 trillion since 2000, three-quarters of it in Asia. As Figure 5.8 shows, this reserve accumulation is still continuing apace.

Exactly what share of these reserves flowed into American assets is a matter of whose statistics you look at. Official American figures show that central banks bought $280 billion of American assets in 2003 and $395 billion in 2004, or around 50% of all American bonds bought by foreigners in those years. But these numbers exclude any bonds that central banks buy in secondary markets abroad, so they surely underestimate the total. The BIS reckons that central banks bought $440 billion-worth of dollar assets in 2003 and 2004.

Whichever numbers you choose, central banks' increases in dollar reserves have been large compared with overall foreign purchases of American bonds, and huge compared with the size of the current-account deficit. Although central banks hold a small share of the stock of America's external liabilities, they have become big marginal buyers. In 2003, they financed the equivalent of 50% of the current-account deficit according to American numbers and 80% according to the BIS. In 2004, the level was 60–70%.

This explains the popular argument that the yield on America's Treasury bonds is determined in Beijing and that America is locked in a "balance of financial terror" with communist China. Estimates of the effect of Asian reserve accumulation on America's interest rates differ wildly. Economists at Goldman Sachs reckon it is worth around 0.4 percentage points; research at the Federal Reserve suggests it could be between 0.5 and 1 percentage points. At the other extreme, Nouriel Roubini and Brad Setser, of Roubini Global Economics, think that American interest rates could rise by up to 2 percentage points if Asian central banks stopped their intervention.

But is that likely? Those in the gloomy camp, epitomised by Messrs Roubini and Setser, put forward several reasons why it will happen sooner rather than later. First, they argue that China is finding itself increasingly alone as a buyer of dollars as other central banks grow wary of a currency that must at some point depreciate. Second, China will have to stop buying because the losses it will face when the dollar eventually falls will be prohibitive (perhaps over 20% of China's GDP by 2008, according to one calculation). Third, large-scale currency intervention will eventually cause inflation in China to rise, forcing a change in policy.

So far, this has not happened. Although the pace of reserve accumulation in China increased in 2005, there was no sign of rising inflation.[3] The country made a first move towards changing its exchange-rate regime, which might eventually imply fewer reserves overall as well as some diversification away from dollar reserves, but nothing suggests that it is in any hurry. And the pessimists probably put too much weight on the "irrationality" of China accumulating reserves on which it will eventually incur losses. China's government appears to worry much less about such losses than about stability in the domestic economy. No doubt its politicians will eventually wean the economy off its heavy reliance on the debt-laden American consumers, but not overnight.

For the past few years, central banks have been acting as cushions.

When private investors have little appetite for American assets, as in 2003 and 2004, central banks buy a lot in order to stop their currencies from appreciating too much against the dollar. When private appetite rises, central banks buy fewer. That is what seems to have been happening in 2005. Although China was accumulating reserves at a rapid rate, few of these appear to have been American bonds and short-term Treasury bills. According to Mr Setser, foreign governments may have bought only about $20 billion-worth of those in the first six months of 2005 – and yet the dollar strengthened. Even if that understates the real picture, it suggests a sharp drop in central-bank purchases of American bonds compared with 2004.

Japan, China and the oil states are likely to continue piling up saving surpluses for some time yet. If Asia's central banks also remain willing swing purchasers of the dollar, that may seem cause for relief: it suggests that things will go on much as they are, avoiding a hard landing. But relief would be the wrong reaction. As long as America can get cheap money from abroad, it has little incentive to rebalance its economy. So when those global economic imbalances are eventually unwound, it will hurt that much more.

Notes

1 The crisis and efforts to contain it eventually sent it up further.
2 There was indeed a bubble and it burst a couple of years later.
3 Currency appreciation eventually ceased and became a flashpoint in 2009–10.

The material on pages 139–59 was first published in *The Economist* in September 2006 (pages 139–46) and September 2005 (pages 147–59)

6   The global slump

When fortune frowned

**The worst financial crisis since the Depression is redrawing
the boundaries between government and markets, says Zanny
Minton Beddoes. Will they end up in the right place?**

AFTER THE STOCKMARKET CRASH of October 1929 it took over three
years for America's government to launch a series of dramatic efforts
to end the Depression, starting with Roosevelt's declaration of a four-
day bank holiday in March 1933. In-between, America saw the worst
economic collapse in its history. Thousands of banks failed, a devastating deflation set in, output plunged by a third and unemployment
rose to 25%. The Depression wreaked enormous damage across the
globe, but most of all on America's economic psyche. In its aftermath
the boundaries between government and markets were redrawn.

During September 2008, little more than a year after the financial storm first struck in August 2007, America's government made
its most dramatic interventions in financial markets since the 1930s.
At the time it was not even certain that the economy was in recession and unemployment stood at 6.1%. In two tumultuous weeks
the Federal Reserve and the Treasury between them nationalised the
country's two mortgage giants, Fannie Mae and Freddie Mac; took
over AIG, the world's largest insurance company; in effect extended
government deposit insurance to $3.4 trillion in money-market funds;
temporarily banned short-selling in over 900 mostly financial stocks;
and, most dramatic of all, pledged to take up to $700 billion of toxic
mortgage-related assets on to its books. The Fed and the Treasury
were determined to prevent the kind of banking catastrophe that
precipitated the Depression. Shell-shocked lawmakers cavilled, but
Congress and the administration eventually agreed.

The landscape of American finance has been radically changed. The independent investment bank – a quintessential Wall Street animal that relied on high leverage and wholesale funding – is now all but extinct. Lehman Brothers has gone bust; Bear Stearns and Merrill Lynch have been swallowed by commercial banks; and Goldman Sachs and Morgan Stanley have become commercial banks themselves. The "shadow banking system" – the money-market funds, securities dealers, hedge funds and the other non-bank financial institutions that defined deregulated American finance – is metamorphosing at lightning speed. And in little more than three weeks America's government, all told, expanded its gross liabilities by more than $1 trillion – almost twice as much as the cost so far of the Iraq war.

Beyond that, few things are certain. In late September 2008 the turmoil spread and intensified. Money markets seized up across the globe as banks refused to lend to each other. Five European banks failed and European governments fell over themselves to prop up their banking systems with rescues and guarantees.

Anatomy of a collapse

That crisis has its roots in the biggest housing and credit bubble in history. America's house prices, on average, are down by almost a fifth. Many analysts expect another 10% drop across the country, which would bring the cumulative decline in nominal house prices close to that during the Depression. Other countries may fare even worse. In Britain, for instance, households are even more indebted than in America, house prices rose faster and have so far fallen by less. On a quarterly basis prices are now falling in at least half the 20 countries in *The Economist's* house-price index.

The credit losses on the mortgages that financed these houses and on the pyramids of complicated debt products built on top of them are still mounting. In October 2008 the IMF reckoned that worldwide losses on debt originated in America (primarily related to mortgages) would reach $1.4 trillion, up by almost half from its previous estimate of $945 billion in April. So far some $760 billion has been written down by the banks, insurance companies, hedge funds and others that own the debt.

Globally, banks alone have reported just under $600 billion of credit-related losses and have raised some $430 billion in new capital. It is already clear that many more write-downs lie ahead. The demise of the investment banks, with their far higher gearing, as well as deleveraging among hedge funds and others in the shadow-banking system will add to a global credit contraction of many trillions of dollars. The IMF's "base case" is that American and European banks will shed some $10 trillion of assets, equivalent to 14.5% of their stock of bank credit in 2009. In America overall credit growth will slow to below 1%, down from a post-war annual average of 9%. That alone could drag Western economies' growth rates down by 1.5 percentage points. Without government action along the lines of America's $700 billion plan, the IMF reckons credit could shrink by 7.3% in America, 6.3% in Britain and 4.5% in the rest of Europe.

Much of the rich world is already in recession, partly because of tighter credit and partly because of the surge in oil prices earlier in 2008. Output is falling in Britain, France, Germany and Japan. Judging by the pace of job losses and the weakness of consumer spending, America's economy is also shrinking.

The average downturn after recent banking crises in rich countries lasted four years as banks retrenched and debt-laden households and firms were forced to save more. This time firms are in relatively good shape, but households, particularly in Britain and America, have piled up unprecedented debts. And because the asset and credit bubbles formed in many countries simultaneously, the hangover this time may well be worse.

But history teaches an important lesson: that big banking crises are ultimately solved by throwing in large dollops of public money, and that early and decisive government action, whether to recapitalise banks or take on troubled debts, can minimise the cost to the taxpayer and the damage to the economy. For example, Sweden quickly took over its failed banks after a property bust in the early 1990s and recovered relatively fast. By contrast, Japan took a decade to recover from a financial bust that ultimately cost its taxpayers a sum equivalent to 24% of GDP.

All in all, America's government has put some 7% of GDP on the line, a vast amount of money but well below the 16% of GDP that

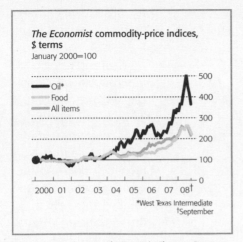

The Economist commodity-price indices, $ terms
January 2000=100

Oil*
Food
All items

*West Texas Intermediate
†September

Sources: *The Economist*; Thomson Datastream

FIG 6.1 Combustible material

the average systemic banking crisis (if there is such a thing) ultimately costs the public purse. Just how America's Troubled Asset Relief Programme (TARP) will work is still unclear. The Treasury plans to buy huge amounts of distressed debt using a reverse auction process, where banks offer to sell at a price and the government buys from the lowest price upwards. The complexities of thousands of different mortgage-backed assets will make this hard. If direct bank recapitalisation is still needed, the Treasury can do that too. The main point is that America is prepared to act, and act decisively.

For the time being, that offers a reason for optimism. So, too, does the relative strength of the biggest emerging markets, particularly China. These economies are not as "decoupled" from the rich world's travails as they once seemed. Their stockmarkets have plunged and many currencies have fallen sharply. Domestic demand in much of the emerging world is slowing but not collapsing. The IMF expects emerging economies, led by China, to grow by 6.9% in 2008 and 6.1% in 2009. That will cushion the world economy but may not save it from recession.

Another short-term fillip comes from the plunge in commodity prices, particularly oil. During the first year of the financial crisis (2007) the boom in commodities that had been building up for five years became a headlong surge. In the year to July 2008 the price of oil almost doubled. *The Economist's* food-price index jumped by nearly 55% (see Figure 6.1). These enormous increases pushed up consumer prices across the globe. In July 2008 average headline inflation was over 4% in rich countries and almost 9% in emerging economies,

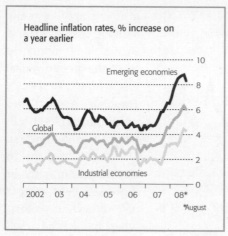

Headline inflation rates, % increase on a year earlier

Emerging economies

Global

Industrial economies

2002 03 04 05 06 07 08*

*August

Source: IMF

FIG 6.2 Danger signals

far higher than central bankers' targets (see Figure 6.2).

High and rising inflation coupled with financial weakness left central bankers with perplexing and poisonous trade-offs. They could tighten monetary policy to prevent higher inflation becoming entrenched (as the European Central Bank did), or they could cut interest rates to cushion financial weakness (as the Fed did). That dilemma is now disappearing. Thanks to the sharp fall in commodity prices, headline consumer prices seem to have peaked and the immediate inflation risk has abated, particularly in weak and financially stressed rich economies. If oil prices stay at mid-2008 levels, headline consumer-price inflation in America may fall below 1% by the middle of 2009.[1] Rather than fretting about inflation, policymakers may soon be worrying about deflation.

The trouble is that because of its large current-account deficit America is heavily reliant on foreign funding. It has the advantage that the dollar is the world's reserve currency, and as the financial turmoil has spread the dollar has strengthened. But this crisis is also testing many of the foundations on which foreigners' faith in the dollar is based, such as limited government and stable capital markets. If foreigners ever flee the dollar, America will face the twin nightmares that haunt emerging countries in a financial collapse: simultaneous banking and currency crises. America's debts, unlike those in many emerging economies, are denominated in its own currency, but a collapse of the dollar would still be a catastrophe.

Tipping point

What will be the long-term effect of this mess on the global economy? Predicting the consequences of an unfinished crisis is perilous. But it is already clear that, even in the absence of a calamity, the direction of globalisation will change. For the past two decades the growing integration of the world economy has coincided with the intellectual ascent of the Anglo-Saxon brand of free-market capitalism, with America as its cheerleader. The freeing of trade and capital flows and the deregulation of domestic industry and finance have both spurred globalisation and come to symbolise it. Global integration, in large part, has been about the triumph of markets over governments. That process is now being reversed in three important ways.

First, Western finance will be re-regulated. At a minimum, the most freewheeling areas of modern finance, such as the $55 trillion market for credit derivatives, will be brought into the regulatory orbit. Rules on capital will be overhauled to reduce leverage and enhance the system's resilience. America's labyrinth of overlapping regulators will be reordered. How much control will be imposed will depend less on ideology than on the severity of the economic downturn. The 1980s savings-and-loan crisis amounted to a sizeable banking bust, but because it did not result in an economic catastrophe, the regulatory consequences were modest. The Depression, in contrast, not only refashioned the structure of American finance but brought regulation to whole swathes of the economy.

That leads to the second point: the balance between state and market is changing in areas other than finance. For many countries a more momentous shock has been the soaring price of commodities, which politicians have also blamed on financial speculation. The food-price spike in late 2007 and early 2008 caused riots in some 30 countries. In response, governments across the emerging world extended their reach, increasing subsidies, fixing prices, banning exports of key commodities and, in India's case, restricting futures trading. Concern about food security, particularly in India and China, was one of the main reasons why the Doha round of trade negotiations collapsed in summer 2008.

Third, America is losing economic clout and intellectual authority.

Just as emerging economies are shaping the direction of global trade, so they will increasingly shape the future of finance. That is particularly true of capital-rich creditor countries such as China. Deleveraging in Western economies will be less painful if savings-rich Asian countries and oil-exporters inject more capital. Influence will increase along with economic heft. China's vice-premier, Wang Qishan, reportedly told his American counterparts at a 2008 Sino-American summit that "the teachers now have some problems."

The enduring attraction of markets

The big question is what lessons the emerging students – and the disgraced teacher – should learn from recent events. How far should the balance between governments and markets shift? Although some rebalancing is needed, particularly in financial regulation, where innovation outpaced a sclerotic supervisory regime, it would be a mistake to blame today's mess only, or even mainly, on modern finance and "free-market fundamentalism". Speculative excesses existed centuries before securitisation was invented, and governments bear direct responsibility for some of today's troubles. Misguided subsidies, on everything from biofuels to mortgage interest, have distorted markets. Loose monetary policy helped to inflate a global credit bubble. Provocative as it may sound in today's febrile and dangerous climate, freer and more flexible markets will still do more for the world economy than the heavy hand of government.

Note

1 By mid-2009 headline inflation in America was negative, and it remained low well into 2010. Commodity prices fell sharply from their mid-2008 levels before rebounding as the world emerged from recession.

Greed – and fear

The golden age of finance collapsed under its own contradictions. Edward Carr asks why it went wrong and what to do next

THE MONUMENT TO Soviet central planning was supposed to have been a heap of surplus left boots without any right ones to match them. The great bull market of the past quarter century is commemorated by millions of empty houses without anyone to buy them. Gosplan drafted workers into grim factories even if their talents would have been better suited elsewhere. Finance beguiled the bright and ambitious and put them to work in the trading rooms of Wall Street and the City of London. Much of their effort was wasted. You can only guess at what else they might have achieved.

When the financial system fails, everyone suffers. Since early 2007 the shock has spread from American housing, sector by sector, economy by economy. Some markets have seized up; others are being pounded by volatility. Everywhere good businesses are going bankrupt and jobs are being destroyed. For the first time since 1991 global average income per head is falling. Even as growth in emerging markets has come to a halt, the rich economies look set to shrink. Alan Greenspan, who as chairman of America's Federal Reserve oversaw the boom, calls the collapse "a once-in-a-half-century, probably once-in-a-century type of event". Financial markets promised prosperity; instead they have brought hardship.

Financial services are in ruins. Perhaps half of all hedge funds will go out of business. Without government aid, so would many banks. Britain has suffered its first bank-run since Disraeli was prime minister in the 1870s. America has stumbled from one rescue to the next. The Wall Street grandees have been humbled. Hundreds of thousands of people in financial services will lose their jobs; many millions of their clients have lost their savings.

For a quarter of a century finance basked in a golden age. Financial globalisation spread capital more widely, markets evolved, businesses were able to finance new ventures and ordinary people had unprecedented access to borrowing and foreign exchange. Modern finance improved countless lives.

But more recently something went awry. Through insurance and saving, financial services are supposed to offer shelter from life's reverses. Instead, financiers grew rich even as their industry put everyone's prosperity in danger. Financial services are supposed to bring together borrowers and savers. But as lending markets have retreated, borrowers have been stranded without credit and savers have seen their pensions and investments melt away. Financial markets are supposed to be a machine for amassing capital and determining who gets to use it and for what. How could they have been so wrong?

Finance is increasingly fragile. Barry Eichengreen of the University of California at Berkeley and Michael Bordo of Rutgers University identify 139 financial crises between 1973 and 1997 (of which 44 took place in high-income countries), compared with a total of only 38 between 1945 and 1971. Crises are twice as common as they were before 1914, the authors conclude.

The paradox is that financial markets can function again only if this lesson is partly forgotten. Financial transactions are a series of promises. You hand your money to a bank, which promises to pay it back when you ask; you invest in a company, which promises you a share of its future profits. Money itself is just a collective agreement that a piece of paper can always be exchanged for goods or services.

Imagine, for a second, how finance began, with small loans within families and between trusted friends. As the circle of lenders and borrowers grew, financial transactions were able to muster larger sums and to spread risk, even as promises became harder to enforce. Paul Seabright, an economist at the University of Toulouse in France, observes that trust in a modern economy has evolved to the miraculous point where people give complete strangers sums of money they would not dream of entrusting to their next-door neighbours. From that a further miracle follows, for trust is what raises the billions of dollars that fund modern industry.

Trust's slow accumulation pushes financial markets forward; its shattering betrayal batters them back. Sometimes this is through bad faith, as when Bernie Madoff, a grand fund manager, allegedly made his investors $50 billion poorer, or mortgage-sellers tempted naive borrowers. But promises made in good faith can be broken too. Indeed, honest failure is even more corrosive of trust than outright criminality. Everyone understands that now.

New order

The failure of finance will affect ideology, too. Many people find capitalism's central planner hard to put up with at the best of times. Free markets shun seemingly worthy causes, whereas the frivolous or apparently undeserving are rewarded. Look at the financial-services industry itself. In America middle-class pay has stalled in recent years but financiers have figured prominently among the tiny number of people who have captured much of the extra income. For as long as the world economy was growing fast, financial markets commanded grudging allegiance. Yet the same financiers who preached the necessity of free markets on the way up have since depended on taxpayers to save their industry at a cost of trillions of dollars.

Financiers will find the arguments for free markets harder to make now that they have lost the benefit of the doubt. Charles Kindleberger's classic study, "Manias, Panics and Crashes: A History of Financial Crises", updated by Robert Aliber in 2005, suggests that financial instability feeds on itself. Japanese savings fled their own bust and sloshed first into the Nordic countries and then into Asia, which suffered contagion in 1997.

Some see today's disaster as a result of that Asian crash. Asian nations – especially China – have been determined to be part of global capital markets but not to run current-account deficits which would leave them vulnerable to sudden currency outflows. So they have been happy to see their money go abroad. In the phrase of Martin Wolf, an economic columnist at the *Financial Times*, they "smoke but do not inhale".

In 2006 America's current-account deficit peaked at 6% of its GDP (see Figure 6.3). Between 2000 and 2008 the country received over $5.7 trillion from abroad to invest, equivalent to over 40% of its 2007 GDP. Over the same period Britain and Ireland absorbed around a fifth of their 2007 GDPs and Spain a vast 50%. The financial system had the job of recycling the money to borrowers. Inevitably, credit

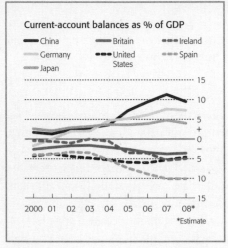

Current-account balances as % of GDP

━━ China　　━━ Britain　　●●● Ireland

━━ Germany　●●● United　━━ Spain
　　　　　　　　States
━━ Japan

Source: IMF

FIG 6.3 The haves and the have-nots

became cheaper and savings declined. In America savings fell from around 10% of disposable income in the 1970s to 1% after 2005.

Not everyone agrees about the cause of this torrent of foreign capital. Although some blame Asian saving, others point to Western extravagance. But there is little doubt about the consequences. All four of the debtor countries in the chart enjoyed housing booms. Jeffry Frieden, a political economist at Harvard University, says about three-quarters of credit booms financed from abroad end up in crashes.

And yet financial services were not so much a victim of the inflows of foreign capital as an eager accomplice. The question is why financial systems are so liable to turn foreign credit into ruinous busts. In particular, why did America, home to the world's most advanced financial system, turn foreign credit into the world's most serious post-war bust?

The suspicion is that American know-how and talent made the disaster worse. Of all the financial instruments to have failed, new-fangled collateralised-debt obligations (CDOs) have turned out to be among the most devastating. One way of thinking about CDOs, says Raghuram Rajan, a professor at the University of Chicago, is as a mechanism for converting mortgage securities and corporate bonds from huge, illiquid assets owned by local investors into liquid financial instruments that could be flogged across the world. Philip Lane, of Trinity College Dublin, thinks that sophisticated American financial services combined dangerously with relatively unsophisticated financial services elsewhere.

Never again, etc

If the price of sophistication is instability, something is wrong. You might conclude that the thing to do is to shackle finance as it was shackled in the 1950s and 60s. If ever there were a moment for this, it would be now. It takes a big upheaval to open the way for radical reform. The structure of financial regulation in America still bears the mark of ideas forged in the Depression.

Reform is certainly needed, yet, for all the excesses and instability of finance, a complete clampdown would be a mistake. For one thing, remember the remarkable prosperity of the past 25 years. Finance deserves some of the credit for that. Note, too, that finance has always been plagued by crises, whether the system is open or closed, simple or sophisticated. Attempts to regulate finance to make it safe often lead to dangerous distortions as clever financiers work around the rules. If there were a simple way to prevent crises altogether, it would already be the foundation stone of financial regulation.

In fact, the aim should be neither to banish finance nor to punish it, but to create a system that supports economic growth through the best mix of state-imposed stability and private initiative. Modern finance is flawed, unstable and prone to excess. But think of those boots and those wasted lives: planned markets are flawed, unstable and excessive too.

The gods strike back

Financial risk got ahead of the world's ability to manage it. Matthew Valencia asks if it can be tamed again

"THE REVOLUTIONARY IDEA that defines the boundary between modern times and the past is the mastery of risk: the notion that the future is more than a whim of the gods and that men and women are not passive before nature." So wrote Peter Bernstein in his seminal history of risk, "Against the Gods", published in 1996. And so it seemed, to all but a few Cassandras, for much of the decade that followed. Finance enjoyed a golden period, with low interest rates, low volatility and high returns. Risk seemed to have been reduced to a permanently lower level.

This purported new paradigm hinged, in large part, on three closely linked developments: the huge growth of derivatives; the decomposition and distribution of credit risk through securitisation; and the formidable combination of mathematics and computing power in risk management that had its roots in academic work of the mid-20th century. It blossomed in the 1990s at firms such as Bankers Trust and JPMorgan, which developed "value-at-risk" (VAR), a way for banks to calculate how much they could expect to lose when things got really rough.

Suddenly it seemed possible for any financial risk to be measured to five decimal places, and for expected returns to be adjusted accordingly. Banks hired hordes of PhD-wielding "quants" to fine-tune ever more complex risk models. The belief took hold that, even as profits were being boosted by larger balance-sheets and greater leverage (borrowing), risk was being capped by a technological shift.

There was something self-serving about this. The more that risk could be calibrated, the greater the opportunity to turn debt into securities that could be sold or held in trading books, with lower capital charges than regular loans. Regulators accepted this, arguing that the "great moderation" had subdued macroeconomic dangers and that securitisation had chopped up individual firms' risks into manageable lumps. This faith in the new, technology-driven order was reflected in the Basel 2 bank-capital rules, which relied heavily on the banks' internal models.

There were bumps along the way, such as the near-collapse of Long-Term Capital Management (LTCM), a hedge fund, and the dotcom bust, but each time markets recovered relatively quickly. Banks grew cocky. But that sense of security was destroyed by the meltdown of 2007–09, which as much as anything was a crisis of modern metrics-based risk management. The idea that markets can be left to police themselves turned out to be the world's most expensive mistake, requiring $15 trillion in capital injections and other forms of support. "It has cost a lot to learn how little we really knew," says a senior central banker. Another lesson was that managing risk is as much about judgment as about numbers. Trying ever harder to capture risk in mathematical formulae can be counterproductive if such a degree of accuracy is intrinsically unattainable.

For now, the hubris of spurious precision has given way to humility. It turns out that in financial markets "black swans", or extreme events, occur much more often than the usual probability models suggest. Worse, finance is becoming more fragile: these days blow-ups are twice as frequent as they were before the first world war, according to Barry Eichengreen of the University of California at Berkeley and Michael Bordo of Rutgers University. Benoit Mandelbrot, the father of fractal theory and a pioneer in the study of market swings, argues that finance is prone to a "wild" randomness not usually seen in nature. In markets, "rare big changes can be more significant than the sum of many small changes," he says. If financial markets followed the normal bell-shaped distribution curve, in which meltdowns are very rare, the stockmarket crash of 1987, the interest-rate turmoil of 1992 and the 2008 crash would each be expected only once in the lifetime of the universe.

This is changing the way many financial firms think about risk, says Greg Case, chief executive of Aon, an insurance broker. Before the crisis they were looking at things like pandemics, cyber-security and terrorism as possible causes of black swans. Now they are turning to risks from within the system, and how they can become amplified in combination.

Cheap as chips, and just as bad for you

It would, though, be simplistic to blame the crisis solely, or even mainly, on sloppy risk managers or wild-eyed quants. Cheap money led to the wholesale underpricing of risk; America ran negative real interest rates in 2002–05, even though consumer-price inflation was quiescent. Plenty of economists disagree with the assertion by Ben Bernanke, chairman of the Federal Reserve, that the crisis had more to do with lax regulation of mortgage products than loose monetary policy.

Equally damaging were policies to promote home ownership in America using Fannie Mae and Freddie Mac, the country's two mortgage giants. They led the duo to binge on securities backed by shoddily underwritten loans.

In the absence of strict limits, higher leverage followed naturally from low interest rates. The debt of America's financial firms ballooned relative to the overall economy (see Figure 6.4). At the peak of the madness, the median large bank had borrowings of 37 times its equity, meaning it could be wiped out by a loss of just 2–3% of its assets. Borrowed money allowed investors to fake "alpha", or above-market returns, says Benn Steil of the Council on Foreign Relations.

The agony was compounded by the proliferation of short-term debt to support illiquid long-term assets, much of it issued beneath the regulatory radar in highly leveraged "shadow" banks, such as structured investment vehicles. When markets froze, sponsoring entities, usually banks, felt morally obliged to absorb their losses. "Reputation risk was shown to have a very real financial price," says Doug Roeder of the Office of the Comptroller of the Currency, an American regulator.

Everywhere you looked, moreover, incentives were misaligned. Firms deemed "too big to fail" nestled under implicit guarantees. Sensitivity to risk was dulled by the "Greenspan put", a belief that America's Federal Reserve would ride to the rescue with lower rates and liquidity support if needed. Scrutiny of borrowers was delegated to rating agencies, who were paid by the debt-issuers. Some products were so complex, and the chains from borrower to end-investor so long, that thorough due diligence was impossible. A proper

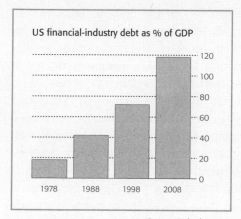

US financial-industry debt as % of GDP

Source: Federal Reserve

FIG 6.4 Borrowed time

understanding of a typical collateralised debt obligation (CDO), a structured bundle of debt securities, would have required reading 30,000 pages of documentation.

Fees for securitisers were paid largely upfront, increasing the temptation to originate, flog and forget. The problems with bankers' pay went much wider, meaning that it was much better to be an employee than a shareholder (or, eventually, a taxpayer picking up the bail-out tab). The role of top executives' pay has been overblown. Top brass at Lehman Brothers and American International Group (AIG) suffered massive losses when share prices tumbled. A study found that banks where chief executives had more of their wealth tied up in the firm performed worse, not better, than those with apparently less strong incentives. One explanation is that they took risks they thought were in shareholders' best interests, but were proved wrong. Motives lower down the chain were more suspect. It was too easy for traders to cash in on short-term gains and skirt responsibility for any time-bombs they had set ticking.

Asymmetries wreaked havoc in the vast over-the-counter derivatives market, too, where even large dealing firms lacked the information to determine the consequences of others failing. Losses on contracts linked to Lehman turned out to be modest, but nobody knew that when it collapsed in September 2008, causing panic. Likewise, it was hard to gauge the exposures to "tail" risks built up by sellers of swaps on CDOs such as AIG and bond insurers. These were essentially put options, with limited upside and a low but real probability of catastrophic losses.

Another factor in the build-up of excessive risk was what Andy

Haldane, head of financial stability at the Bank of England, has described as "disaster myopia". Like drivers who slow down after seeing a crash but soon speed up again, investors exercise greater caution after a disaster, but these days it takes less than a decade to make them reckless again. Not having seen a debt-market crash since 1998, investors piled into ever riskier securities in 2003–07 to maintain yield at a time of low interest rates. Risk-management models reinforced this myopia by relying too heavily on recent data samples with a narrow distribution of outcomes, especially in subprime mortgages.

A further hazard was summed up by the assertion in 2007 by Chuck Prince, then Citigroup's boss, that "as long as the music is playing, you've got to get up and dance." Performance is usually judged relative to rivals or to an industry benchmark, encouraging banks to mimic each other's risk-taking, even if in the long run it benefits no one. In mortgages, bad lenders drove out good ones, keeping up with aggressive competitors for fear of losing market share. A few held back, but it was not easy: when JPMorgan sacrificed five percentage points of return on equity in the short run, it was lambasted by shareholders who wanted it to "catch up" with zippier-looking rivals.

An overarching worry is that the complexity of today's global financial network makes occasional catastrophic failure inevitable. For example, the market for credit derivatives galloped far ahead of its supporting infrastructure. Only now are serious moves being made to push these contracts through central clearing-houses which ensure that trades are properly collateralised and guarantee their completion if one party defaults.

Network overload

The push to allocate capital ever more efficiently over the past 20 years created what Till Guldimann, the father of VAR and vice-chairman of SunGard, a technology firm, calls "capitalism on steroids". Banks got to depend on the modelling of prices in esoteric markets to gauge risks and became adept at gaming the rules. As a result, capital was not being spread around as efficiently as everyone believed.

Big banks had also grown increasingly interdependent through the boom in derivatives, computer-driven equities trading and so

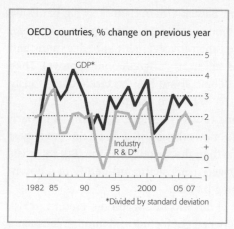

OECD countries, % change on previous year

GDP*

Industry
R & D*

5
4
3
2
1
+
0
−
1

1982 85   90   95   2000   05 07
*Divided by standard deviation

Source: OECD

FIG 6.5 In lockstep

on. Another bond was cross-ownership: at the start of the crisis, financial firms held big dollops of each other's common and hybrid equity. Such tight coupling of components increases the danger of "non-linear" outcomes, where a small change has a big impact. "Financial markets are not only vulnerable to black swans but have become the perfect breeding ground for them," says Mr Guldimann. In such a network a firm's troubles can have an exaggerated effect on the perceived riskiness of its trading partners. When Lehman's credit-default spreads rose to distressed levels, AIG's jumped by twice what would have been expected on its own, according to the IMF.

Mr Haldane has suggested that these knife-edge dynamics were caused not only by complexity but also – paradoxically – by homogeneity. Banks, insurers, hedge funds and others bought smorgasbords of debt securities to try to reduce risk through diversification, but the ingredients were similar: leveraged loans, American mortgages and the like. From the individual firm's perspective this looked sensible. But for the system as a whole it put everyone's eggs in the same few baskets, as reflected in their returns (see Figure 6.5).

Efforts are now under way to deal with these risks. The Financial Stability Board, an international group of regulators, is trying to co-ordinate global reforms in areas such as capital, liquidity and mechanisms for rescuing or dismantling troubled banks. Its biggest challenge will be to make the system more resilient to the failure of giants. There are deep divisions over how to set about this, with some favouring tougher capital requirements, others break-ups, still others – including America – a combination of remedies.

In January 2010 President Barack Obama shocked big banks by proposing a tax on their liabilities and a plan to cap their size, ban "proprietary" trading and limit their involvement in hedge funds and private equity. The proposals still need congressional approval. They were seen as energising the debate about how to tackle dangerously large firms, though the reaction in Europe was mixed.

Regulators are also inching towards a more "systemic" approach to risk. The old supervisory framework assumed that if the 100 largest banks were individually safe, then the system was too. But the crisis showed that even well-managed firms, acting prudently in a downturn, can undermine the strength of all.

The banks themselves will have to find a middle ground in risk management, somewhere between gut feeling and number fetishism. Much of the progress made in quantitative finance was real enough, but a firm that does not understand the flaws in its models is destined for trouble. The rules will have to be both tightened and better enforced to avoid future crises – but all the reforms in the world will never guarantee total safety.

The nuts and bolts come apart

As global demand contracts, trade is slumping and
protectionism rising

COMPARISONS TO THE DEPRESSION feature in almost every discussion of the global economic crisis. In world trade, such parallels
are especially chilling. Trade declined alarmingly in the early 1930s
as global demand imploded, prices collapsed and governments
embarked on a destructive, protectionist spiral of higher tariffs and
retaliation.

Trade is contracting again, at a rate unmatched in the post-war
period. In March 2009 the World Trade Organisation (WTO) predicted
that the volume of global merchandise trade would shrink by 9% in
2009. This would be the first fall in trade flows since 1982. Between
1990 and 2006 trade volumes grew by more than 6% a year, easily
outstripping the growth rate of world output, which was about 3%
(see Figure 6.6). Now the global economic machine has gone into
reverse: output is declining and trade is tumbling at a faster pace. The
turmoil has shaken commerce in goods of all sorts, bought and sold
by rich and poor countries alike.

It is too soon to talk of a new protectionist spiral. Nevertheless,
errors of policy risk making a bad thing worse – despite politicians'
promises to keep markets open. When they met in November 2008,
the leaders of the G20 rich and emerging economies declared that
they would eschew protectionism. But this pledge was not honoured.
According to the World Bank, 17 members of the group had taken a
total of 47 trade-restricting steps since November.

Modern protectionism is more subtle and varied than the 1930s
version. In the Depression tariffs were the weapon of choice. America's Smoot-Hawley act, passed in 1930, increased nearly 900 American import duties – which were already high by today's standards
– and provoked widespread retaliation from America's trading partners. A few tariffs have been raised this time, but tighter licensing
requirements, import bans and anti-dumping (imposing extra duties

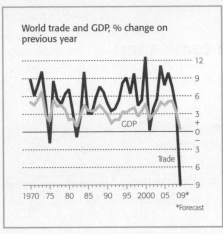

World trade and GDP, % change on previous year

12
9
6
3
+
0
−
3
6
9

GDP

Trade

1970 75 80 85 90 95 2000 05 09*

*Forecast

Sources: IMF; World Bank; WTO

FIG 6.6 Over the edge

on goods supposedly dumped at below cost by exporters) have also been used. Rich countries have included discriminatory procurement provisions in their fiscal-stimulus bills and offered subsidies to ailing national industries. These days, protectionism comes in 57 varieties.

There are good reasons for thinking that the world has less to fear from protectionism than in the past. International agreements to limit tariffs, built over the post-war decades, are a safeguard against all-out tariff wars. The growth of global supply chains, which have bound national economies together tightly, have made it more difficult for governments to increase tariffs without harming producers in their own countries.

But these defences may not be strong enough. Multilateral agreements provide little insurance against domestic subsidies, fiercer use of anti-dumping or the other forms of creeping protection. Most countries are able to raise tariffs, because their applied rates are below the maximum allowed by their WTO commitments. They may choose to do so despite the possible disruption to global supply chains. And because global sourcing amplifies the effect of tariff rises, even action that is permissible under WTO rules could cause a lot of damage. The subtler variants of protection may be similarly disruptive.

The gears of globalisation

The immediate cause of shrinking trade is plain: global recession means a collapse in demand. The credit crunch adds an additional squeeze, thanks to an estimated shortfall of $100 billion in trade finance, which lubricates 90% of world trade.

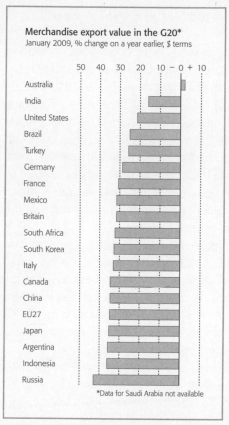

Merchandise export value in the G20*
January 2009, % change on a year earlier, $ terms

*Data for Saudi Arabia not available

Australia, India, United States, Brazil, Turkey, Germany, France, Mexico, Britain, South Africa, South Korea, Italy, Canada, China, EU27, Japan, Argentina, Indonesia, Russia

Sources: World Bank; National statistics

FIG 6.7 Australia fair, others foul

Just as striking as the speed of the downturn in trade is its indiscriminate nature. The World Bank has trade data for 45 countries (figures for G20 countries in January 2009 are shown in Figure 6.7). These are values, expressed in American dollars, and so have been depressed not only by lower volumes but also by falling prices and a stronger dollar. The exports of 37 of these 45 countries were more than a quarter lower than in January 2008. Countries as diverse as Ecuador, France, Indonesia, the Philippines and South Africa saw exports drop by 30% or more. Commodity exporters, such as Argentina, have suffered with sellers of sophisticated manufactures, such as Germany and Japan.

Kei-Mu Yi, an economist at the Federal Reserve Bank of Philadelphia, argues that trade has fallen so fast and so uniformly around the world largely because of the rise of "vertical specialisation", or global supply chains. This contributed to trade's rapid expansion in recent decades. Now it is adding to the rate of shrinkage. When David Ricardo argued in the early 19th century that comparative advantage was the basis of trade, he conceived of countries specialising in products, like wine or cloth. But Mr Yi points out that countries now specialise not so much in final products as in steps in the process of production.

Trade grows much faster in a world with global sourcing than in a world of trade in finished goods because components and part-finished items have to cross borders several times. The trade figures are also boosted by the practice of measuring the gross value of imports and exports rather than their net value. For example, a tractor made in America would once have been made from American steel and parts; it would have touched the trade data only if it was exported. Now, it may contain steel from India, and be stamped and pressed in Mexico, before being sold abroad. As a result, changes in demand in one country now affect not just the domestic economy but also the trade flows and economies of several countries.

Mr Yi points out that this mechanism can be seen at work in data such as those for the American automotive trade for the last three months of 2008. Imports from everywhere fell by about 20%. On the export side, sales to America's partners in the North American Free Trade Agreement (NAFTA) fell by 20% whereas those to non-NAFTA countries rose slightly. This, he argues, is because three-quarters of exports to non-NAFTA countries consist of finished vehicles, whereas 60% of exports to NAFTA partners consist of parts and components, most of which return to the United States embodied in imported vehicles. So American exports to other NAFTA countries are to a large extent determined by America's own demand for cars.

By making trade flows more sensitive to falls in output, vertical specialisation may provide some insurance against widespread protectionism. Manufacturers that rely on imported inputs may resist higher tariffs because they push up the prices of those inputs, making domestic industry less competitive.

Governments using tariffs as trade weapons now have to calculate the consequences far more carefully. This is borne out, for example, by Mexico's response in March 2009 to the suspension by America of a NAFTA programme that allowed some Mexican truckers to carry goods north of the border. Mexico raised some tariffs, but by less than NAFTA rules allowed, and chose the goods carefully in order to limit the damage to its own industries.

Nevertheless, there is plenty of evidence that developing countries, at least, continue to use tariffs extensively. In the World Bank's study, tariff increases accounted for half of the protective measures by these countries. Ecuador raised duties on 600 goods. Russia increased them on used cars. India put them up on some kinds of steel. Developing countries have more scope for raising tariffs without breaking WTO rules than richer ones do, because the gap between their applied rates and the ceilings they agreed to is greater than for developed countries.

When governments do impose tariffs, vertical supply chains amplify their effects. Because tariffs are typically levied on the gross value crossing the border (with some exceptions, such as exports from Mexican *maquiladoras*), trade responds more to changes in tariffs – down or up – with global supply chains than without.

But there is another, more subtle reason to worry about even small rises in tariffs. Theoretical models that incorporate vertical specialisation find that it takes off only when tariffs fall below a threshold level. Once this happens, however, trade explodes, so that a slight lowering of trade barriers can cause a huge increase in trade. By the same token, if tariffs rose above a certain point – which might be below the maximum agreed on at the WTO – global supply chains would disintegrate. Trade would drop even more steeply than it has in recent months.

That said, supply chains need not snap so easily. Even if tariffs go up, other costs that determine the viability of supply chains may go down: the price of oil (and hence the cost of transport) fell a long way in 2008. Firms have invested a lot in their supply chains and will be loth to abandon them. And if global supply chains do survive, vertical specialisation could help trade recover speedily when demand returns.

Although increased tariffs are a cause for concern, they are far from the only form of protection being used in this crisis. Two-thirds of the trade-restricting measures documented by the World Bank are non-tariff barriers of various kinds. As with tariffs, developing countries are the principal wielders of these weapons.

Indonesia has specified that certain categories of goods, such as clothes, shoes and toys, may be imported through only five ports. Argentina has imposed discretionary licensing requirements on car parts, textiles, televisions, toys, shoes and leather goods; licences for all these used to be granted automatically. Some countries have imposed outright import bans, often justified by a tightening of safety rules or by environmental concerns. For example, China has stopped imports of a wide range of European food and drink, including Irish pork, Italian brandy and Spanish dairy products. The Indian government has banned Chinese toys.

In addition, anti-dumping is on the increase. The number of anti-dumping cases initiated at the WTO had been declining, but it started to pick up in the second half of 2007. Chad Bown, an economist at Brandeis University, estimated that the 2008 number would be 31% higher than in the previous year. The number of cases ending with extra duties went up by 20%. India was the biggest initiator of anti-dumping action, and America and the European Union imposed duties most frequently.

Rich countries' weapon of choice so far is neither tariffs nor non-tariff barriers to imports. They have been keen users instead of subsidies to troubled domestic industries, particularly carmakers. Some economists, such as Gene Grossman, of Princeton University, cite this as evidence that global sourcing has changed the political economy of protection. The American automotive industry no longer lobbies for direct protection, as it used to, because it imports much of its value-added and competes with foreign firms that assemble their cars in America. Carmakers now prefer explicit subsidies, and the world is replete with examples. Besides America, Argentina, Australia, Brazil, Britain, Canada, China, France, Germany, Italy and Sweden have all also provided direct or indirect subsidies to carmakers. The World Bank reckons that proposed subsidies for the car industry amount to $48 billion. Nearly 90% of this is in rich countries, where it can easily be slipped into budgetary packages to stimulate demand.

The worry about such subsidies is that they could cause production to switch from more efficient plants (eg, in central and eastern Europe) to less efficient ones in rich countries with deep pockets (eg, in western Europe). Whether the location of output is shifting is not yet clear, but politicians plainly hope it will. On March 19th 2009 Luc Chatel, the French industry minister, boasted that Renault's plans to create 400 jobs at a factory near Paris by "repatriating" some production from Slovenia was the result of government aid. Renault denied this, saying that it was at full capacity in Slovenia.

There are some international rules to prevent distorting subsidies. The EU has regulations to limit state aid, and is looking into its members' assistance to carmakers. Gary Hufbauer, of the Peterson Institute for International Economics in Washington, DC, argues that American subsidies transgress WTO norms.

Helpful ambiguity

However, WTO action against subsidies is not straightforward. To complain successfully, a country has to show that a subsidy meets several criteria. Then there is a pots-and-kettles problem: having subsidies of your own does not stop you from challenging someone else's, but if you pick a fight they may have a go at yours. This uncertainty and ambiguity only adds to subsidies' attraction. Governments can aid their carmakers and at the same time criticise others for their protectionist ways.

Protectionist urges are also being bolstered by countries' seeming inability to co-ordinate their fiscal stimulus programmes. Some countries have been reluctant to work the budgetary pump for fear that their extra demand will leak abroad to the benefit of foreigners. To stop the seepage, some governments have inserted discriminatory conditions into their fiscal programmes, the prime example being the "Buy American" procurement rules. These were weakened after protests and threats of retaliation from abroad, but not before the prospects for global co-operation had been dented. Greater co-ordination of fiscal expansion would ease governments' worries about leakage, because everyone else would be leaking too: all would gain from each other's spending.

What should world leaders do to stop protection fraying the threads that tie the world economy together? The pious declaration at the January 2009 G20 meeting has had little effect. The difficulty lies in devising something comprehensive and detailed enough to address the variety of protectionist measures that are being deployed in the crisis, and doing it quickly enough to maintain open trade.

Many argue that the most important thing for world leaders to do is to pledge a quick completion of the Doha round of trade talks, which stalled for the umpteenth time in summer 2008. By reducing tariff ceilings, this would place tighter limits on countries' ability to increase tariffs. It would also ban export subsidies in agriculture, which are being used with greater vigour, especially as prices of farm goods fall. The EU, for example, has announced new export subsidies for butter, cheese and milk powder. Most important, completing Doha would be the clearest and most tangible evidence possible of a commitment to consolidating and building on the gains from more open trade secured in successive rounds since the second world war.

Some economists disagree. Aaditya Mattoo, of the World Bank, and Arvind Subramanian, of the Peterson Institute, argue that the Doha round is too ambitious given the state of the world economy, because it seeks to open markets for rich countries' manufactured goods just when the politics are against it. At the same time, they point out that Doha would not restrict the use of some non-tariff measures causing most concern, such as the Buy American provisions or subsidies for failing industries. Messrs Mattoo and Subramanian suggest a new "crisis round" of world trade talks. In the first instance, WTO members could commit themselves to a standstill on all forms of protectionism.

Several other economists have also proposed a standstill. However, Messrs Mattoo and Subramanian suggest that in order to give governments a political reason to agree to this, they should also be allowed to postpone further liberalisation for the duration of the crisis. They would then embark on a new round instead of Doha, which would address the forms of protection that now look most pressing.

But the appetite for starting yet another series of talks is likely to be limited. Even if the crisis round's agenda were more realistic than Doha's (which isn't obvious), there would be no guarantee that it could be concluded quickly enough to stop the bleeding in global trade.

Whatever they think about Doha or about the idea of a crisis round, most economists will agree that a simple promise to resist protectionism will not suffice. Some thing more specific is needed. A good start would be for governments, beginning with the leaders of the G20, to draw up a comprehensive list of protectionist measures that goes beyond tariffs and export subsidies. They could then agree to go no further with these than they have already.

Next, an agreement on co-ordinating fiscal policy would go a long way towards making such a standstill commitment credible, because it would alleviate worries about leakages abroad. Finally, empowering the WTO to name those who break the standstill would help to underpin it. The threat of embarrassment may make some countries think twice.

During the Depression, the volume of world trade shrank by a quarter. Nothing like that has been seen or forecast so far. Yet one lesson from the worldwide economic distress of three-quarters of a century ago is that once trade barriers come up, they take years of negotiation to dismantle. Preventing protectionism from getting worse is preferable to having to repair the damage afterwards. And even if a full-blown trade war can be ruled out, death by a thousand cuts cannot. The costs of myriad piecemeal measures could still add up to damaging protectionism. And when demand does eventually revive, if the world economy is supported by an open system of trade, it will recover all the faster.

When jobs disappear

The world economy faces the biggest rise in unemployment in decades. How governments react will shape labour markets for years to come

IN FEBRUARY 2009 America's unemployment rate climbed to 8.1%, the highest in a quarter of a century. For those newly out of a job, the chances of finding another soon are the worst since records began 50 years ago. In China 20m migrant workers (maybe 3% of the labour force) have been laid off. Cambodia's textile industry, its main source of exports, has cut one worker in ten. In Spain the building bust has pushed the jobless rate up by two-thirds in a year, to 14.8% in January 2009. And in Japan, where official unemployment used to be all but unknown, tens of thousands of people on temporary contracts are losing not just their jobs but also the housing provided by their employers.

The next phase of the world's economic downturn is taking shape: a global jobs crisis. Its contours are only just becoming clear, but the severity, breadth and likely length of the recession, together with changes in the structure of labour markets in both rich and emerging economies, suggest the world is about to undergo its biggest increase in unemployment for decades.

In the last three months of 2008 America's GDP slumped at an annualised rate of 6.2%. This quarter may not be much better. Output has shrunk even faster in countries dependent on exports (such as Germany, Japan and several emerging Asian economies) or foreign finance (notably central and eastern Europe). The IMF said this week that global output will probably fall for the first time since the second world war. The World Bank expects the fastest contraction of trade since the Depression.

An economic collapse on this scale is bound to hit jobs hard. In its latest quarterly survey Manpower, an employment-services firm, finds that in 23 of the 33 countries it covers, companies' hiring intentions are the weakest on record (see Figure 6.8). Because changes in

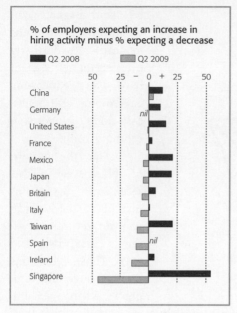

% of employers expecting an increase in hiring activity minus % expecting a decrease

■ Q2 2008   ▨ Q2 2009

China
Germany
United States
France
Mexico
Japan
Britain
Italy
Taiwan
Spain
Ireland
Singapore

Source: Manpower

FIG 6.8 The jobs crunch

unemployment lag behind those in output, jobless rates would rise further even if economies stopped contracting today. But there is little hope of that. And several features of this recession look especially harmful.

The credit crunch has exacerbated the impact of falling demand, pressing cash-strapped firms to cut costs more quickly. The asset bust and unwinding of debt that lie behind the recession mean that eventual recovery is likely to be too weak to create jobs rapidly. And when demand does revive, the composition of jobs will change. In a post-bubble world indebted consumers will save more and surplus economies, from China to Germany, will have to rely more on domestic spending. The booming industries of recent years, from construction to finance, will not bounce back. Millions of people, from Wall Street bankers to Chinese migrants, will need to find wholly different lines of work.

For now the damage is most obvious in America, where the recession began earlier than elsewhere (in December 2007, according to the National Bureau of Economic Research) and where the ease of hiring and firing means changes in the demand for workers show up quickly in employment rolls. The economy began to lose jobs in January 2008. At first the decline was fairly modest and largely confined to construction (thanks to the housing bust) and manufacturing (where employment has long been in decline). But since September 2008 it has accelerated and broadened. Of the 4.4m jobs lost since the

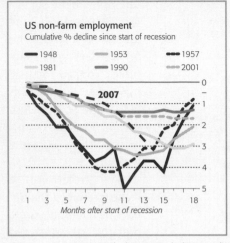

US non-farm employment
Cumulative % decline since start of recession

━━ 1948   ▨▨▨ 1953   ●━● 1957
━━ 1981   ━━ 1990   ▨▨➤ 2001

Months after start of recession

Source: Federal Reserve Bank of Minneapolis

FIG 6.9 Compare and contrast

recession began, 3.3m went in the six months to March 2009. Virtually every sector has been hit hard. Only education, government and health care added workers in February 2009.

So far, the pattern of job losses in this recession resembles that of the early post-war downturns (starting in 1948, 1953 and 1957). Those recessions brought huge, but temporary, swings in employment, in an economy far more reliant on manufacturing than today's. As a share of the workforce, more jobs have been lost in this recession than in any since 1957. The pace at which people are losing their jobs, measured by the share of the workforce filing for weekly jobless claims, is much quicker than in the downturns of 1990 and 2001 (see Figure 6.9).

The worry, however, is that the hangover from excess debt and the housing bust will mean a slow revival – looking more like the jobless recoveries after the past two downturns than like the vigorous V-shaped rebounds from the early post-war recessions. Ominous signs are a sharp increase in permanent-job losses and a rise in the number of people out of work for six months or more to 1.9% of the labour force, near a post-war high.

Official forecasts can barely keep up. In its budget in February 2009 the Obama administration expected a jobless rate of 8.1% for the year. That figure was reached within the month. Many Wall Street seers think the rate will exceed 10% by 2010 and may surpass the post-1945 peak of 10.8%. Past banking crises indicate an even gloomier prognosis. A study by Carmen Reinhart of the University of Maryland and Ken Rogoff of Harvard University suggests that the unemployment

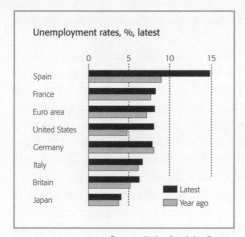

Unemployment rates, %, latest

| | 0 | 5 | 10 | 15 |
Spain
France
Euro area
United States
Germany
Italy
Britain
Japan

■ Latest
■ Year ago

Sources: National statistics; Eurostat

FIG 6.10 Sooner or later

rate rose by an average of seven percentage points after other big post-war banking busts. That implies a rate for America of around 12%.

Moreover, the official jobless rate understates the amount of slack by more than in previous downturns. Many companies are cutting hours to reduce costs. At 33.3 hours, the average working week is the shortest since at least 1964. Unpaid leave is becoming more common, and not only at the cyclical manufacturing firms where it is established practice. A recent survey by Watson Wyatt, a firm of consultants, finds that almost one employer in ten intends to shorten the work week in coming months. Compulsory unpaid leave is planned by 6% of firms. Another 9% will have voluntary leave.

Europe's jobs markets look less dire, for now. That is partly because the recession began later there, partly because joblessness had been unusually low by European standards and partly because Europe's less flexible labour markets react more slowly than America's. The euro area's unemployment rate was 8.2% in January 2009, up from 7.2% a year before. That of the whole European Union was 7.6%, up from 6.8%. For the first time in years American and European jobless rates are roughly in line (see Figure 6.10).

Within the EU there are big variations. Ireland and Spain, where construction boomed and then subsided most dramatically, have already seen heavy job losses. Almost 30% of Ireland's job growth in the first half of this decade came from the building trade. Its unemployment rate almost doubled in 2008. In Britain, another post-property-bubble economy, the rate is also rising markedly. At the end of 2008 6.3% of workers were jobless, up from 5.2% the year before. In

March 2009 British unemployment rose above 2m for the first time in more than a decade.

In continental Europe's biggest economies, the consequences for jobs of shrivelling output are only just becoming visible. Although output in Germany fell at an annualised rate of 7% in the last quarter of 2008, unemployment has been only inching up. In March 2009 the rate was still lower than it was a year earlier. Even so, no one doubts the direction in which joblessness is heading. In January the European Commission forecast the EU's jobless rate to rise to 9.5% in 2010. As in America, many private-sector economists expect 10% or more.

Structural changes in Europe's labour markets suggest that jobs will go faster than in previous downturns. Temporary contracts have proliferated in many countries, as a way around the expense and difficulty of firing permanent workers. Much of the reduction in European unemployment earlier this decade was due to the rapid growth of these contracts. Now the process is going into reverse. In Spain, Europe's most extreme example of a "dual" labour market, all the job loss of 2008 was borne by temps. In France employment on temporary contracts has fallen by a fifth. Permanent jobs have so far been barely touched.

Although the profusion of temporary contracts has brought greater flexibility, it has laid the burden of adjustment disproportionately on the low-skilled, the young and immigrants. The rising share of immigrants in Europe's workforce also makes the likely path of unemployment less certain. As Samuel Bentolila, an economist at CEMFI, a Spanish graduate school, points out, the jump in Spain's jobless rate is not due to fewer jobs alone. Thanks to continued immigration, the labour force is still growing apace. In Britain, in contrast, hundreds of thousands of migrant Polish workers are reckoned to have gone home.

Despite having few immigrants, Japan is also showing the strains of a dual labour market. Indeed, its workforce is more starkly divided than that of any other industrial country. "Regular" workers enjoy strong protection; the floating army of temporary, contract and part-time staff have almost none. Since the 1990s, the "lost decade", firms have relied increasingly on these irregulars, who now account for one-third of all workers, up from 20% in 1990.

As Japanese industry has collapsed, almost all the jobs shed have been theirs. Most are ineligible for unemployment assistance. A labour-ministry official estimates that a third of the 160,000 who lost work during 2007 lost their homes as well, sometimes with only a few days' notice. In January 2009 several hundred homeless temporary workers set up a tent village in Hibiya Park in central Tokyo, across from the labour ministry and a few blocks from the Imperial Palace. Worse lies ahead. Overall unemployment, 4.1% in March 2009, was widely expected to surpass the post-war peak of 5.8% within the year. In Japan too, some economists talk of double digits.

In emerging economies the scale of the problem is much harder to gauge. Anecdotal evidence abounds of falling employment, particularly in construction, mining and export-oriented manufacturing. But official figures on both job losses and unemployment rates are squishier. Estimates from the International Labour Organisation suggest the number of people unemployed in emerging economies rose by 8m in 2008 to 158m in early 2009, an overall jobless rate of around 5.9%. In a 2008 report the ILO projected several scenarios for 2009. Its gloomiest suggested there could be an additional 32m jobless in the emerging world in 2009. That estimate seems all too plausible. Millions will return from formal employment to the informal sector and from cities to rural areas. The World Bank reckons that another 53m people were pushed into extreme poverty in 2009.

History implies that high unemployment is not just an economic problem but also a political tinderbox. Weak labour markets risk fanning xenophobia, particularly in Europe, where this is the first downturn since immigration soared. China's leadership is terrified by the prospect of social unrest from rising joblessness, particularly among the urban elite.

Given these dangers, politicians will not sit still as jobs disappear. Their most important defence is to boost demand. All the main rich economies and most big emerging ones have announced fiscal stimulus packages.

Since most emerging economies lack broad unemployment insurance, the main way they help the jobless is through labour-intensive government infrastructure projects as well as conditional cash transfers for the poorest. China's fiscal boost includes plenty of money for infrastructure; India is accelerating projects worth 0.7% of GDP. However, a few emerging economies have more creative unemployment-insurance schemes than anything in the rich world. In Chile and Colombia formal-sector workers pay into individual unemployment accounts, on which they can draw if they lose their jobs. Many more countries have created prefunded pension systems based on individual accounts. Robert Holzmann of the World Bank thinks people should be allowed to borrow from such accounts while unemployed. Several countries are considering the idea.

In developed countries, governments' past responses to high unemployment have had lasting and sometimes harmful effects. When joblessness rose after the 1970s oil shocks, Europe's governments, pressed by strong trade unions, kept labour markets rigid and tried to cut dole queues by encouraging early retirement. Coupled with generous welfare benefits this resulted in decades of high "structural" unemployment and a huge rise in the share of people without work. In America, where the social safety net was flimsier, there were far fewer regulatory rigidities and people were more willing to move, so workers responded more flexibly to structural shifts. Less than six years after hitting 10.8%, the post-war record, in 1982, America's jobless rate was close to 5%.

Policy in America still leans towards keeping benefits low and markets flexible rather than easing the pain of unemployment. Benefits for the jobless are, if anything, skimpier than in the 1970s. Unemployment insurance is funded jointly by states and the federal government. The states set the eligibility criteria and in many cases have not kept up with changes in the composition of the workforce. In 32 states, for instance, part-time workers are ineligible for benefits. All told, fewer than half of America's unemployed receive assistance. The benefits they get also vary a lot from state to state, but overall are among the lowest in the OECD when compared with the average wage.

America's recent stimulus package strengthened this safety net. Jobless benefits have increased modestly, their maximum duration has been extended, and states have been given a large financial incentive to broaden eligibility. The package also includes temporary subsidies to help pay for laid-off workers' health insurance. Even so, benefits remain meagre.

Housing is a far bigger drag on American job mobility. Almost a fifth of American households with mortgages owe more than their house is worth, and house prices are set to fall further. "Negative equity" can lock in homeowners, making it hard to move to a new job. A study suggests that homeowners with negative equity are 50% less mobile than others.

Europe's governments, at least so far, are trying hard to avoid the mistakes of the 1970s and 1980s. As Stefano Scarpetta of the OECD points out, today's policies are designed to keep people working rather than to encourage them to leave the labour force. Several countries, from Spain to Sweden, have temporarily cut social insurance contributions to reduce labour costs.

A broader group, including Austria, Denmark, France, Germany, Hungary, Italy and Spain, are encouraging firms to shorten work weeks rather than lay people off, by topping up the pay of workers on short hours. Germany, for instance, has long had a scheme that covers 60% of the gap between shorter hours and a full-time wage for up to six months. The government recently simplified the required paperwork, cut social-insurance contributions for affected workers, and extended the scheme's maximum length to 18 months.

Britain has taken a different tack. Rather than intervening to keep people in their existing jobs, it has focused on deterring long-term joblessness with a package of subsidies to encourage employers to hire, and train, people who have been out of work for more than six months.

Of all rich-country governments, Japan's has flailed the most. Forced to confront the ugly reality of its labour market, it is trying a mixture of policies. In 2008 it proposed tax incentives for companies to turn temps into regular employees – a futile effort when profits are scarce and jobs being slashed. The agriculture ministry suggested sending the jobless to the hinterland to work on farms and fisheries. As Naohiro Yashiro, an economist at the International Christian University in Tokyo, puts it: "Although temporary and part-time workers are everywhere in Japan, they are thought to be a threat to employment practices and – like terrorists – have to be contained."

Recently, a more ambitious strategy has emerged. The government is considering shortening the minimum work period for eligibility to jobless benefits. It is providing newly laid-off workers with six-month loans for housing and living expenses. It is paying small-business owners to allow fired staff to remain in company dorms. It is subsidising the salaries of workers on mandatory leave. It is paying firms for rehiring laid-off staff, and offering grants to anyone willing to start a new business.

Whether these policies will be enough depends on how the downturn progresses. For by and large they are sticking-plasters, applied in the hope that the recession will soon be over and the industrial restructuring that follows will be modest. Subsidising shorter working weeks, for instance, props up demand today, but impedes long-term reordering. The inequities of a dual labour market will become more glaring the higher unemployment rises. Politicians seem to be hoping for the best. Given the speed at which their economies are deteriorating, they would do better to plan for the worst.

The material on pages 160–96 was first published in *The Economist* in October 2008 (pages 160–6), January 2009 (pages 167–71), February 2010 (pages 172–8) and March 2009 (pages 188–96).

7   Crisis-time economics

Putting the air back in

Staring at recession, policymakers in rich economies are considering how to avoid a prolonged slump. Here are some options – and some obstacles

DEBT IS OUT; cash is in. Financial institutions are finding it hard to borrow from anyone but the state – and they are reluctant to lend to anyone else. Firms, aware that credit is drying up, are striving to raise cash. They have already run down their inventories and are trimming investment and jobs. Householders whose homes are worth less than their mortgages must save hard to reduce their debts. Those that cannot service their mortgages will default, causing more trouble for banks and, via lower house prices, other homeowners.

In mid-2008, the main worry of policymakers in many economies was whether, as the prices of oil and other commodities shot up, they could contain inflation. But the flight from debt and the dash for cash, inelegantly called "deleveraging", means a bludgeoning for demand. Now central banks and governments are facing a new set of questions. First, can they stop deleveraging from gaining momentum and wrecking their economies? And second, will the tools of conventional macroeconomic policy – cutting interest rates, lowering taxes and increasing public spending – be enough?

The standard response to a demand shock is to use monetary policy: cut interest rates and increase the money supply. Lower interest rates spur spending by making saving less rewarding. Banks able to borrow more cash at lower cost from the central bank will usually offer more and cheaper loans to firms and households, to pay for new equipment, buildings and consumer goods, or to cover running costs.

Central banks are powerful because they control the "monetary base". This comprises the notes and coins in wallets, purses, petty-cash trays and tills, plus the cash reserves that commercial banks hold with the central bank. When interest rates are cut, the cost of holding money goes down; and more money in circulation means more spending. A boost to bank reserves has a less direct, but usually larger effect. Just as individuals carry cash to cover incidental spending, banks hold reserves to cover cash withdrawals, cheque payments and bank transfers. So bank reserves matter because they are the foundation for other, "broader" kinds of money – current (checking) accounts, interest-bearing deposits and so on. Because most deposits lie fallow on any one day, banks are safe in holding only a fraction of them in reserve. The ratio of broad to base money is known as the "money multiplier".

The banks are the conduit between central-bank policy and the wider economy. The trouble is, the conduit is blocked. Despite deep cuts in interest rates by the Federal Reserve, the cost of bank credit for American firms and households has not dropped by much. Investors are wary of lending to banks for even a few months, because of the risk that they may go bust or run out of cash. Banks are loth to lend to each other for the same reason (and fear of their own demise is leading them to hoard cash). The spread between what banks pay for overnight central-bank cash and what they pay to borrow for three months is therefore far above pre-crisis levels. The latter rate is the reference point for loans to customers.

One route around this blockage is for central banks to lend directly to firms by purchasing their short-term debt at fixed rates, as the Fed started to do in October 2008. A drawback, however, is that it essentially turns the central bank into a commercial bank, exposing the taxpayer to lending risk. And the fix helps only big firms.

The monetary base in big economies has been swollen by lots of liquidity from central banks. In the euro area, for instance, it has grown by one-third since the eve of the crisis in August 2007, even though interest rates are barely lower now than then. Most of the increase is accounted for by a doubling of bank reserves.

Some fear that such a rapid expansion of the monetary base will stoke inflation. If the ratio of broad to base money were constant, such fears would be warranted. But because banks are using central-bank liquidity to plug holes in their short-term funding, the money multiplier is collapsing: even as reserves swell, broad-money and credit growth is wilting. In the year to September 2008 bank lending to British households rose by only 0.9%. Mortgage lending fell. If money is not circulating, but is stashed in reserves or under mattresses, it cannot boost spending or push up inflation.

Indeed, if scared banks, firms and households cling more tightly to cash rather than lend it or spend it, the downturn will deepen. The more confidence weakens and asset prices fall, the more eager is the rush into cash. At the extreme, the demand for cash is so strong that not even interest rates at zero can get the economy moving. When standard monetary-policy responses reach their limit, fiscal options, such as cutting taxes and increasing public spending, come into play.

To some extent, government budgets in rich countries stabilise the economy automatically in booms and busts. When the economy slows and jobs are shed, the state spends more on unemployment benefits, helping to support aggregate demand. At the same time, tax receipts shrink faster than GDP: this hurts public finances in recessions but helps ease the pain for firms and their employees. The power of these automatic stabilisers is greater in Europe, where state benefits are more generous and the tax take higher, than in America.

The use of fiscal policy to fine-tune the business cycle in any more than this passive way went out of fashion around 30 years ago. Policymakers have since preferred to tweak aggregate demand via interest rates rather than taxes. One reason is that although it may be easy to increase public spending in bad times it is hard to reduce it when the economy revives. Tax cuts might be saved, or spent on imports. And continued budget deficits harm private enterprise by soaking up savings, pushing up interest rates and "crowding out" private investment.

But when skittish banks and investors are turning away from funding private spending, there is a strong case for a more active fiscal policy to prop up demand. The dash into safe assets has cut the cost of public borrowing for most rich countries (see Figure 7.1). Low bond yields may be a market signal to "crowd in" public spending. A well-judged budgetary stimulus would help fill the shortfall in demand while debt-laden firms and consumers get their finances in order. It

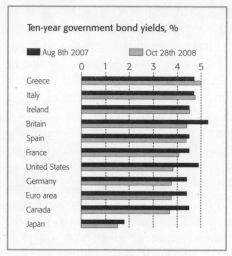

Ten-year government bond yields, %

■ Aug 8th 2007   ☐ Oct 28th 2008

0   1   2   3   4   5

Greece
Italy
Ireland
Britain
Spain
France
United States
Germany
Euro area
Canada
Japan

Source: Thomson Datastream

FIG 7.1 Choose your harbour

may prevent a recession from turning into a rout. A good package would minimise the drawbacks of fiscal policy: a road-building programme, for example, would cease on completion; tax cuts could be aimed at the poor, who would be more likely to spend the extra cash than the rich.

However, fiscal policy has its limits. A run of big budget deficits increases the risk that a government will default or repay its debts only by forcing its central banks to print money, creating inflation. If public debt spirals upwards as the economy stagnates, investors will worry that future taxpayers will be unable to shoulder the burden. Looser fiscal policy will stretch the public finances of countries that went into the downturn with big debts and budget deficits and have since had to fund bank bail-outs. Markets could choke on the extra bond sales required to finance huge deficits, driving interest rates up and worsening the downturn.

They are not choking yet. Financing government deficits is hard when investors are keen on rival uses for their money – such as companies' shares and bonds. In fact, investors are shying away from such assets. The omens for business investment from company reports and confidence surveys remain poor. Job cuts, slumping asset prices and a worsening credit drought augur ill for consumer spending too. If firms fear that others will cut their spending, it will make them still more cautious. The rot could easily feed on itself, leaving equipment and workers idle, and depressing tax revenues. A pre-emptive fiscal stimulus may help prevent that – and shore up the government's tax base.

If conventional monetary and fiscal policy fail, what then?

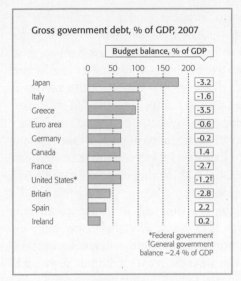

Gross government debt, % of GDP, 2007

Budget balance, % of GDP

Japan	-3.2
Italy	-1.6
Greece	-3.5
Euro area	-0.6
Germany	-0.2
Canada	1.4
France	-2.7
United States*	-1.2†
Britain	-2.8
Spain	2.2
Ireland	0.2

*Federal government
†General government
balance −2.4 % of GDP

Sources: Eurostat; IMF; OECD; US O ce of Management and Budget

FIG 7.2 The state of the state

Pessimists point to Japan's travails as a lesson in how a deflating asset-price bubble and a vast overhang of debt can defeat all that monetary and fiscal policy can throw at it. Since 1993 Japan's economy has been kept afloat by heavy government borrowing: the average annual budget deficit since then has been more than 5% of GDP. The economy flowered after 2003, thanks partly to a big intervention to weaken the exchange rate, but it is now close to recession again and threatened further by the rise of the yen. Japan's gross public debt has reached 180% of GDP, according to the OECD (see Figure 7.2).

The sobering lesson is that conventional policy may not prevent a prolonged deflationary slump. This lesson has not been lost on policymakers. The nuclear option, conceived in America but untried in Japan, is to finance public spending or tax cuts by printing money. This requires the central bank to go along with the fiscal authorities (which may prove easier in America than in Europe). It could work like this: the government announces a tax rebate and issues bonds to finance it. But instead of selling them to private investors, it lodges them with the central bank in exchange for a deposit. It draws on this account to clear the cheques mailed to taxpayers. This scheme is essentially the same as the proverbial "helicopter drop" of money, but with neater accounting and a less erratic distribution of cash. It bypasses banks and money markets, and puts money directly into people's pockets.

Monetising a slug of public debt in this way is bound to be

inflationary. But by this stage, inflation would be a blessing: an economy where conventional policy tools had failed would suffer from falling prices. A burst of inflation would lift asset prices, ease the weight on debtors (whose real burdens are increased by deflation) and improve public finances. Some central bankers will shudder at the thought. Some, but not all. Ben Bernanke, now the Fed chairman, recommended this course of action to Japan's policymakers in 2003 (when he was a Fed governor). Indeed, he went further. One way out of a slump, he argued, is for policymakers to commit themselves to a period of catch-up inflation, to break deflationary expectations and heal the wounds from past price falls.

If all else fails, it seems, the one sure way to secure solvency in the private and public sectors is to inflate away debts and buoy up asset prices. That nuclear option is the ultimate bail-out: rescuing the indebted by hurting those with savings. In essence, if not degree, it is not so different from conventional policy. Interest-rate cuts are a salve for debtors and a penalty on savers. Fiscal-stimulus schemes impose a cost on all taxpayers, even those well placed to endure a downturn. But the cost of a prolonged slump, in terms of idle resources, lost income, decaying skills and an erosion in the trust that keeps civil society going, would be far higher.

A stimulating notion

The idea of giving flagging economies a fiscal boost is back in fashion

"I AM A KEYNESIAN NOW," Richard Nixon declared in 1971. With the benefit of hindsight, his quip marked the high point of fiscal fine-tuning. Inspired by John Maynard Keynes's "General Theory", many economists in the 1960s and early 1970s viewed government tax and spending decisions as the prime tool for smoothing the economic cycle. That confidence was later shattered by stagflation and rising budget deficits. The modern consensus has been that monetary policy, administered by an independent central bank, makes a better first weapon against recession than the whims of politicians.

But now, after more than three decades in the wilderness, Keynesian-style fiscal policy seems to be staging a comeback. On February 13th 2008 George Bush signed into law individual tax rebates and temporary investment incentives worth $152 billion (just over 1% of GDP) that year, and $168 billion in total. Passed in record time by the normally sluggish Congress – and before recession was even a certainty – the stimulus was aimed at cushioning America's downturn by getting cash into consumers' pockets and encouraging firms to invest.

Meanwhile debate has begun on the merits of a fiscal boost well beyond America. The IMF, traditionally a fierce guardian of budget probity, is pushing for broad fiscal loosening if the global economic outlook darkens. Monetary policy may be less effective in this downturn, argues the fund's managing director, Dominique Strauss-Kahn, and many countries are in unusually strong fiscal positions. At the G7 finance ministers' gathering in Tokyo on February 9th 2008, he said that, in addition to America, countries making up a quarter of global GDP had the potential to cut taxes or increase spending – and urged them to begin contingency planning now.

A few non-American politicians are already thinking along those lines. Spain's government is putting together a fiscal-stimulus package as its economy slows in the wake of a construction bust.[1] But many others are sceptical. Jean-Claude Trichet, president of the European Central Bank, has said bluntly that discretionary fiscal policy should be "avoided". Joaquín Almunia, the European Commission's top man on economic matters, has given warning against "succumbing to the Sirens' songs". Ken Rogoff, the IMF's former chief economist, says Mr Strauss-Kahn's plan seems "dubious". A fair few economists within the fund agree.

Who is right depends on the answer to two questions. Do countries have more room to use counter-cyclical fiscal policy than they used to? And what is the evidence that it works?

Bold or barmy?

Many of the world's rich economies have healthier budgets than before other recent downturns. In 2007 almost half of the countries within the OECD ran structural fiscal surpluses (that is, adjusted for the state of the business cycle). The euro zone's public finances have improved dramatically, from a combined structural deficit of 2.1% of GDP before the 2001 recession to a deficit of only 0.7% of GDP in 2007. Germany's budget is now virtually in balance. Spain, Ireland and Finland are all running surpluses.

Judging by fiscal deficits alone, it is America and Britain that should fret. In 2000 America ran a structural surplus; in 2007 it had an underlying deficit of 3% of GDP. At 3.1% of GDP, Britain's was slightly bigger (see Figure 7.3).

Although cyclically adjusted budget positions give a better picture of a country's fiscal health than headline surpluses or deficits, they tell only a partial story. Countries have varying underlying debt burdens and face differing pressures from ageing populations. Japan has a big deficit, a large debt and the oldest population in the OECD. Britain has a bigger structural budget deficit than Italy, but much less debt (43% of GDP versus 105%).

Outside the OECD the fiscal situation has vastly improved. Thanks to better economic management and the boom in commodity prices, several emerging economies have enviably strong public finances. Measured properly, China's budget is in surplus. High oil revenues have brought double-digit budget surpluses to the Gulf oil producers

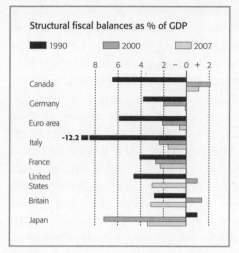

Structural fiscal balances as % of GDP

■ 1990   ■ 2000   □ 2007

8   6   4   2 – 0 + 2

Canada
Germany
Euro area
Italy   -12.2 ■
France
United
States
Britain
Japan

Source: OECD

FIG 7.3 High-wire balancing act

and pushed Russia's surplus over 6% of GDP. Brazil and Mexico both have deficits of less than 2% of GDP, a far cry from the fiscal laxness of a few years ago.

The news is not all good: India's budget deficit is still large. Countries such as Turkey and Hungary have large current-account deficits that would make fiscal expansions risky. But no longer is the option of countering a downturn with fiscal tools confined to rich countries.

But should that option be exercised? Sceptical economists argue that counter-cyclical stimulus often does more harm than good. Politicians traditionally fail to recognise recessions in time, and then take too long to enact stimulus. By the time tax cuts and spending increases arrive, the downturn is often over, and the extra stimulus simply adds inflationary pressure. Moreover, since politicians are usually unwilling to tighten fiscal policy enough in a boom, any loosening of the budget reins tends to result in permanently higher debt. Others argue that temporary stimulus, even if well timed, will not work because people will hardly adjust their spending in response to a one-off tax cut.

There is evidence to support all these worries. Most analyses of America's stimulus efforts in the 1970s conclude that they were badly timed. In continental Europe, the record suggests that activist fiscal policy brought permanently higher public spending and debt – a point Mr Trichet has been quick to note. Japan's experience is salutary. It tried to break deflationary stagnation in the 1990s with several fiscal packages. Debt soared but the country did not recover for a decade. Milton Friedman famously used Japan to argue that fiscal pump-priming didn't work.

But not all the evidence is negative. An influential study in 2001 by Adam Posen of the Peterson Institute and Ken Kuttner, now at Oberlin College, argued that Japan's debt burden stemmed from its stagnant economy not the stimulus packages. Stimulus appeared to fail because it was fitfully implemented. When tax cuts and spending boosts were enacted properly, their analysis suggests, they worked.

More recently, the post-mortems on America's 2001 fiscal boost have been positive. By luck more than design, the income-tax rebate was well timed (Mr Bush had promised to cut taxes long before the recession hit). It also seemed to work. One study suggested that people spent between 20–40% of their rebate in the quarter in which it was received, and over 60% of it within six months. Poorer, more credit-constrained people spent a higher share of their rebates.

Such studies have informed America's recent debate. Politicians have been urged to act quickly and keep the stimulus "targeted and temporary". Two-thirds of the boost will come from tax rebates, which 130m American families were due to receive starting in May 2008. If people spend roughly the same share of their rebate as they did in 2001, Morgan Stanley reckons output could grow at an annual rate of more than 4% in the third quarter of 2008.

That is a big boost but it will not last long. By the beginning of 2009, Morgan Stanley's economists expect GDP growth to slip back to 1.3%. A growing group of forecasters is now fretting about a "W" shaped, or double-dip, recession.

To Keynesian converts that outcome would simply call for more stimulus. Even before Mr Bush had signed the February 2008 package, some Congressmen were talking about a second round, focused on extending unemployment insurance. Laurence Seidman of the University of Delaware says America has had "an excellent first dose" of stimulus and should be planning for a second if necessary. Traditionally, such talk would have sent shudders though the IMF. Now at least some within the fund's upper ranks seem to agree.

Less clear, however, is how far America's experience is applicable elsewhere. With stingier unemployment benefits and a lower federal tax take, America has fewer "automatic stabilisers" than other rich countries do. Since many American states are forced, by law, to run balanced budgets they cut spending or raise taxes in a downturn – the opposite of Keynesian pump-priming. Federal-stimulus packages, in part, counter those trends. With higher tax burdens and more generous jobless benefits, European countries get a bigger fiscal boost without any change in policy.

A few euro-zone economies, notably Spain and Ireland, may use the fiscal lever. But others seem content to rely on automatic stabilisers. Germany's finance minister has ruled out new counter-cyclical measures. France and Italy have headline deficits that could soon nudge against the 3% of GDP limit prescribed by the European Union's stability and growth pact.

Nor, for now, is there much enthusiasm for action in emerging markets. The economies with the strongest fiscal positions, such as China, need to worry about overheating more than slumping. But what if the outlook darkens? Many emerging economies, often at the IMF's behest, have limited their fiscal flexibility by introducing clear budget rules.

Nor are the mechanisms for swift stimulus obvious. Emerging economies, in general, have fewer automatic stabilisers than rich ones do. In China, for instance, personal income tax was paid by only 30% of workers in 2008 and accounted for just 7% of government revenue. Some poor countries, particularly those with excess household saving, could do with a better social safety net. But revamping health, education and pension systems takes time.

In many developing countries, infrastructure spending may be the most promising way for governments to support output – and boost the economy's long-term potential. Keynes argued that governments, *in extremis*, could boost demand by digging holes. Until now, few emerging economies had the luxury to contemplate his advice. Now that they do, roads, bridges and electricity grids would be a better bet.

Note

1   This article was written in February 2008. Since then most rich countries and some emerging ones have used fiscal stimulus, with a broad consensus on its desirability being reached at the G20 summit in London in April 2009.

Pay for delay

Wage subsidies and fatter jobless benefits have softened the impact of the recession but may yet hurt recovery

AMERICA MAY LEAD the rich world in periods of prosperity, but Europe has shown a greater talent for dealing with recession. Unemployment in the euro area has risen by 30% from its pre-crisis levels. America's jobless rate has more than doubled. In Germany, the largest country in the euro zone, output fell far harder than America's during the worst months of the crisis but Germany's unemployment rate barely rose. Consumer spending has held up surprisingly well in a country where high saving is the norm even in good times. "Germany is calm," says one official with satisfaction. By comparison, America is deeply troubled.

What explains the resilience of continental Europe? Some of it was already built-in. Job-protection laws make it costly for firms to lay off workers, and where posts are sacrificed, the newly unemployed are preserved from penury. They receive benefits worth around two-thirds of their lost salaries in most countries. Only in Italy are benefits anywhere near as skimpy as in America and Britain, where new claimants receive just 28% of their previous earnings. European governments also have fewer qualms about intervention. A 2009 report from the OECD identifies 14 kinds of job-market initiatives put in place since recession struck. France ticks 12 of those boxes, more than any other country.

One policy in particular has helped keep a lid on unemployment. Schemes that subsidise the wages of employees working fewer hours than normal were introduced or expanded in 22 of the 29 countries surveyed by the OECD. Germany had around 1.4m workers on its short-time working scheme by summer 2009, equivalent to a cull of 400,000–500,000 full-time workers. That would add one percentage point to the jobless rate. Countries without these arrangements, such as America, Britain and Spain, have tended to suffer bigger rises in unemployment (see Figure 7.4).

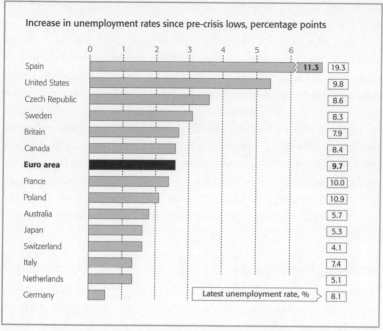

Increase in unemployment rates since pre-crisis lows, percentage points

	Increase (pp)	Latest unemployment rate, %
Spain	11.3	19.3
United States		9.8
Czech Republic		8.6
Sweden		8.3
Britain		7.9
Canada		8.4
Euro area		**9.7**
France		10.0
Poland		10.9
Australia		5.7
Japan		5.3
Switzerland		4.1
Italy		7.4
Netherlands		5.1
Germany		8.1

Sources: National statistics; Eurostat

FIG 7.4 The price of flexibility

In normal times, wage subsidies would be frowned upon. But in a credit crunch they can be a smart use of fiscal resources. Firms worried about future sales, low on cash and deprived of credit, may too readily fire workers without a subsidy. That would only add to a downward spiral of confidence and spending. In Europe, the state funds generous jobless benefits in any case. Why not instead make it easier for firms to hoard workers and keep a skilled workforce intact for when the economy turns?

All policies have drawbacks, and those that help economies to absorb a shock will also tend to make the damaging effects linger. Subsidising jobs that are no longer viable will hold back recovery. The flow of workers from dying industries to new ones may be blocked. If sustained for too long, short-time working schemes can become artificial props for industries that need to shrink. A scheme in Spain, say, to pay construction firms to hoard workers would be madness when there is a glut of empty homes.

Firms may also be tempted to use wage subsidies as a cheap way of keeping their options open at the government's expense. A well-designed scheme can curb this. In the Netherlands, businesses that lay off workers within three months of the scheme's end have to pay back half the subsidy. The more workers that firms register for support, the sooner the subsidy runs out. A Swedish policy to prevent lay-offs due to weak cashflow looks even smarter. Instead of wage support, Sweden gives its firms the option to delay their social-security contributions. A punitive interest charge for firms receiving such help would root out all but the truly distressed. Other countries have trimmed their taxes on jobs in addition to (or instead of) wage subsidies.

Working hypothesis

Another way of softening recession is to expand the welfare system. Around half of the rich countries in the OECD survey have done so since the crisis began – by raising benefits, making it easier to claim them or providing for longer. Extra money for the jobless is an effective stimulus measure since cash-starved households are likely to spend it. But if benefits are kept high for too long they will make the jobless less keen to search for work. One way of striking a balance between short-term stimulus and long-term incentives is to increase the value of benefits but withdraw them sooner. That is what Poland and the Czech Republic have done. The recession's length has forced America's government to do the opposite. It used to offer just six months of jobless benefits, but has extended its support to stop people falling into poverty.

It may seem heartless to counsel against too much support for the unemployed but incentives matter even when unemployment is high. Firms in rich countries make hires equivalent to some 14–15% of all employment in deep recessions, according to the OECD. (Net job creation falls because there are more lay-offs.) More generous benefits will mean vacancies are filled less quickly, pushing up unemployment. Active help for those on benefits – training, counselling and so on – can also be neglected in recession. Switzerland and Denmark link spending on such policies to their jobless rates to ensure that a fixed amount of spending is not shared between a larger pool of unemployed.

Evidence from past deep recessions suggests that unemployment is unlikely to fall as quickly as it has risen. Indeed further increases seem likely in Europe, because jobs have not adjusted much to a lower level of GDP. In those circumstances, the temptation to prolong wage subsidies and buttress benefits will be great. It should be resisted. The unemployment rate in the euro area has risen far less than in America, but both are now close to 10%. Pre-crisis rates in Europe were higher precisely because of its rigid jobs markets. It would be a shame if measures that have helped mitigate crisis were left to spoil prospects for recovery.

The material on pages 197-211 was first published in *The Economist* in November 2008 (pages 197-202), February 2008 (pages 203-7) and November 2009 (pages 208-11).

8 Recovery, repair and rebalancing

How to grow

Without faster growth the rich world's economies will be stuck. But what can be done to achieve it?

WHAT WILL TOMORROW'S HISTORIANS see as the defining economic trend of the early 21st century? There are plenty of potential candidates, from the remaking of finance in the wake of the crash of 2008 to the explosion of sovereign debt. But the list will almost certainly be topped by the dramatic shift in global economic heft.

In 2000 rich countries dominated the world economy, contributing around two-thirds of global GDP after allowing for differences in purchasing power. Since then that share has fallen to just over half. In another decade it could be down to 40%. The bulk of global output will be produced in the emerging world.

The pace of the shift testifies to these countries' success. Thanks to globalisation and good policies, virtually all developing countries are catching up with their richer peers. In 2002–08 more than 85% of developing economies grew faster than America's, compared with less than a third between 1960 and 2000, and virtually none in the century before that.

This "rise of the rest" is a remarkable achievement, bringing with it unprecedented improvements in living standards for the majority of people on the planet. But there is another, less happy, explanation for the rapid shift in the global centre of economic gravity: the lack of growth in the big rich economies of America, western Europe and Japan.

The next few years could be defined as much by the stagnation of the West as by the emergence of the rest, for three main reasons. The first is the sheer scale of the recession of 2008–09 and the weakness of

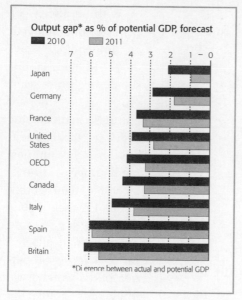

Output gap* as % of potential GDP, forecast
■ 2010   ▨ 2011

Japan
Germany
France
United States
OECD
Canada
Italy
Spain
Britain

*Di erence between actual and potential GDP

Source: OECD

FIG 8.1 Yawning

the subsequent recovery. For the advanced economies as a whole, the slump that followed the global financial crisis was by far the deepest since the 1930s. It has left an unprecedented degree of unemployed workers and underused factories in its wake. Although output stopped shrinking in most countries by the end of 2009, the recovery is proving too weak to put that idle capacity back to work quickly (see Figure 8.1). The OECD, the Paris-based organisation that tracks advanced economies, does not expect this "output gap" to close until 2015.

The second reason to worry about stagnation has to do with slowing supply. The level of demand determines whether economies run above or below their "trend" rate of growth, but that trend rate itself depends on the supply of workers and their productivity. That productivity in turn depends on the rate of capital investment and the pace of innovation. Across the rich world the supply of workers is about to slow as the number of pensioners rises. In western Europe the change will be especially marked. Between 2010 and 2020 the region's working-age population, which until now has been rising slowly, will shrink by some 0.3% a year. In Japan, where the pool of potential workers is already shrinking, the pace of decline will more than double, to around 0.7% a year. America's demography is far more favourable, but the growth in its working-age population, at some 0.3% a year between 2010 and 2030, will be less than a third of the post-war average.

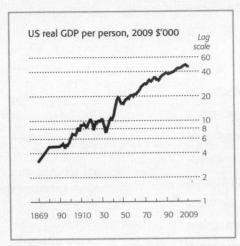

US real GDP per person, 2009 $'000

Log scale

Sources: US Department of Commerce; BLS; *The Economist*

FIG 8.2 Onwards, ever upwards

With millions of workers unemployed, an impending slowdown in the labour supply might not seem much of a problem. But these demographic shifts set the boundaries for rich countries' medium-term future, including their ability to service their public debt. Unless more immigrants are allowed in, or a larger proportion of the working-age population joins the labour force, or people retire later, or their productivity accelerates, the ageing population will translate into permanently slower potential growth.

Calculations by Dale Jorgenson of Harvard University and Khuong Vu of the National University of Singapore make the point starkly. They show that the average underlying annual growth rate of the G7 group of big rich economies between 1998 and 2008 was 2.1%. On current demographic trends, and assuming that productivity improves at the same rate as in the first decade of the 21st century, that potential rate of growth will come down to 1.45% a year between 2010 and 2020, its slowest pace since the second world war.

Faster productivity growth could help to mitigate the slowdown, but it does not seem to be forthcoming. Before the financial crisis hit, the trend in productivity growth was flat or slowing in many rich countries even as it soared in the emerging world. Growth in output per worker in America, which had risen sharply in the late 1990s thanks to increased output of information technology, and again in the early 2000s as the gains from IT spread throughout the economy, began to flag after 2004. It revived during the recession as firms slashed their labour force, but that boost may not last. Japan's productivity slumped after its bubble burst in the early 1990s. Western Europe's, overall, has also weakened since the mid-1990s.

The third reason to fret about the rich world's stagnation is that the hangover from the financial crisis and the feebleness of the recovery could themselves dent economies' potential. Long periods of high unemployment tend to reduce rather than augment the pool of potential workers. The unemployed lose their skills, and disillusioned workers drop out of the workforce. The shrinking of banks' balance-sheets that follows a financial bust makes credit more costly and harder to come by.

Optimists point to America's experience over the past century as evidence that recessions, even severe ones, need not do lasting damage. After every downturn the economy eventually bounced back so that for the period as a whole America's underlying growth rate per person remained remarkably stable (see Figure 8.2). Despite a lack of demand, America's underlying productivity grew faster in the 1930s than in any other decade of the 20th century. Today's high unemployment may also be preparing the ground for more efficient processes.

Most economists, however, reckon that rich economies' capacity has already sustained some damage, especially in countries where much of the growth came from bubble industries like construction, as in Spain, and finance, as in Britain. The OECD now reckons that the fallout from the financial crisis will, on average, knock some 3% off rich countries' potential output. Most of that decline has already occurred.

The longer that demand remains weak, the greater the damage is likely to be. Japan's experience over the past two decades is a cautionary example, especially to fast-ageing European economies. The country's financial crash in the early 1990s contributed to a slump in productivity growth. Soon afterwards the working-age population began to shrink. A series of policy mistakes caused the hangover from the financial crisis to linger. The economy failed to recover and deflation set in. The result was a persistent combination of weak demand and slowing supply.

To avoid Japan's fate, rich countries need to foster growth in two ways, by supporting short-term demand and by boosting long-term supply. Unfortunately, today's policymakers often see these two strategies as alternatives rather than complements. Many of the Keynesian economists who fret about the lack of private demand think that concerns about economies' medium-term potential are beside the point at the moment. They include Paul Krugman, a Nobel laureate and commentator in the *New York Times*, and many of President Barack Obama's economic team.

Stimulus v austerity

European economists put more emphasis on boosting medium-term growth, favouring reforms such as making labour markets more flexible. They tend to reject further fiscal stimulus to prop up demand. Jean-Claude Trichet, the president of the European Central Bank, is a strong advocate of structural reforms in Europe. But he is also one of the most ardent champions of the idea that cutting budget deficits will itself boost growth. All this has led to a passionate but narrow debate about fiscal stimulus versus austerity.

Both sides are blinkered. Governments should think more coherently about how to support demand and boost supply at the same time. The exact priorities will differ from country to country, but there are several common themes. First, the Keynesians are right to observe that, for the rich world as a whole, there is a danger of overdoing the short-term budget austerity. Excessive budget-cutting poses a risk to the recovery, not least because it cannot easily be offset by looser monetary policy. Improvements to the structure of taxation and spending matter as much as the short-term deficits.

Second, there is an equally big risk of ignoring threats to economies' potential growth and of missing the opportunity for growth-enhancing microeconomic reforms. Most rich-country governments have learned one important lesson from previous financial crises: they have cleaned up their banking sectors reasonably quickly. But more competition and deregulation deserve higher billing, especially in services, which in all rich countries are likely to be the source of most future employment and productivity growth.

Instead, too many governments are determined to boost innovation by reinventing industrial policy. Making the jobless more employable should be higher on the list, especially in America, where record levels of long-term unemployment suggest that labour markets may not be as flexible as many people believe.

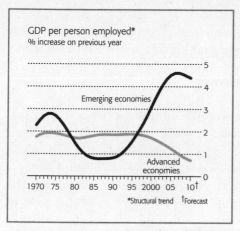

GDP per person employed*
% increase on previous year

Emerging economies

Advanced
economies

1970 75   80   85   90   95 2000 05   10†

*Structural trend   †Forecast

Source: The Conference Board

FIG 8.3 All right for some

Faster growth is not a silver bullet. It will not eliminate the need to trim back unrealistic promises to pensioners; no rich country can simply grow its way out of looming pension and health-care commitments. Nor will it stop the relentless shift of economic gravity to the emerging world. Since developing economies are more populous than rich ones, they will inevitably come to dominate the world economy. But whether that shift takes place against a background of prosperity or stagnation depends on the pace of growth in the rich countries. For the moment, worryingly, too many of them seem to be headed for stagnation.

Withdrawal symptoms

After the stimulus, the hangover

SOME AMERICANS HAVE ALWAYS TAKEN the national debt personally. During the 1940 census (according to the late David McCord Wright, an American economist) a housewife was asked if she had a mortgage on her home. "Yes," she replied. "For $40 billion."

That figure (about 40% of 1940 GDP) now seems quaint. The federal debt held by the public was $8.9 trillion in August 2010, or about 60% of GDP. Add to that the Treasury debt held by America's public-pension scheme, and the national debt reached $10 trillion back in September 2008. The extra digit obliged the national debt clock near New York's Times Square to move its dollar sign to make room.

Many of today's Americans feel as indignant about the debt as that 1940s housewife did. But they are just as profligate as their government (see Figure 8.4). Their mortgages and other debts also amount to around $13 trillion, almost 120% of their annual disposable income.

The most remarkable thing about that figure, though, is not how big it is, but that it is smaller than it was in 2008. For over 60 years after the second world war, household debt moved in only one direction: upwards. Then, in the second quarter of 2008, it started to fall – not just as a proportion of income, or after allowing for inflation, but in everyday dollars and cents. Between March 1st 2008 and June 30th 2010 households reduced their debts by $473 billion. Businesses and banks joined in later. Although the federal debt displayed on the Times Square clock is ticking remorselessly upwards, the true national debt, including households, banks and firms, is now lower than it was in the first quarter of 2009.

In 2008–09, for the first time since the 1930s Depression, consumer spending in real terms fell for two years in a row. Households are now saving 6% of their disposable income, compared with just 2.7% in the years before the crisis. Combined with the stockmarket's fitful rallies, this frugality has helped American households rebuild some

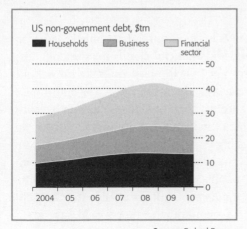

US non-government debt, $trn

■ Households   ▨ Business   ☐ Financial
                                sector

Source: Federal Reserve

FIG 8.4 Chipping away at the mountain

of the wealth washed away by the recession. Their net worth is now about 490% of their disposable income, compared with just 440% in the worst months of the crisis. As a cushion against a riskier world, American households will probably try to set aside a stash of assets worth some 540–550% of their income, according to Martin Sommer of the IMF and Jirka Slacalek of the European Central Bank. If that figure is right, their balance-sheet repairs are currently only half completed.

This new thrift is not confined to America. Household debt is also falling in Spain. In Britain households saved 6.3% of their disposable income in 2009 (though less in the first half of 2010), compared with 2% in 2008. Nor is the frugality limited to households. In the wake of the financial crisis, companies across the rich world have been piling up cash. Small firms have been unable, and many big firms have been unwilling, to borrow. In Japan and Britain corporate investment fell by about a quarter from peak to trough. The pace of investment has recovered somewhat, but companies are still not rushing to add new factories and machinery when so much of their existing capacity lies idle.

All told, across the OECD households and businesses are forecast to spend $2.6 trillion less than their incomes in 2010, the equivalent of 7% of GDP. This follows another huge private-sector surplus, of 7.2%, in 2009. In 2007, by contrast, the rich world's households and businesses ran a combined deficit. This astonishing rise in private saving is the main reason why the recession was so deep and the recovery is so muted. After two years of private-sector austerity in the rich countries, the biggest macroeconomic controversy now facing their governments is whether to embrace some austerity of their own.

Squirrel it away

Squirrels save by burying nuts in the ground. In sophisticated economies, people save by amassing financial claims on someone else. Savers therefore need borrowers. In textbook economics households save and banks use those savings to lend to firms. For both households and firms to run a surplus, someone else must run a deficit. That someone else could be a foreign nation. But none of the economies outside the OECD is big enough to absorb the excess private saving of the rich world. China would have to run a current-account deficit of over 40% of GDP to offset a $2.6 trillion surplus. Even if the task were spread across all the Asian countries outside the OECD (of which Japan and South Korea are members), they would have to run deficits of over 25% each.

The only other possibility is governments. That is why the rich world's private surpluses have been mirrored by equally vast public deficits. In 2009 the OECD's governments ran a combined deficit of 7.9% of GDP, and in 2010 it was expected to be only marginally less. Among the big economies, Britain's deficit will be the largest, at 11.5%, with America not far behind. In an accounting sense, these eye-popping deficits are simply the counterpart of private surpluses. In an economic sense, their remarkable increase is less the outcome of government profligacy than private thrift.

According to the IMF, when the final bill for the budgetary cost of the crisis is calculated a few years hence, the unpopular bank bailouts and fiscals splash-outs will account for less than 30% of it. The rest will be down to the crisis itself, which squeezed revenues and reduced growth.

Regardless of its source, borrowing on this scale plays havoc with the public finances. According to the IMF, gross government debt in the world's big rich economies reached 97% in 2009 and is rising at its fastest pace in modern history. By 2015 the IMF expects them to have a combined debt burden of 110% of GDP, against less than 70% in 2007.

At the start of 2010 fears about soaring public deficits and debt in some countries seemed about to bring on another financial meltdown, thanks to Greece's brush with default. More than 200 years ago America's first treasury secretary, Alexander Hamilton, warned of the "extravagant premium" countries must pay if their credit is "questionable". In spring 2010 Greece's credit was severely questioned. The premium, or spread, it had to pay on its bonds, relative to German bunds, rose extravagantly, from about 2% at the start of the year to almost 10% at the height of the crisis in May. Spreads on Irish, Portuguese and, to a lesser extent, Spanish debt also spiked. These fears re-emerged in September, particularly in Ireland.

Greece had to be bailed out by the EU and the IMF. Along with other wobbly euro-zone borrowers, it was forced to make radical budget cuts. But the Greek crisis had a palpable effect even on countries under no obvious pressure from financial markets, especially Britain, where the new coalition government announced tax increases and dramatic cuts in spending. According to the Institute for Fiscal Studies, these are even tougher than the cuts imposed on Britain by the IMF in 1976.

In America bond yields are near record lows and the economy is slowing, but the government's efforts to introduce a second stimulus have foundered. Much of the political debate in Washington, DC, is about the scale of fiscal tightening; in particular, whether to allow any of the Bush tax cuts to expire at the end of 2010, as scheduled.

Even though the rich world's economies continue to operate below capacity, in 2011 they are heading for what is likely to be their biggest collective budget squeeze in at least four decades. The appetite for government releveraging is coming to an end before private deleveraging is over.

Too soon to tighten?

Is this a mistake? Economists are deeply divided. Many Keynesians think the answer is yes. They fret that the costs and risks of higher public debt are wildly exaggerated, and that as long as households are cutting back and economies are operating so far below their potential, governments should not try to trim public deficits.

Nonsense, say the advocates of austerity, pointing to the fickleness of financial markets and to the dangers government debt poses to long-term growth. Many claim that fiscal austerity could even boost growth in the short term. By reducing the spectre of massive government debt, it would lift private confidence and unlock spending. Entrepreneurs would be emboldened to invest and households might feel freer to spend, without fear of future tax increases to help repay the debt.

Keynesians are right that deficits, so far, have been more a symptom than a source of economic distress. The fiscal swing undoubtedly helped to contain the damage from the crisis. Without it the private sector's determination to save would have depressed spending across the economy even further. That would have caused a correspondingly steeper fall in incomes, making it harder for households to repair their balance-sheets.

Nor are most rich countries anywhere close to the limits of what they can borrow. A 2010 study from the IMF suggests that most advanced economies still have plenty of "fiscal space". In America and Britain, for instance, the fund's economists calculate that public debt will not reach its absolute limit until it hits 160% of GDP or more, far higher than its current levels. The wolf is not at the door.

But termites are in the woodwork, as Charles Schultze, a former White House official, once put it. Governments have big underlying structural budget gaps that will not be filled by economic recovery. Rising health-care and pension spending will put relentless pressure on government debt. Eventually the rich world's economies will return to full employment, and when they do, public borrowing will crowd out private investment and hurt growth.

How much damage can these termites do, and when does it get serious? Carmen Reinhart of the University of Maryland and Ken Rogoff of Harvard University have examined the effects of a couple of centuries of sovereign debt. Their verdict is that public debt does little discernible harm until it reaches about 90% of a country's GDP, but then the effect on growth can be sudden and big.

So far and no farther

Other scholars reach somewhat grimmer conclusions. Looking at 99 countries since 1980, Mehmet Caner and Thomas Grennes of North Carolina State University with Fritzi Koehler-Geib of the World Bank

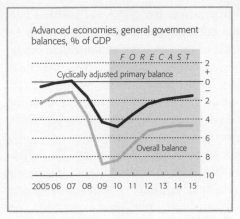

Advanced economies, general government balances, % of GDP

FORECAST

Cyclically adjusted primary balance

Overall balance

2005 06 07 08 09 10 11 12 13 14 15

Source: IMF

FIG 8.5 Recovery position

identified a threshold of 77% of GDP. Every member of the G7 will breach that limit in 2010. If the authors have got it right, these debts will knock half a percentage point off the collective growth rate of the G20's rich members.

The IMF says governments should aspire to cut their debt ratios back to 60% by 2030. To do so they will have to perform some fiscal heroics. Their budgets will have to swing from a projected underlying primary deficit of 4.9% of GDP in 2010 (see Figure 8.5) to a surplus of 3.8% by 2020 and stay there for a decade, even as ageing populations add 4–5% of GDP to their fiscal costs. In America, Britain, Greece, Ireland, Japan and Spain a swing of 9% or more of GDP is required.

Given the scale of the task, it seems best not to put it off for too long, especially since economies are no longer shrinking, just growing slowly. Numerous studies suggest that consolidation based on spending cuts is more likely to stick, and will do more to boost medium-term growth, than measures involving tax increases. Cutting public-sector wages and welfare payments is better than cutting government investment.

Putting in place reforms that slow down the rise in pension and health-care spending ought to be a particular priority, since the net present value of governments' promises to the elderly dwarf today's debts. Raising the retirement age is a particularly good idea because it simultaneously cuts governments' liabilities and boosts future growth and tax revenue as people work longer. If revenues must be raised, taxes on consumption and property are less harmful to growth than those on income or saving.

By these standards most rich-country fiscal-consolidation plans score reasonably well. Britain's government plans to squeeze three-quarters of its budget adjustment from spending cuts. In Greece the share is 51% and in Spain 62%. Several European countries are raising their statutory retirement ages, albeit in small steps. Where there have been tax increases, they have mostly been on VAT. By comparison, America's fiscal plans – a rise in taxes on income and capital if the Bush cuts expire, and no progress on reforming pensions or health-care spending – are much worse.

However, the advocates of austerity tend to exaggerate the beneficial effect on short-term growth of such contractions (even if properly designed). Alberto Alesina and Silvia Ardagna of Harvard University have identified many examples of economies that expanded even as their deficits were squeezed through spending cuts (though not tax increases), yet a study in the IMF's October 2010 *World Economic Outlook* shows that in some of their examples the deficits were not really squeezed.

For instance, in 1998 Japan's government injected over ¥24 trillion into Japan National Railway; in the following year it did not. Between those two years its budget balance appeared to improve by about 4.8% of GDP even though it had neither cut spending nor raised taxes. Similarly, in 1995 Germany's government took on east German housing and industrial debts worth about 6.8% of GDP. The following year its budget seemed to improve dramatically after that one-off event – even though there had been no squeeze.

The IMF's researchers looked at countries that actually raised taxes or cut spending and found no evidence that such measures boosted growth. In fact, they reckon that a fiscal contraction worth 1% of GDP typically cuts output by about 0.5% after two years. To cut public debt below 60% by 2030, as the IMF advocates, America would have to endure that kind of fiscal pain every year for ten years.

Ration the morphine

Fiscal tightening hurts less if offset by monetary easing. Central banks typically cut interest rates and the currency weakens when governments tighten fiscal policy. These lower interest and exchange rates roughly halve the pain of budgetary repairs, the IMF calculates.

But governments cannot expect as much monetary morphine

this time. If households are paying back debt, cheaper credit may provide less of a stimulus than at other times. Since so many governments are tightening at once, and not every country's currency can cheapen against every other's, they may not benefit from much of a depreciation.

Moreover, central banks cannot cut their policy rates by as much as governments might like. Rates in America, Britain and Japan are already at or near zero. In such cases a fiscal contraction of 1% of GDP is more damaging to growth, knocking about 1% off output in the following year, according to the IMF's researchers.

This lack of leeway is a real constraint on recovery. But although central banks cannot lower their policy rates any further, they are not impotent. They can, and do, ease monetary policy in other ways. Some have tried to steer inflationary expectations with words. The Fed has promised to keep rates "exceptionally low" for an "extended period". Several have swelled their balance-sheets by printing money to buy assets, such as government bonds, a process known as "quantitative easing".

The biggest easer, relative to the size of the economy, has been the Bank of England. Since March 2009 it has bought almost £200 billion-worth of government bonds, or gilts, equivalent to 14% of GDP, as well as a smattering of corporate bonds. The bank's research shows that its purchases of gilts raised their price, as well as that of other securities that compete with government paper. When prices go up, yields go down: they fell by about one percentage point on gilts and 0.7 points on the safest corporate bonds and by 1.5 points on riskier junk bonds.

But it is not clear whether quantitative easing on its own changes people's expectations of monetary policy and inflation. A more direct way to do so would be to raise the bank's inflation target, currently set at 2%. A figure of 4–5% might make central bankers' lives easier, according to some economists. But most central bankers do not like the idea. They think that the costs of higher, and possibly more volatile, inflation would outweigh any gains. A less-discussed but potentially more useful innovation would be price-level targeting (PLT), meaning that a central bank targets the level of prices, not their rate of change. Targeting a price level that rises by 2% a year is different from targeting an inflation rate of 2% a year because rather than washing its hands of past mistakes, the central bank has to make up for past errors, returning prices to their prescribed path.

That should make inflation expectations a more powerful stabilising force. In a slump, inflation often falls uncomfortably low: prices might rise by only 1% over the year, for example. Under PLT, the central bank has to make up this lost ground, so prices might rise faster than 2% to catch up. With a conventional inflation target, by contrast, the central bank must promise inflation no higher than 2% in each and every year, regardless of the rate the year before.

In central banking, as in many industries, the most innovative outfits are often the small ones. Inflation-targeting was pioneered by New Zealand's central bank 20 years ago before being taken up by bigger institutions such as the Bank of England. America's Federal Reserve is still suspicious of it. Similarly, much of the best research on PLT is being conducted at the Bank of Canada. It will take time to catch on even if its theoretical appeal survives contact with reality.

What seems clear is that if the economic weakness persists and inflation rates fall further, central banks may become more willing to experiment. Policies that look outré today may seem necessary tomorrow. It is worth recalling that less than two years after it began quantitative easing in March 2001 the Bank of Japan was buying equities. And in 2003 it was advised to adopt price-level targeting by none other than Ben Bernanke, now the Fed's chairman.

Beware self-fulfilling prophecies

Some economists argue that central banks' determination to avoid deflation could have the opposite effect. The Fed's pledge to keep interest rates low for "an extended period", for instance, suggests that it believes the economy will remain underemployed (and inflation subdued) for an extended period. If its pessimism spreads, it may become self-fulfilling. People will hoard cash because they expect prices to fall and investments to fail, thus prolonging the economy's weakness.

This is the "peril" that befell Japan, according to James Bullard of the St Louis Fed. The private sector came to expect deflation and its expectations were duly fulfilled. The central bank could not cut rates below zero, and it did not raise them because inflation was already too low. Mr Bullard argues that America "is closer to a Japanese-style outcome today than at any time in recent history".

Others worry not that the Fed will prolong the slump but that it may sow the seeds of the next crisis. Low rates are supposed to help the economy mobilise its resources, but they can also cause it to misallocate them. After the 2001 recession they generated "excessive growth of sectors that rely on either fixed-asset investment or credit", argues Raghuram Rajan of the University of Chicago. He fears that by setting rates at zero the Fed may "merely pump up growth in the short term only to see it collapse later". Low rates subsidise borrowers at the expense of savers. If this transfer were easier for voters to see, they might find a lot to dislike. But "because the Fed picks investors' pockets silently and forcibly ... no one asks questions about cost," he writes.

Given that the main reason for the recession and the weakness of the recovery is the dramatic increase in private thrift, this seems an odd short-term concern. The rich world is short of private borrowing and awash with saving. Overall credit has been shrinking. Nonetheless, Mr Rajan's worries about the medium term are reasonable. Years of ultra-loose monetary policy are likely to have unwelcome side-effects. That is a reason for governments to beware of overly fast fiscal tightening. It is also a reason to look for antidotes to stagnation beyond macroeconomic policy. The longer-term remedy must be creating new jobs and increasing productivity, but the most urgent need is to hurry up the repairs to a broken financial system.

The cost of repair

A battered finance sector means slower growth

ALL RECESSIONS ARE PAINFUL, but the hangovers that follow financial crises are particularly long and grim. Growth is substantially lower than it is during "normal" recoveries as households and firms reduce their debt burdens. That is the depressing conclusion from a growing body of research on the aftermath of big financial busts. In one such study, Prakash Kannan, an economist at the IMF, looked at 83 recessions in 21 countries since 1970. He found that in recessions that followed financial crises, growth was a lot slower and credit growth stagnated – whereas after normal recessions it soared (see Figure 8.6).

So far the current recovery is following this post-crisis script. Output is sluggish and credit is growing weakly or shrinking across much of the rich world. But is this because over-leveraged households and firms have become less willing to borrow, or because banks have become less willing to lend? In other words, is the credit problem one of demand or supply? The answer will make a difference to the rich world's growth prospects and to the way policymakers should respond. People's unwillingness to borrow bodes ill for short-term demand. Firms' reluctance to invest also risks denting productivity growth. But a broken financial system's inability to allocate capital efficiently has bigger long-term consequences.

In practice, both supply and demand probably play a role. There is plenty of evidence that consumers and firms have become less willing to borrow. A study by Atif Mian of the University of California at Berkeley and Amir Sufi of the University of Chicago, for instance, shows a close correlation between American car sales and the level of household debt. In places where households had heavier debt burdens at the start of the recession, subsequent car sales were weaker.

Across the rich world, companies, particularly big ones, have been piling up cash. Firms' cash stockpiles are at, or near, record levels, and bond investors are clamouring for more corporate debt. In August

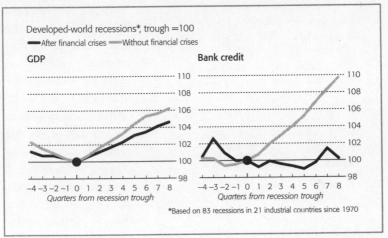

Developed-world recessions*, trough =100
━━After financial crises ━━Without financial crises

Source: Prakash Kannan, IMF

FIG 8.6 The worst kind

2010 Johnson & Johnson, a top-rated American pharmaceutical, medical device and consumer-products company, issued $1.1 billion in bonds at the lowest yields then on record for ten- and 30-year corporate debt, even though its operating cash flow far exceeds its investment needs.

The historical record suggests that the lack of demand for credit is likely to persist. In a 2010 paper Carmen and Vincent Reinhart estimate that in past crises it took an average of seven years for households and businesses to bring their debts and debt service back to tolerable levels relative to income. In many countries that process has yet to begin. In America, where progress has been fastest, the Reinharts reckon that about half the rise in the ratio of credit to GDP accumulated during the boom era has been unwound.

At the same time the supply of credit is clearly constrained. Banks in the euro zone continue to tighten credit standards, and in America they have only just begun to ease standards after several years of tightening. Most worrying is the potential damage that starving companies of credit will do to productivity.

Credit crunches do not affect all companies the same way. In a paper in 1996, Mr Rajan and Luigi Zingales, also of the University of Chicago, argued that the more a company depends on external

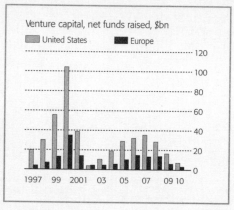

Venture capital, net funds raised, $bn
- United States
- Europe

Source: Thomson Reuters

FIG 8.7 Nothing ventured, nothing gained

financing such as bank loans or issues of stocks and bonds, rather than internal cashflow, the more sensitive its fortunes are to the health of the financial system. Mr Kannan of the IMF came to the same conclusion in his study. In the 13 recessions caused by financial crises, the industries most dependent on external finance grew 0.8 percentage points more slowly, on average, than those least dependent. There was no such gap after other kinds of recession.

Cash conundrum

The latest recession is likely to have similar effects. For example, Luc Laeven, an economist at the IMF, and Randy Kroszner of the University of Chicago have found that listed biotech companies, which make up 10% of America's total stockmarket listings, are heavily dependent on external finance and their growth is likely to suffer far more from a withdrawal of credit than that of the overall economy. As Mr Laeven says, "we may only see the real impact five years from now when, without a crisis, some of those investments would have paid off and generated new products."

Venture-capital raising, which never fully recovered from the bursting of the internet bubble in 2000, has been "harmed immensely" by the latest crisis, says Steve Jurvetson at Draper Fisher Jurvetson, a venture-capital firm (see Figure 8.7). Endowments, foundations and pension funds, enthusiastic participants in venture capital before the crisis, pulled back after their stock and private-equity holdings were clobbered. The moribund IPO market makes it harder for venture funds to cash in their investments.

If the bear market in IPOs proves transitory (which is what usually happens), the harm will be small. A prolonged drought would be another matter. In the mid-1970s the dearth of venture capital and IPOs set back the development of computer and network technologies that would prove to have such a revolutionary impact in the 1980s and 1990s, says Josh Lerner of Harvard University. Venture-capital firms raise only about a third as much money in Europe as in America. The aftermath of the crisis could widen the gap by reinforcing continental mistrust of free-wheeling Anglo-Saxon finance.

What will ultimately be more important, though, is the health of banks. Early-stage entrepreneurs are generally thought to rely on them less than on friends, family, venture capitalists and angel investors. But Alicia Robb at the University of California at Santa Cruz and David Robinson of Duke University, who examined the sources of finance of 4,000 American start-ups, found that bank loans are far more important than other sources of finance. On average, new firms borrow seven times as much from banks as they do from friends and family.

Mr Robinson says the damage to start-up financing from the crisis is "potentially quite severe". The collapse in house prices has undercut the many entrepreneurs who rely on home-equity loans. This will also depress jobs growth, which over time depends disproportionately not on either small or large firms but on small firms that become large, according to work by the Kauffman Foundation.

Japan offers a sobering case history. Regulators were slow to force banks to recognise the problem of collapsed collateral values, but they did require banks to meet new international standards for capital. Banks that acknowledged non-performing loans risked falling below those standards, so they kept zombie borrowers alive on a drip-feed of fresh money. They continued to "extend credit to insolvent borrowers, gambling that somehow these firms would recover or that the government would bail them out", according to Ricardo Caballero, Takeo Hoshi and Anil Kashyap in a 2006 paper.

They estimate that zombie companies – those getting by on subsidised credit – which had made up 5–15% of banks' borrowers in the early 1990s, increased their share to 25% later that decade. The effects were variable. Zombies were much less prevalent in manufacturing, which was constantly exposed to international competition, than in construction and retailing, where job turnover and productivity growth were lower.

Policymakers have laboured to learn these lessons. In America and Europe they have imposed stress tests to see how vulnerable their banks are to bad loans. Ireland and Germany have set up "bad banks" to shift bad loans to the public sector, as Sweden and Korea successfully did after their respective crises in the 1990s. Still, there is a widespread belief that banks have not fully owned up to their problems, partly because of political pressure. Germany's *Landesbanken*, which have ties to local politicians and firms, are widely thought to be in deeper trouble than the stress tests suggest.

In America, banks and Fannie Mae and Freddie Mac, the nationalised mortgage companies, have been discouraged by federal and state governments from foreclosing on homeowners unable to keep up their payments. Banks do not mind all that much since it allows them to put off recognising losses. But the non-performing loans may come to constitute a drain on banks' resources that inhibits lending to more productive borrowers.

In Japan bad loans were to corporations rather than households, but the problem is essentially the same. Despite their noble intent, federal subsidies that keep stressed owners in their homes delay the necessary reallocation of capital away from property. "Fortunately we've been pretty unsuccessful," says Dale Jorgenson, a productivity expert at Harvard University, noting the small number of temporary mortgage modifications that have become permanent.

Weak banks are not the only reason for a credit squeeze. There is also uncertainty over the effect of new regulations on the financial system's ability to channel savers' funds into investments. In July 2010 America passed its biggest overhaul of financial rules since the 1930s, known as the Dodd-Frank act after its leading congressional sponsors. In September the Basel Committee of international bank regulators agreed on a new set of requirements for banks' liquidity and capital. These rules, known as Basel 3, will require global banks to have common equity equal to at least 7% of their risk-weighted assets, against 2% now. That includes a minimum common-equity standard of 4.5% plus a countercyclical buffer of another 2.5%.

Experience shows that higher capital requirements do dent credit growth, at least in the short term. The first Basel agreement on bank capital contributed significantly to a steep decline in loan growth in America in the early 1990s, according to a 2000 study by the Bank for International Settlements (BIS).

Bankers say the new rules will also hurt lending. The Institute of International Finance, which is backed by the world's big banks, argued in a report published in June that the rules then being contemplated would trim annual economic growth by 0.5 percentage points in America, 0.9 in the euro area and 0.4 points in Japan over five years. But in a study of its own the BIS predicted a far more modest effect: less than 0.2 percentage points in most countries, though in the medium term there would be a gain from greater stability.

Make me virtuous, but not yet

Compelling banks to set aside a lot more capital without much warning is clearly risky. The Federal Reserve found it would have to lower short-term interest rates by 40 basis points to soften the impact of bigger capital buffers on growth – an impossibility now that rates are, in effect, at zero. To deal with this concern, the new Basel rules have a long lead time. The minimum level for common equity is not due to take effect until 2015, and the additional buffer not until 2019.

Equally contentious is the effect of the post-crisis regulatory clampdown on high-octane finance. America's new financial rules compel banks to trim their holdings of private equity and hedge funds. They require greater transparency in derivatives markets and demand greater disclosure from hedge funds. These new rules are as yet imperfectly understood, but are already having an effect. For example, Ford Motor's credit arm pulled an asset-backed bond deal because credit-rating agencies, fearful of new liabilities under the Dodd-Frank act, forbid the use of their opinions in the deal document. The deal went ahead when the Securities and Exchange Commission temporarily suspended the requirement that deal documents include such ratings.

In Britain and America sophisticated finance is ingrained enough to survive tighter regulation. Continental Europe, however, has never had America's breadth of financing options for fast-growing companies such as junk bonds, mezzanine debt and private equity, note Thomas Philippon and Nicolas Véron in a 2008 report for Bruegel, a Brussels-based think-tank.

So far the European response has been less draconian than many feared. New rules currently being negotiated by the European parliament and EU finance ministers could stop foreign hedge funds and private-equity funds from marketing themselves to EU investors unless they accept certain restrictions. But Mr Véron notes that they have yet to pass, and Britain has raised objections. New proposals for regulating derivatives trading, released by the European Commission in September, were less onerous than expected, and in some ways less likely to discourage innovation than America's new rules.

Nonetheless, increased regulation is likely to slow the pace of financial innovation. How much that matters depends on whether such innovation boosts growth. It has become fashionable to say it does not. Paul Volcker, a former Fed chairman, has caustically called the ATM cash dispenser the only worthwhile financial innovation of recent decades, a sentiment widely shared by venture capitalists and non-financial businesses. "I can't think of any financial or banker product or service that's ever helped us," says Mr Jurvetson. "Engineers contribute to the economy, lawyers and bankers ... subtract."

In a new book Amar Bhidé, a professor at Tufts University, argues that modern banks reduced loan decisions to arm's-length algorithms based on credit scores and asset values, biasing them towards homogeneous loans such as residential mortgages. Yet the prospects of young, innovative businesses are not easily summarised in a credit score; a bank manager must sample its wares, kick the delivery van's tyres and meet the founders. Mr Bhidé says that is how banks worked before deregulation in the 1980s and 1990s, and thinks a return to that old model would boost credit to young businesses.

The uses of novelty

However, this too easily dismisses the contribution of financial innovation. Work by Mr Laeven of the IMF with Ross Levine and Stelios Michalopoulos suggests that finance innovates to meet the changing needs of the economy as it evolves; whether that innovation is beneficial depends on the economic purpose it serves. Subprime CDOs helped facilitate a reckless overinvestment in property, whereas preferred shares, a 19th-century innovation, financed that era's railroad boom.

Financial innovation may even help the economy cope with the aftermath of the crisis. Lloyds Banking Group and Rabobank have led the way in issuing "contingent convertible bonds" which can be converted to equity if the bank is about to become undercapitalised. In theory, this lessens the risk of future insolvency and taxpayer bail-out and lowers the cost of raising fresh equity capital. Private-equity firms are currently dabbling in buying deeply discounted "underwater" mortgages from banks, then restructuring the terms to prevent foreclosure. There is even a fledgling market in bonds explicitly backed by delinquent mortgages. Meanwhile, American local governments are issuing "property assessed clean energy" or PACE bonds, then lending the proceeds to homeowners to make their homes more energy-efficient. Homeowners repay the loans through their property tax.

There are many more ideas on the drawing board. Robert Shiller of Yale University, whose theories led to the development of property derivatives, has proposed their use in developing home-equity insurance for homeowners. Mr Caballero and Pablo Kurlat of the Massachusetts Institute of Technology would like to see governments sell "tradable insurance credits" which give any financial institution the right to buy a government guarantee in a financial crisis.

Nothing may come of these ideas, yet their potential should not be dismissed. In the early 1990s America's Resolution Trust Corporation used securitisation to offload billions of dollars in property loans inherited from busted banks more quickly and at better prices than if it had disposed of them one at a time. It would be ironic if financial innovation, so reviled for helping to bring on the latest crisis, were to play a part in cleaning up the mess.

Smart work

Faster productivity growth will be an important part of rich economies' revival

PRODUCTIVITY GROWTH is the closest economics gets to a magic elixir, especially for ageing advanced economies. When workers produce more for every hour they toil, living standards rise and governments have more resources to service their debts and support those who cannot work. As the rich world emerges from the financial crisis, faster productivity growth could counteract the drag from adverse demography. But slower productivity growth could make matters worse.

Workers' productivity depends on their skills, the amount of capital invested in helping them to do their jobs and the pace of "innovation" – the process of generating ideas that lead to new products and more efficient business practices. Financial crises and deep recessions can affect these variables in several ways. Workers' skills may erode if long-term unemployment rises. The disruption to the financial sector and the reluctance of businesses to invest in the face of uncertain demand may also reduce the rate of capital formation, delaying the factory upgrades and IT purchases that would boost workers' efficiency.

Financial crises can affect the pace of innovation, too, though it is hard to predict which way. Deep recessions can slow it down as firms slash their spending on research and development. But they can also boost the pace of efficiency gains as weak demand forces firms to rethink their products and cost structures and the weakest companies are winnowed out. According to Alexander Field of Santa Clara University, the 1930s saw the fastest efficiency improvements in America's history amid large-scale restructuring.

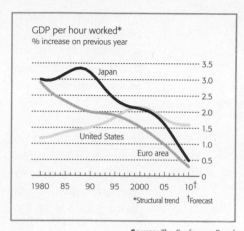

GDP per hour worked*
% increase on previous year

Japan

United States

Euro area

1980 85 90 95 2000 05 10†

*Structural trend †Forecast

Source: The Conference Board

FIG 8.8 It's getting harder

Here we go again

Almost every government in the rich world has a spanking new "innovation strategy". Industrial policy – out of fashion since its most credible champion, Japan, lost its way in the 1990s – is staging a comeback. But mostly such policies end up subsidising well-connected industries and products. "Green technology" is a favourite receptacle for such subsidies.

In 2008 France created a sovereign-wealth fund as part of its response to the financial crisis; it promises to promote biotechnology ventures, though it has also sunk capital into conventional manufacturers that happened to need money. In 2009 Britain followed suit with a "strategic investment fund". The Japanese too are back in the game. In June 2010 the newly invigorated Ministry of Economy, Trade and Industry (METI) unveiled a plan to promote five strategic sectors, ranging from environmental products to robotics. However, past experiments with industrial policy, from France's Minitel, an attempt to create a government-run national communications network, to Spain's expensive subsidies to jump-start solar power, suggest that governments are not much good at picking promising sectors or products.

More important, the politicians' current focus on fostering productivity growth via exciting high-tech breakthroughs misses a big part of what really drives innovation: the diffusion of better business processes and management methods. This sort of innovation is generally the result of competitive pressure. The best thing that governments can do to foster new ideas is to get out of the way. This is especially true in the most regulated and least competitive parts of the economy, notably services.

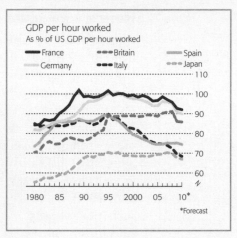

GDP per hour worked
As % of US GDP per hour worked

- France
- Germany
- Britain
- Italy
- Spain
- Japan

Source: The Conference Board

FIG 8.9 Not catching up

To see why competition matters so much, consider the recent history of productivity in the rich world. On the eve of the recession the rate of growth in workers' output per hour was slowing. So, too, was the pace of improvement in "total factor productivity" (a measure of the overall efficiency with which capital and workers are used which is economists' best gauge of the speed of innovation). But that broad trend masks considerable differences.

Since the mid-1990s America's underlying productivity growth – adjusted for the ups and downs of the business cycle – has outperformed most other rich economies' by a wide margin (see Figure 8.8). Workers' output per hour soared in the late 1990s, thanks largely to investment in computers and software. At first this advance was powered by productivity gains within the technology sector. From 2000 onwards efficiency gains spread through the wider economy, especially in services such as retailing and wholesaling, helped by the deregulated and competitive nature of America's economy. The improvements were extraordinary, though they slowed after the middle of the decade.

The recent history of productivity in Europe is almost the mirror image of America's. Up to the mid-1990s the continent's output per hour grew faster than America's (see Figure 8.9), helped by imports of tried and tested ideas from across the water. Thanks to this process of catch-up, by 1995 Europe's output per hour reached over 90% of the American level. But then Europe slowed, and by 2008 the figure was back down to 83%. This partly reflected Europe's labour-market reforms, which brought more low-skilled workers into the workforce.

That seemed a price well worth paying for higher employment. But the main reason for Europe's disappointing productivity performance was that it failed to squeeze productivity gains from its service sector.

A forthcoming history of European growth by Marcel Timmer and Robert Inklaar of the University of Groningen, Mary O'Mahony of Birmingham University and Bart Van Ark of the Conference Board, a business-research organisation, carefully dissects the statistics for individual countries and industries and finds considerable variation within Europe. Finland and Sweden improved their productivity growth whereas Italy and Spain were particularly sluggish. Europe also did better in some sectors than in others; for example, telecommunications was a bright spot. But overall, compared with America, European firms invested relatively little in services and innovative business practices. A 2010 McKinsey study suggests that around two-thirds of the differential in productivity growth between America and Europe between 1995 and 2005 can be explained by the gap in "local services", such as retail and wholesale services.

Europe's service markets are smaller than America's, fragmented along national lines and heavily regulated. The OECD has tracked regulation of product and services markets across countries since 1998. It measures the degree of state control, barriers to competition and obstacles to starting a new company, assigning a score to each market of between 0 and 6 (where 0 is the least restrictive). Overall the absolute level of product regulation fell between 1998 and 2008, and the variation between countries lessened. America and Britain score joint best, with 0.84. The EU average is 1.4. But when it comes to services, the variation is larger and Europe has made much less progress.

In professional services, the OECD's score for Europe is fully twice as high as for America (meaning it is twice as restrictive). As the McKinsey report notes, many European countries are rife with anti-competitive rules. Architects' and lawyers' fees in Italy and Germany are subject to price floors and ceilings. Notaries in France, Spain and Greece and pharmacies in Greece are banned from advertising their services. Such restrictions limit the ability of efficient newcomers to compete for market share, cosseting incumbents and raising costs across the economy.

In Japan productivity growth slumped after the country's asset bubble burst at the start of the 1990s. One reason was the failure to deal decisively with the bad loans clogging its banks, which propped up inefficient "zombie" companies rather than forcing them into liquidation. That meant less capital was available to lend to upstart firms. Another problem was the lack of competition. Japan's service sector, unlike its world-class manufacturers, is fragmented, protected from foreign competition and heavily regulated, so it failed to capture the gains of the IT revolution.

Over the years Japan made various efforts at regulatory reform, from freeing up the energy market and mobile telephony in the mid-1990s to liberalising the financial sector in the late 1990s. These have borne some fruit. Japan's total factor productivity growth, unlike Europe's, began to improve after 2000. But coupled with the continuing weakness of investment, the reforms were too modest to bring about a decisive change in the country's overall productivity prospects.

Learn Swedish

Sweden offers a more encouraging lesson. In the aftermath of its banking bust in the early 1990s it not only cleaned up its banks quickly but also embarked on a radical programme of microeconomic deregulation. The government reformed its tax and pension systems and freed up whole swaths of the economy, from aviation, telecommunications and electricity to banking and retailing. Thanks to these reforms, Swedish productivity growth, which had averaged 1.2% a year from 1980 to 1990, accelerated to a remarkable 2.2% a year from 1991 to 1998 and 2.5% from 1999 to 2005, according to the McKinsey Global Institute.

Sweden's retailers put in a particularly impressive performance. In 1990, McKinsey found, they were 5% less productive than America's, mainly because a thicket of regulations ensured that stores were much smaller and competition less intense. Local laws restricted access to land for large stores, existing retailers colluded on prices and incumbent chains pressed suppliers to boycott cheaper competitors. But in 1992 the laws were changed to weaken municipal land-use restrictions, and Swedish entry into the EU and the creation of a new

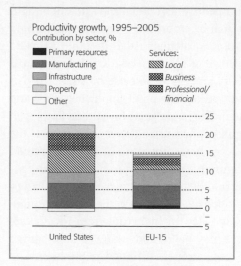

Productivity growth, 1995–2005
Contribution by sector, %

■ Primary resources
■ Manufacturing
■ Infrastructure
□ Property
□ Other

Services:
▧ Local
▨ Business
▨ Professional/
financial

25
20
15
10
5
+
0
–
5

United States   EU-15

Source: McKinsey Global Institute

FIG 8.10 Services with a smile

competition authority raised competitive pressures. Large stores and vertically integrated chains rapidly gained market share. By 2005 Sweden's retail productivity was 14% higher than America's.

The restructuring of retail banking services was another success story. Consolidation driven by the financial crisis and by EU entry increased competition. New niche players introduced innovative products like telephone and internet banking that later spread to larger banks. Many branches were closed, and by 2006 Sweden had one of the lowest branch densities in Europe. Between 1995 and 2002 banking productivity grew by 4.6% a year, much faster than in other European countries. Swedish banks' productivity went from slightly behind to slightly ahead of American levels.

All this suggests that for many rich countries the quickest route to faster productivity growth will be to use the crisis to deregulate the service sector. A study by the Bank of France and the OECD looked at 20 sectors in 15 OECD countries between 1984 and 2007. It found that reducing regulation on "upstream" services would have a marked effect not just on productivity in those sectors but also on other parts of the economy. The logic is simple: more efficient lawyers, distributors or banks enable firms across the economy to become more productive. The size of the potential gains calculated by the Bank of France is stunning. Getting rid of all price, market-entry and other competition-restricting regulations would boost annual total factor productivity growth by one percentage point in a typical country in their sample, enough to more than double its pace.

Getting rid of all anti-competitive regulation may be impossible, but even the more modest goal of embracing "best practice" would yield large benefits. The IMF has calculated that if countries could reduce regulation to the average of the least restrictive three OECD countries, annual productivity growth would rise by some 0.2 percentage points in America, 0.3 percentage points in the euro area and 0.6 percentage points in Japan. The larger gains for Europe and Japan reflect the amount of deregulation left to be done. In both cases the productivity gains to be achieved from moving to best practice would all but counter the drag on growth from unfavourable demography.

Even in America there would be benefits. But, alas, the regulatory pendulum is moving in the opposite direction as the Obama administration pushes through new rules on industries from health care to finance. So far the damage may be limited. Many of Mr Obama's regulatory changes, from tougher fuel-efficiency requirements to curbs on deep-water drilling, were meant to benefit consumers and the environment, not to curb competition and protect incumbents. Some of the White House's ideas, such as the overhaul of broadband internet access, would in fact increase competition. The biggest risk lies in finance, where America's new rules could easily hold back innovation.

An unlikely role model

The country that is grasping the challenge of deregulation most energetically is Greece, whose debt crisis has earned it a reputation for macroeconomic mismanagement. Under pressure from the IMF and its European partners, the Greek government has embarked on one of the most radical reforms in modern history to boost its productive potential.

Again, this involves freeing up an historically cushioned service sector. So far the main battleground has been trucking. Before Greece descended into crisis, its lorry drivers required special licences, and none had been granted for several decades. So a licence changed hands in the secondary market for about €300,000, driving up the costs of everything that travelled by road in Greece. But under a reform recently passed by the Greek government, the number of licences is due to double. Greek lorry drivers went on strike in protest, but the government did not budge. Lawyers and pharmacists too are slated for deregulation.

If Greece can stick to its plans, it will, like Sweden, show that crises can offer valuable opportunities. Without the country's brush with default and the conditions attached to the resulting bail-out, its leaders would have been unlikely to muster the necessary political will.

The sluggish progress of reform elsewhere underlines this point. Germany, which ranks 25th out of 30 OECD countries on the complications of its licence and permit system, approaches deregulation on tiptoes: it recently reduced restrictions on price-setting by architects and allowed chimney-sweeps easier market access.

Two French economists, Jacques Delpla and Charles Wyplosz, have argued that incumbent service providers should be paid off in exchange for accepting competition. They reckon that compensating French taxi drivers for deregulation would cost €4.5 billion. But buying off the losers from reforms may not hold much appeal.

Boosting European integration could be another way to cut through national resistance to deregulation. As Mario Monti, a former EU competition commissioner, pointed out, 70% of the EU's GDP is in services but only 20% of those services cross borders. The EU's Services Directive, which is supposed to boost cross-country competition in services, has proved fairly toothless.

How governments can help

Activism on the part of governments is not always misguided. Their investment in basic research is important. The grants doled out by America's National Institutes of Health, for example, generate the raw ideas that pharmaceutical firms turn into profitable medicines. America's Defence Department created the beginnings of the internet. Public spending on building and maintaining infrastructure also matters, though economists argue about how much. Governments can encourage private R&D spending with tax credits and subsidies, and the evidence suggests that more R&D spending overall boosts growth. Other research shows that firms which spend more on R&D are also often quicker to adopt other innovations.

But these traditional ways of encouraging innovation may be less relevant now that research has become more global and more concentrated on software than on hardware. Since the mid-1990s China alone has accounted for a third of the increase in global spending on research and development. Big firms maintain research facilities in many countries. Dreaming up new products and services, as well as better ways of producing old ones, increasingly involves collaboration across borders and companies. As Dale Jorgenson of Harvard University puts it: "Think Google, not lab coats."

In this more fluid world the old kind of government incentives, such as tax credits and subsidies, may do less to boost innovation than more imaginative inducements, such as offering firms prizes for breakthrough innovations. Bigger efforts to remove remaining barriers to collaboration, from limitations on high-skilled immigration to excessively rigid land-use rules, should also help.

A smart innovation agenda, in short, would be quite different from the one that most rich governments seem to favour. It would be more about freeing markets and less about picking winners; more about creating the right conditions for bright ideas to emerge and less about promises of things like green jobs. But pursuing that kind of policy requires courage and vision – and most of the rich economies are not displaying enough of either.

A better way

The rich world should worry about growth-promoting reforms more than short-term fiscal austerity

"ONCE YOU START THINKING about growth", said Robert Lucas, a Nobel prize-winning economist, "it's hard to think about anything else." Judging by their rhetoric, the world's policymakers are indeed thinking about little else. The statement released after the meeting of G20 leaders in Toronto in June 2010 mentioned the word "growth" 29 times in nine pages. Mr Obama says his economic policy is all about "laying the foundations for long-term growth". Britain's prime minister, David Cameron, used his first speech in office to lay out a "strategy for economic growth". Japan's government unveiled a ten-year "new growth strategy" in June.

The task is immense. The rich world's nascent recoveries are losing momentum even though joblessness remains worryingly high. The slowdown has been most obvious in America. The housing market has turned down again and the pace of job creation remains painfully slow.

Led by a surge in German GDP, the euro area fared relatively better in the first half of 2010, but as the rebound in global trade wanes, Germany's export-dependent economy slowed again. The country's latest figures for investor confidence look a lot feebler than they did earlier in 2010. Japan's economy, too, is weakening for much the same reason.

The OECD's September 2010 forecast reckoned that the annual rate of GDP growth in the G7 group of big rich economies would fall to 1.5% in the second half of the year, a full percentage point below its forecast in May. Gloomier analysts worry about a "double-dip" recession. Even optimists no longer expect anything more than tepid growth in 2011 (see Figure 8.11).

Looking further ahead, towards 2015, the picture remains dark as first debt and then ageing populations will weigh heavily on the rich world's prospects. The fall-out of the financial bust will weigh

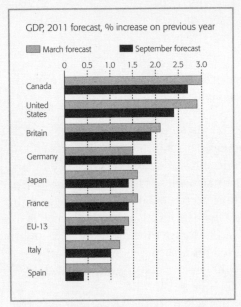

GDP, 2011 forecast, % increase on previous year

March forecast   September forecast

Source: *The Economist* poll of forecasters

FIG 8.11 Don't hang your hopes too high

on private spending for several more years as banking systems are repaired and households and firms pay down their debts. Even in America, where households are moving out of the red faster than elsewhere, they have at best got only halfway there.

According to the analysis by Carmen and Vincent Reinhart (see page 229), GDP per head, on average, grows 1% a year more slowly in the decade after big crises than in the decade before. Since rich economies as a group grew by an average of 2.5% a year before the financial crisis and then slumped by more than 3% during the recession, that suggests they might grow by less than 1.7% a year over the next few years.

Slower growth in advanced economies will mean lower private investment, higher unemployment and higher public debt, all of which will hurt their longer-term capacity to grow. At the same time the adverse effect of ageing (and in many cases shrinking) populations on growth will become much more noticeable, especially in Europe, where a big rise in the share of women in the labour force has hitherto concealed the demographic drag.

The overall effect of these various elements is likely to be big. The grimmest predictions of the consequences of demography, higher public debt and lower private investment suggest that the potential growth rate of the big advanced economies as a group could halve, from above 2% before the crisis to around 1% over the next few years. Small wonder that Jean-Claude Trichet, the president of the European

Central Bank and a man not normally given to hyperbole, worries that the next ten years could be a "lost decade".

Are today's growth strategies good enough to prove him wrong? There are three big reasons to doubt it. First, rich countries, collectively, are relying too much on foreign demand as a source of growth. Second, they are at risk of both overdoing and mismanaging short-term fiscal austerity. Third, most are paying far too little attention to structural reforms that would speed up the pace of debt reduction, make high unemployment less likely to become entrenched and boost productivity growth.

Begin with the wishful thinking on foreign demand. At every international economic gathering there is talk of the importance of "rebalancing" the pattern of global demand. The world economy must rely less on spending by over-indebted Anglo-Saxon consumers and cajole more spending out of thriftier Germans and Japanese, as well as firms and households in fast growing emerging economies, notably China. Yet there is little sign that these efforts have done any good so far.

The rich world's deficit countries, such as America and Britain, certainly want to push exports to counter weak consumer demand. The Obama administration has said it would like to double America's exports in five years. Britain's new government has put export promotion at the heart of its foreign policy. But the surplus economies, particularly Germany and Japan, are equally determined to go on focusing on trade. In September 2010 Japan intervened in currency markets for the first time in six years to stem the yen's rise.

Nor is there much sign of a rapid rebalancing towards the emerging world. China, as the biggest saver, should bear the brunt of such a shift. Its current-account surplus declined sharply between 2008 and 2009, but it rose again in 2010. Although the government promised a more flexible currency in June, the yuan barely moved in subsequent months.

More important, the structural barriers that get in the way of higher domestic spending – from government monopolies in many services to taxes, subsidies and corporate-governance rules that favour profits over wages – will take years to remove. Nor is there much sign that other emerging economies are keen to run big deficits for now. In the longer term faster growth in poorer countries' demand is bound to be good for the advanced economies, but it will take time.

A dangerous squeeze

The rich countries also seem to underestimate the risks that fiscal austerity poses to domestic demand. Virtually all the advanced economies are planning some combination of tax increases and spending cuts in 2011 as their stimulus packages expire and budget consolidation begins. Collectively, says the IMF, these will amount to a tightening of some 1.25% of GDP. That would be the biggest simultaneous fiscal squeeze since modern records began. The IMF's own analyses, which refute the idea that fiscal contractions boost growth in the short term, suggest that such a tightening might reduce the rich world's already weak growth in 2011 by a percentage point or so.

Is this a sensible trade-off? Countries in which financial markets have lost confidence, such as Ireland or Spain, have no choice. Others must weigh the costs of slower growth against the benefits of greater prudence, particularly the reduced risk of a sudden jump in bond yields and the prospect of lower public debt later. For many individual economies, particularly open and indebted ones, that points towards earlier austerity. But what makes sense for individual countries may not make sense for the rich world as a whole.

More important, policymakers' obsession with cutting deficits in the short term has deflected attention from the more important question of how to do it. Some countries are setting about it the right way. France, for instance, is pushing through pension reform; and in Britain three-quarters of the fiscal adjustment will come from spending cuts. But America, if Mr Obama has his way and the Bush tax cuts for high earners are eliminated, is heading for the worst possible outcome: raising taxes on income and capital but failing to trim the country's pension liabilities and rising health-care costs.

In most rich countries the detailed plans for fiscal austerity contrast sharply with a lamentable lack of microeconomic ambition. Greece is the only rich economy that is responding to the crisis with broad and radical reforms to boost its productive potential. In Britain, whose economy is already relatively deregulated, spending cuts will help reduce the role of the state. But elsewhere progress has been limited. Spain has gone some way towards freeing its labour markets, and Japan's "growth strategy" proposes a series of small liberalising steps, such as cutting rules around nursing care. But Germany's politicians are far keener to denounce deficits than to deregulate domestic services. And in America the policy debate revolves almost entirely around demand, the wisdom of stimulus and the Bush tax cuts. Most officials barely acknowledge that supply-side reforms, such as an overhaul of training schemes to help combat long-term joblessness, or bigger efforts to reduce household debts, might even be necessary.

The economic case for a growth strategy that combines hefty fiscal cuts with timid structural reforms is not obvious, especially when private demand is likely to stay weak. In the long run bold productivity-enhancing reforms will do more to boost the rich world's growth prospects than short-term fiscal austerity. And better growth prospects will, themselves, make government debt less onerous. In a 2010 study, economists at the IMF analysed the respective impact of deficit reduction, global rebalancing and productivity-enhancing structural reforms on the growth prospects of big rich economies and found that by far the strongest positive effect came from structural reforms.

There is also a political logic to favouring a bigger prop for demand along with bolder action on structural reforms. The contrasting stories of Sweden and Japan suggest that although big crises can offer an opportunity to overhaul an entire economy, a prolonged period of sluggish growth makes structural reforms increasingly difficult. Both politicians and voters become accustomed to gradual decline. In many rich countries an extended bout of high unemployment could easily lead to policies such as protectionism that will further hurt long-term growth.

All told, there is a case for changing the debate about growth in the rich world. Fiscal consolidation should be more nuanced and supply-side reforms should be given greater prominence. This is particularly true for America. In an ideal world, America's politicians would come up with a package of medium-term spending cuts and tax reforms to fill the country's fiscal gap. But since that is impossible, given that Republicans refuse to countenance any tax increases and Democrats refuse to cut any spending on entitlements, the best short-term remedy would be to extend the Bush tax cuts for another three years.

America's structural reforms ought to focus on encouraging households to reduce their debts more quickly and tackling entrenched joblessness. By the standards of previous financial crises America's banks have been recapitalised remarkably quickly, but much less has been done to deal with the $800 billion-worth of American mortgages (almost 25% of the total) where the house is worth less than the outstanding loan. Legal reforms that made it easier to reduce this debt overhang would allow a more efficient allocation of capital and hence boost investment. They would help to deal with high unemployment, too, by making it easier for workers to move to new jobs. A comprehensive strategy to counter structural joblessness would also include things like hiring subsidies for the hard-to-employ and an overhaul of training schemes.

Outside America the design of fiscal consolidation is more sensible, though the scale may be excessive. In both continental Europe and Japan reform should concentrate on boosting growth by freeing up labour markets and services. Rules that stifle competition should be struck out in industries from health care to road transport.

The to-do list is familiar, not least because the OECD has spent years cataloguing and comparing the rich world's supply-side rigidities. It even produces a handy annual publication, called "Going for Growth", that sets out priorities. But rich-world governments have found it hard to summon up the political courage to act. The recession and its grim aftermath offer an opportunity to do better.

If the rich world really wants to go for growth, it must get away from its narrow focus on public debt and embark on a broader economic overhaul. Instead of promising to halve their budget deficits by 2013, for instance, big rich economies could decide to raise their retirement ages or free up their professional services. Fiscal consolidation would not be ignored: it would just not be the only priority.

An American official famously quipped after the 2007–08 debacle that you should "never let a serious crisis go to waste". It is advice that the rich world would do well to heed.

Dropping the shopping

Can America wean itself off consumption?

GENERAL ELECTRIC has historically been a manufacturer, but in the long boom leading up to the financial crisis it became more like a bank. Half its profit came from its finance arm, GE Capital, which among other things had a lucrative business issuing mortgages and credit cards to American consumers. GE's chief executive, Jeffrey Immelt, now talks like a man chastened. With GE Capital acting as a drag on the company, he vows that in the future finance will be a smaller part of the company. In its place GE touts its manufacturing and exporting prowess. Mr Immelt boasts of record aircraft engine orders at the Paris Air Show in June 2009, none of them to American airlines.

Like GE, the entire American economy is at an inflection point. For decades, its growth has been led by consumer spending. Thanks to rising asset prices and ever easier access to credit, Americans went on a seemingly unstoppable spending binge, fuelling the global economy as they bought ever bigger houses and filled them with ever more stuff. Consumer spending and residential investment rose from 67% of GDP in 1980 to 75% in 2007 (see Figure 8.12, left-hand side). The household saving rate fell from 10% of disposable income in 1980 to close to zero in 2007; household indebtedness raced from 67% of disposable income to 132%. As Americans spent more than they produced, the country's current-account balance went from a surplus of 0.4% of GDP in 1980 to a deficit of almost 6% in 2006 (see Figure 8.12, right-hand side).

Economists had hoped that these imbalances would unwind gradually as Americans saved more and the rest of the world spent more. But they had long fretted that the process would end in tears. Most worried about a dollar crash, as investors balked at America's rising foreign borrowing. Instead the financial crisis felled America's consumers. The destruction of more than $13 trillion of consumer wealth and the implosion of the shadow banking system, a once

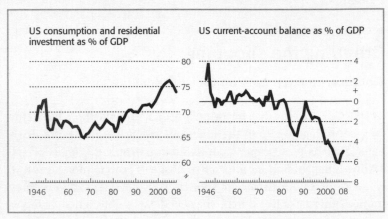

Source: US Bureau of Economic Analysis

FIG 8.12 Anatomy of a boom

plentiful source of credit, has triggered a shift to thrift, which in turn has plunged the economy into its deepest recession in decades. Americans now save more than 5% of their after-tax income, still well below the post-war average but hugely up from July 2008. The current-account deficit has shrunk dramatically: the IMF projects that it will shrivel to less than 3% of GDP in 2009 and 2010 as Americans spend and invest less.

The collapse in consumption has dramatically changed the composition of America's economy. A huge increase in private saving has been offset by a leap in the budget deficit. The combination of Barack Obama's big fiscal stimulus package, as well as the natural consequence of declining tax revenues, means that the 2009 federal budget deficit is likely to be 13% of GDP, about 12 percentage points more than in 2007. That has cushioned the slump. GE is among those taking advantage. It is aggressively pursuing stimulus-related sales, while tapping federal, state and local incentives. In June 2009 the company said that it would create 400 jobs at a plant in Louisville, Kentucky, making a low-energy water heater that is now made in China and that it would hire 1,100 people to staff a software research centre on the site of an auto plant in Van Buren, Michigan. Both investments were helped along by government incentives.

But despite the government's largesse, America's recession has been deep and its impact on the rest of the world profound. Though America is still a source of demand for the rest of the world, its waning appetite has been a hefty drag on world economic growth. In the years before the financial crisis kicked in, American demand contributed to global growth. In 2009 it will subtract from it.

As the boost from fiscal stimulus takes effect there are signs that America's economy is stabilising. An index of leading indicators compiled by the Conference Board, a research group, rose for the third consecutive month in June 2009. In testimony to Congress on July 21st 2009, Ben Bernanke, the chairman of the Federal Reserve, struck an undeniably upbeat tone about the state of the economy. But the bigger issue – for America and for the world – is where growth will come from in the medium term. The answer is not entirely in America's hands – the world's big surplus economies, China, Germany and Japan, may also boost their domestic demand. But as the world's biggest economy America is the right place to start. Three questions stand out. Can America continue to rely on government stimulus to drive growth? Will the consumer recover? Or can exports take up the slack?

The answer to the first question is "not for ever". In the short term, policymakers are committed to using a mixture of fiscal stimulus and aggressive monetary policy to hasten the end of the recession and prevent inflation from turning into deflation. But the contribution of the stimulus is due to start ebbing in 2010. The lesson of Japan in the 1990s is that the after-effects of a bubble suppress demand for longer than most expect, necessitating extended government stimulus. Unlike Japan, though, America is already in hock to the foreigners. Mohamed El-Erian of Pimco, a fund manager, predicts that policymakers will be reluctant to stimulate any further for fear of feeding suspicions that America will inflate away its debts, which could push long-term interest rates much higher. Even if they do not withdraw the stimulus in 2010, they must at some point if the federal debt, projected to double to 82% of GDP by 2019, is to stop rising.

The prospect of a withdrawal of government support need not spell disaster. As America looked forward to the end of the second world war, policymakers were deeply anxious that as war spending shrank, the economy would slip back into 1930s-like stagnation. "All alike expect and fear a post-war collapse," Alvin Hansen of Harvard University, a leading economist of the time, wrote in 1942. Yet the collapse never came. Thanks to rising productivity and rapid recovery in Europe and Japan, the post-war years witnessed strong, balanced growth. From 1946 until 1980, American households saved 8–10% of their disposable income and the country usually ran small trade surpluses.

An historic challenge

Perhaps productivity can accelerate again, boosting incomes enough to support robust spending as well as more saving. But an obvious difference from the post-war period is the need for American consumers to reduce their debts. Richard Berner of Morgan Stanley notes that in the past decade the proportion of income that American households devoted to servicing debt rose from 12% to 14%. He calculates that it would have risen to only around 12.5% but for a dramatic loosening of lending standards during the recent bubble. He thinks the ratio will revert to around 12% through a combination of lower interest rates, debt repayments and write-offs. That can be done, he says, with consumer spending growing at just over 2% a year, still far below its average of 3.4% from 1993 to 2007.

The implication is that demand from abroad must take the place of a splurging domestic consumer and a free-spending government. As Larry Summers, Mr Obama's chief economic adviser, said on July 17th 2009: "The rebuilt American economy must be more export-oriented and less consumption-oriented."

Take California, where the consumption and housing bubbles were especially pronounced. The shortage of land on the coasts drove many first-time homebuyers inland, fuelling a huge building boom. According to Jerry Nickelsburg of the Anderson Forecast at the University of California, Los Angeles, home-building permits tripled between the 1990s and 2005. The growth of new housing developments triggered a boom in new retail stores, lured by local government incentives. Meanwhile, America's ravenous appetite for imports from Asia fuelled business at the ports of Long Beach, Los Angeles and Oakland and their supporting infrastructure of railroads, transport and warehouses.

California's disproportionate exposure to the boom explains why its bust has been especially painful. Mr Nickelsburg says home-building permits have plunged by 85% since 2005 and that the value of new retail-construction permits has fallen by half. Import volumes have dropped sharply. Most big subprime lenders have gone bankrupt or left the business.

The first glimmers of an export-led revival are apparent. The state's manufacturing employment has shrunk by less than in most of the big manufacturing states, reflecting less dependence on carmakers and greater exposure to Asia. The seasonally adjusted number of containers loaded at its ports for export, many with agricultural products and other raw materials, has risen from the lows of early 2009.

But it is one thing for exports to grow (and imports to fall) but another entirely for trade to compensate for the retrenchment of the much larger consumer sector. A cheaper currency may help. The trade deficit narrowed sharply in the late 1980s with the help of a dramatic fall in the dollar against the currencies of America's largest trading partners. The dollar has come down considerably since 2002 but has rallied over the past 12 months (August 2008–July 2009) as investors have repatriated money from abroad. Its decline is likely to resume but its contribution to rebalanced growth will be constrained if China does not let the yuan appreciate against the dollar.

Turning circle

Nor is it clear how quickly America can shift resources into tradable products. Its economy is adept at moving workers and capital from dying to growing industries. But the scale of the adaptation needed now is daunting. Robert DiClemente, an economist at Citigroup, estimates that credit-sensitive industries – housing, finance and cars – have shed 2m jobs, or one-third of all those lost, since the recession began (see Figure 8.13). It is not clear how quickly mortgage brokers and structured-finance whizzes can retrain in more productive industries. The fact that so many homeowners are sunk in negative equity will also constrain mobility.

The American economy is like a supertanker that, even in calm waters, changes direction very slowly. It is now being forced to do so

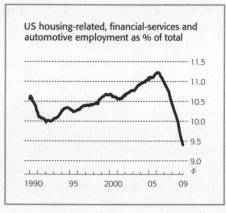

US housing-related, financial-services and automotive employment as % of total

11.5
11.0
10.5
10.0
9.5
9.0

1990   95   2000   05   09

Source: Citigroup

FIG 8.13 Nice while it lasted

in a gale. With the help of still sturdy growth in emerging markets America should be able to re-orient itself. But come what may, changing direction means losing speed. On the demand side foreign spending is unlikely to compensate for the freewheeling American consumer. On the supply side investment has slumped and will take time to right its course. Pimco's Mr El-Erian reckons that the transition from consumption to export-oriented expansion will lead to prolonged subpar growth and high unemployment.

That will heighten political risks such as protectionism. The House of Representatives, for example, has passed a bill aimed at capping American carbon emissions that would slap tariffs on countries that do not do likewise. The steelworkers' union has attacked Mr Immelt as a hypocrite for touting GE's new focus on manufacturing while opposing "Buy American" provisions in the stimulus package. Mr Obama's support for free trade remains lukewarm, a failing that could yet undermine hopes for export-led growth.

Writing America off is always a dangerous thing to do. Most probably, however, it faces years of painfully high unemployment and sluggish growth. GE's union at its plant in Louisville had to agree to a wage freeze until 2011 and to let new employees start for just $13 an hour. Like GE's workers, Americans will find the new, export-driven model of growth much less comfortable than the old one.

The spend is nigh

Can China reduce its trade surplus by consuming more?

A REBALANCED GLOBAL ECONOMY requires America to consume less and save more. That means the world's three big surplus economies – China, Germany and Japan – will have to save less and spend more. None is under more scrutiny than China, whose vast current-account surplus has been fingered by some as the ultimate cause of the financial crisis. The case against China is exaggerated but a surplus of more than $400 billion in 2008, or 10% of GDP, was clearly too big. Can China right its trade imbalances, and if so, how will it achieve rapid growth in future?

The good news is that the surplus is already shrinking. The strong rebound in China's economy in the second quarter of 2009 – pushing GDP 7.9% higher than a year earlier – came entirely from domestic demand. This sucked in more imports, while exports continued to slump. China's merchandise trade surplus narrowed to $35 billion in the same quarter, 40% down on a year earlier. Yu Song and Helen Qiao of Goldman Sachs calculate that the decline is even more impressive in real terms (adjusting for changes in export and import prices), with the surplus shrinking to less than one-third of its level a year earlier (see Figure 8.14). They even suggest that a monthly trade deficit is possible within the next 12 months.

Another way to look at the huge swing in China's trade is that net exports (exports minus imports) contributed 2.6 percentage points of the country's GDP growth in 2007, but shaved almost three points off its growth in the first half of 2009.

Most economists think that China's trade surplus will remain large. The jump in imports in the second quarter of 2009 included heavy stockpiling of commodities, which will not last; copper imports, for example, were 150% higher than a year earlier. Yet the underlying surplus is clearly shrinking. Paul Cavey of Macquarie Securities forecasts that China's current-account surplus will fall to under 6% of GDP in 2009 and 4% in 2010, down from a peak of 11% in 2007. Exports

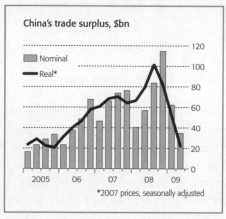

China's trade surplus, $bn

Nominal
Real*

120
100
80
60
40
20
0

2005   06   07   08   09

*2007 prices, seasonally adjusted

Source: Goldman Sachs

FIG 8.14 Shrinking at last

amounted to 35% of GDP in 2007; in 2009, reckons Mr Cavey, that ratio will drop to 24.5%.

On the surface, therefore, China is fulfilling the long-standing demand of Western governments that it shift its engine of growth from exports to domestic demand. Thanks to the biggest fiscal stimulus and loosening of credit of any large economy, China's real domestic demand is likely to grow by at least 10% in 2009. In fact, the popular perception that China has always relied on export-led growth is rather misleading. Its current-account surplus did soar from 2005 onwards but until then was rather modest. And over the past ten years net exports accounted, on average, for only one-tenth of its growth.

The problem is more that the mix of domestic demand between consumption and investment is unbalanced, and becoming even more so. In 2008 private consumption accounted for only 35% of GDP, down from 49% in 1990 (see Figure 8.15). By contrast, investment had risen from 35% to 44% of GDP. In 2009 the bulk of the government's stimulus went into infrastructure, further swelling investment's share. Chinese capital spending could exceed that in America for the first time, while its consumer spending will be only one-sixth as large. This is China's most glaring economic imbalance.

Spending lots of money on building railways, roads and power grids is the most effective way for the government to prop up demand in the short term – especially since China, as a poor country, needs better infrastructure. However, the pace of investment is unsustainable. Even before 2009's infrastructure boom capital spending was too great, causing many economists to worry about excess capacity and the risk that bank loans could sour.

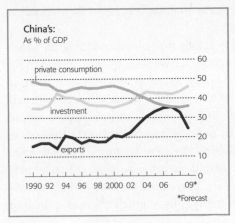

China's:
As % of GDP

private consumption

investment

exports

1990 92 94 96 98 2000 02 04 06 09*

*Forecast

Sources: CEIC; *The Economist* estimates

FIG 8.15 Unconsuming passion

China deserves credit for the speed with which it responded to the global downturn. Now it needs to focus on structural reforms not just to keep domestic demand growing strongly and to reduce its trade surplus further, but also to derive more of its growth from consumption and less from investment.

Before exploring how China can do so, it is important first to clear up a misunderstanding. It is often argued that China runs a current-account surplus because its consumer spending has been sluggish. On the contrary, China has the world's fastest-growing consumer market, increasing by 8% a year in real terms in the past decade. Retail sales have leapt by 17% in real terms in the 12 months to August 2009, although this figure may be inflated by government purchases. Even so, China's consumer spending has grown more slowly than the overall economy. As a result consumption as a share of GDP has fallen and is extremely low by international standards: only 35%, compared with 50–60% in most other Asian economies and 70% in America.

Economists disagree about the main reason why the consumption ratio has fallen – and hence about the best way to lift it. The most popular explanation is that Chinese households have been saving a bigger slice of their income because of an inadequate social safety net. They have squirrelled away more money to cover the future cost of health care, education and pensions. According to Eswar Prasad, an economist at Cornell University, the saving rate of urban households has jumped from 20% to 28% of their disposable income over the past decade. After exploring all the possible causes, he concludes that uncertainty about the private burden of health care and education is indeed the main culprit. The effect has been worsened by an undeveloped financial system, making it hard for households to borrow.

The Beijing government is acting: it doubled spending on health care, education and social security between 2005 and 2008. But the total amount remains low at only 6% of GDP, compared with an average of around 25% in OECD countries. In 2009 the government increased pensions coverage and payments to low-income households. It has also pledged to provide basic health care for 90% of the population by 2011, although the new spending appears to be less than 0.5% of GDP each year. If such measures ease households' worries about future health care, they could encourage them to save less. But it will take years for them to have much effect on consumer behaviour.

Slicing up saving

More to the point, an inadequate welfare state does not fully explain why consumption has fallen as a share of GDP. The first niggle is that most workers lost their state-provided health care and education almost a decade ago, after the reform of state-owned firms, so this cannot really explain why saving has continued to rise more recently. Louis Kuijs, an economist at the World Bank in Beijing, suggests that the extra saving may owe as much to greater income inequality as to the lack of a welfare state. Rich people save a lot more and their numbers have increased.

A second flaw in the thesis is that although urban households have been saving more, rural households have become less thrifty over the past decade. As a result China's average household-saving rate has risen more modestly. Mr Kuijs calculates that total household saving has risen from 21% of GDP in 1998 to 24% in 2008. Households accounted for only one-fifth of the increase in total domestic saving over the period. Most of the increase in saving came from companies (see Figure 8.16).

This matters for two reasons. First, if anyone saves too much, it is companies, not households. Second, you need to look elsewhere for the cause of China's falling consumption ratio. The drop in consumer spending as a share of GDP over the past decade has been almost four times larger than the rise in household saving.

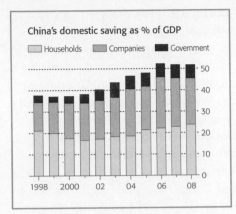

China's domestic saving as % of GDP

Households   Companies   Government

50
40
30
20
10
0

1998   2000   02   04   06   08

Source: Louis Kuijs, World Bank

FIG 8.16 The world's biggest squirrels

The more important reason why consumption has fallen is that the share of national income going to households (as wages and investment income) has fallen, while the share of profits has risen. Workers' share of the cake has dwindled because China's rapid growth has generated surprisingly few jobs. Growth has been capital-intensive, focusing on heavy industries such as steel rather than more labour-intensive services. Profits (the return to capital) have outpaced wage income.

Capital-intensive production has been encouraged by low interest rates and by the fact that most state-owned firms do not pay any dividends, allowing them to reinvest all their profits. The government has also favoured manufacturing over services by holding down the exchange rate as well as by suppressing the prices of inputs such as land and energy.

Simply urging households to spend a bigger slice of their income will not be enough to shift China's growth towards consumption. Beefing up the welfare state is important but policy also needs to focus on how to lift household income and reduce corporate saving, says Mr Kuijs. Making growth more labour-intensive will require lots of difficult reforms. China needs financial-sector liberalisation to lift the cost of capital for state-owned companies and improve access to credit for private ones, especially in services. Higher deposit rates would also boost household income. Distortions in the tax system which favour manufacturing and barriers to private-sector participation in some service industries should be scrapped. State-owned firms ought to be forced to pay bigger dividends. The prices of subsidised industrial inputs should be raised. Land reform and the removal of restrictions on migration from rural to urban areas would also help to lift incomes and thus consumption.

China has barely started on these important reforms. That may be because they involve much harder political decisions than creating a welfare state. They require the government to loosen its control over the economy, something which Beijing will do slowly and reluctantly.

Last but not least, China needs to allow its exchange rate to rise. This would lift consumers' real purchasing power, discourage excessive investment in manufacturing and help to reduce the trade deficit further. It would also alleviate the risk of a protectionist backlash abroad. From July 2005 (when China abandoned its dollar peg) to February 2009, the yuan rose by 28% in real trade-weighted terms, according to the Bank for International Settlements. But alarmed by the collapse of exports, China has virtually repegged the yuan to the dollar over the 12 months to August 2009. As the greenback fell during 2009, it dragged the yuan down with it. Since February 2009 the yuan's real trade-weighted value has lost 8%.

Economists disagree about the extent to which the yuan is undervalued. In the IMF's "Article IV" assessment of China, published on July 22nd 2009, officials were split over whether the currency was "substantially undervalued". Morris Goldstein and Nicholas Lardy, of the Peterson Institute for International Economics, have done some of the most extensive work on China's exchange rate. In a study, they estimate that the yuan is undervalued by 15–25%, based on the adjustment needed to eliminate the current-account surplus.

The American government has softened its demands for revaluation, largely because it needs China to keep buying Treasury bonds to fund its own stimulus spending. At the Strategic and Economic Dialogue meeting between American and Chinese officials on July 27th and 28th 2009 in Washington, DC, the yuan's exchange rate was barely discussed. However, the case for appreciation remains strong.

China's recent efforts to boost domestic spending have helped to maintain robust growth and reduce its trade surplus. But excessive levels of investment are not a recipe for sustained rapid growth. Unless it is prepared to embrace difficult structural reforms and to allow the yuan to climb, China's commitment to rebalancing will remain half-hearted. In the long run that will be bad news for China itself as well as for the rest of the world.

The lives of others

Can Germany wean itself from its export dependence?

THERE WAS A TIME not so long ago when European policymakers believed trade imbalances were only a problem for America and China. For much of 2008, a stock phrase in the press statement agreed each month by the European Central Bank's rate-setters was "the euro area does not suffer from major imbalances". As the year wore on, the claim was repeated but seemed more and more desperate, as if it were a spell to ward off recession. It was only when the collapse of Lehman Brothers in September 2008 sparked a global slump that the formulation was quietly dropped.

In a narrow sense the claim was true. Until the crisis struck, the euro area's current account was roughly in balance. That contrasted with America, where a spending boom and falling savings drove the current-account deficit as high as 6% of GDP in 2006. But Europe looked steadier only because Germany's huge trade surplus offset deficits elsewhere – notably in Spain but also in France, Greece, Italy and Portugal.

These imbalances were not trifling. In 2007 Spain had the largest current-account deficit in the world outside America. The surplus chalked up by Germany that year, at $263 billion, was second only to China's hoard of $372 billion. Germany's saving glut allowed others to spend freely and to run up large debts. Its economy benefited from strong export sales to other euro-zone countries, as well as to America and Britain. The common currency allowed imbalances to grow unchecked by fears of an exchange-rate crisis.

But the skewed pattern of demand only made recession worse when it came. The biggest slumps in demand were in Spain and Ireland, where growth had been consumer-led. The impact on output was felt most in Germany, where a collapse in exports and investment drove GDP down by 7% from its peak. The question now, with its main customers pulling back, is whether Germany can kick its export addiction and encourage more demand at home.

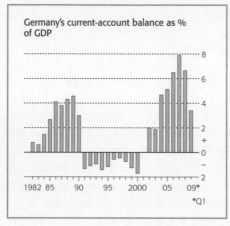

Germany's current-account balance as % of GDP

Source: Thomson Datastream

FIG 8.17 Back to black

A rebalancing of world demand requires high-savers, such as China and Germany, to spend more and run smaller trade surpluses so that the trade deficits of countries such as America and Spain can narrow as savings are rebuilt. Recession has forced that adjustment to begin in the most painful way. Germany's current-account surplus shrank dramatically, to 3.4% of GDP, in the three months to the end of March 2009, from 6.6% of GDP during 2008 (see Figure 8.17). The change in its external balance has made Germany the world economy's main shock absorber, says Hans-Werner Sinn of the Ifo Institute for Economic Research in Munich.

Much of the adjustment reflects a collapse in exports. Germany specialises in machinery and durable goods, purchases that businesses and consumers will put off when times are uncertain. It also reflects the resilience of domestic demand. German consumer spending has been broadly flat. That would count as a boom in many places where consumers are cutting back.

Fiscal policy has been a stabilising force, too. Germany's budget deficit should rise from around zero to 4% of GDP in 2009, and to 6% in 2010. Although it was a late convert to the need to do more, Germany's stimulus has worked well. Consumers have kept up their spending because most have held on to their jobs. A government scheme that allows firms to put underused employees on short-time working, and which subsidises their pay, has stopped unemployment rising sharply. Around 1.4m workers are on the short-time register, many of them in the depressed car and capital-goods industries. Cash incentives from government for older cars that are traded in for new ones have helped boost sales.

The short-time arrangements mean that workers stay in employment and keep their skills fresh. Firms are not panicked into laying off workers they might otherwise have to hire back again at great cost. "There is a certain accord with government to keep our core workforce intact for as long as possible," says Matthias Wissmann of the German Association of the Automotive Industry (VDA).

The drawback of the short-time working scheme is that it prevents a broader economic restructuring. When Spain's fiscal-stimulus package provided funds to build low-cost housing, it was criticised for spurring more construction in a country that had already seen too much. Germany's schemes to prop up demand for cars and car workers have the same weakness. They fossilise an industrial structure that needs to change.

Officials see these initiatives as a "bridge" over global recession and they are candid about what they hope is on the other side: a return to export-led growth. Some point out that Germany's economy cannot quickly change its orientation towards domestic demand. It has a comparative advantage in producing specialist goods that require a global market. "You cannot put power plants in the supermarket," notes one German economist. There is also widespread concern about the long-term costs of today's fiscal props for a rapidly ageing economy. Fingers are crossed that foreign demand will revive quickly so that Germany can get back to a balanced budget soon. Fine, except that it was Germany's export dependency and manufacturing bent that made its economy so vulnerable in the first place.

The presumption that what is good for exports is good for the economy partly explains why consumer spending in Germany has historically been weak. Its typical response to a faltering economy is to trim manufacturing costs, including wages, in order to keep exports keenly priced against other countries. That was the path taken in the early 1970s, when the D-mark rose after the collapse of the Bretton Woods system of fixed exchange rates. It was followed again after the 1990s when Germany's reunification boom and devaluations by some trading partners pushed up its relative wage costs.

The wage discipline was remarkable. German pay was more or less frozen for a decade from the mid-1990s, at a time when it was rising quickly in the rest of Europe. That wage restraint tilted

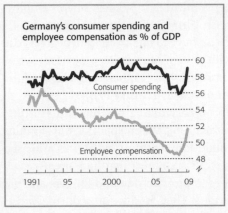

Germany's consumer spending and employee compensation as % of GDP

Source: Thomson Datastream

FIG 8.18 Too skint to spend

demand in favour of exports and away from consumption. The share of employee pay in GDP drifted steadily downward until the eve of recession in 2008 (see Figure 8.18). So even as exports boomed and jobs were created, sluggish wages meant the gains from national income growth went mostly to profits. Consumer spending suffered, falling to a low of 56% of GDP – well below America's 70%. The increase in the rate of value-added tax (VAT), from 16% to 19%, at the start of 2007 was a further check on spending. It says something that the increase was sold as a way to boost competitiveness (VAT is a tax that hurts consumption but not exports).

This tale of export fetishism tells us how Germany looks abroad for demand to kick-start its recoveries and explains why its trade balance rises in the early phase of the cycle. But it cannot fully account for the vast and enduring current-account surpluses that Germany piled up year after year. They also reflect a persistent excess of domestic saving over domestic investment. The share of income that households put aside has been broadly stable for years but the investment share in GDP has declined (see Figure 8.19). That is partly because Germany's mature export industries do not have great scope or appetite to expand capacity. It is also because capital is not finding its way to new ventures.

Some analysts believe that Germany's deep-rooted preference for equality in pay lies behind both its bent for export-led growth and the seemingly endless surpluses. In this view, a welfare policy designed to maintain a narrow gap between the best- and worst-paid employees has limited the earnings of the most skilled workers across all sectors, tempting many of them abroad. This "wage compression" has also

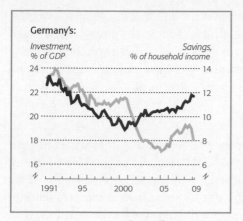

Germany's:

Investment,
% of GDP

Savings,
% of household income

Source: Thomson Datastream

FIG 8.19   Invested disinterest

stunted the emergence of a low-wage service sector that could cater for the home market. Wage floors prop up the pay of unskilled workers and make services expensive to supply. If personal services were on tap cheaply, consumers might spend more. Since investment in service industries is less attractive the pool of domestic savings leaks abroad.

Whenever firms are reluctant to invest, economists are quick to blame "inflexible" product and job markets. It is hard to start a business in Germany: it was ranked 102nd out of 181 countries on that criterion in the World Bank's 2009 *Doing Business* survey. Such regulatory barriers stop the economy's broader industrial structure from changing. Yet within manufacturing, businesses are flexible in their use of labour and in their control of costs. Germany's small capital-goods firms are famously nimble. If exporters were too rigid, they would not be quite so successful.

That suggests the standard wish-list of reforms might not make the economy any less dependent on exports and manufacturing. Germany's export addiction has deep roots. There is a wariness about services, particularly personal services, and a pride in being the world's biggest exporter. "Why does it take so long to start a company? Why are there so few links between universities and business? We have been wedded to the export model for so long we have ceased to look for alternatives," says Thomas Mayer of Deutsche Bank.

Germany may never again run as large a current-account surplus as it did before the crisis, if only because many of its main export markets will not easily regain their former buoyancy. German makers of plant and machinery may feel they have a decent chance of bouncing back, thanks to China's state-sponsored recovery. Durable-goods manufacturers (especially carmakers) will find the going far tougher, as consumers in America, Britain and Spain struggle. If foreign demand does not fully return, jobs will go once short-time working schemes expire. The government will have to keep supporting the economy while the private sector restructures.

Cars for clunkers

A shift from export dependency to an economy that serves its own consumers better would be painful but would be good for Germany, and the world, in the longer run. Its big saving surpluses required big deficits somewhere else; the deeper Germany's customers fell into debt, the less their IOUs were worth. German banks ended up with toxic American assets because they had excess savings to recycle. When carmakers reached capacity limits at home, they used cash piles to make poor acquisitions abroad (Daimler and Chrysler; BMW and Rover).

"It made no sense for Germany to sell Porsches for Lehman certificates," says Ifo's Mr Sinn. Those loaned funds could instead have been used to finance new ventures at home. Soon many Germans will reach retirement age; they will need a richer array of services than is on offer now. As some export industries shrink, new service industries will be needed to create jobs. That may even lift Germany's long-term growth rate. The export model left Germany at the mercy of changes in global demand. Yet there was no real growth dividend to compensate for that exposure. Growth in GDP per person in the past decade has been slower than in France and well below that in Britain or America.

There is a danger that Germany takes the wrong lesson from the crisis. It could decide the episode only shows the folly of relying on finance and services to drive growth, as America and Britain have. It could simply reinforce its long-standing export bias. But thoughtful Germans may conclude that a crisis that has created such a burden for future taxpayers stems partly from the ill use of their own savings. They may well end up wishing they had spent the money on themselves.

Stuck in neutral

Japan's long-standing inability to rebalance its economy is bad for the world and even worse for its own people

NO CITIZENS IN THE RICH WORLD take as few holidays as the Japanese. No wonder. In mid-August 2009, as millions left the cities for an annual pilgrimage to villages where they venerate the souls of their ancestors, many were likely to be stuck in 40-mile traffic jams on oven-like expressways, cursing the midsummer heat.

Such misery is common during the Buddhist festival of Obon, but it was worse in 2009. One of the government's aggressive measures to alleviate the economic crisis is to encourage people to spend money on hotels, transport cafés and other forms of leisure. To do that, it has slashed the cost of toll roads to almost one-tenth of their normal level, attracting yet more people on to fume-choked roads.

This is not the first time Japan's leaders have tried to emphasise the fun side of life to strengthen Japan's domestic economy and leave it less vulnerable to the vagaries of world trade. In 1986, when Japan's bulging current-account surplus was a huge source of tension with America, the Maekawa report, written by a panel of Japanese experts, preached the virtues of more time off as a means for workaholics to let their hair down and spend, spend, spend.

It never happened. Instead, what Japan gave the world in the late 1980s was a lesson in how tricky it is to rebalance economies. The country first mollified America and evened out its trade books by raising the value of the yen. But as the dollar slid, it reversed course and cut interest rates, which boosted spending on everything from golf-club memberships at home to splashy buildings in Manhattan. Cheaper credit had the effect of stoking the vast stockmarket and land bubble that popped with disastrous consequences in the 1990s and beyond.

Fast forward to this decade and Japan's current-account surplus was higher than ever, reaching a record 4.8% of GDP in 2007 (see Figure 8.20). That is because the impact of foreign trade on the growth of the

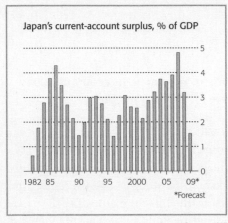

Japan's current-account surplus, % of GDP

1982 85   90   95   2000   05   09*

*Forecast

Source: IMF

FIG 8.20 Entrenched

economy is still much larger than in many other, more open economies. Export growth increased from 4% a year in the decade beginning in 1992 to nearly 10% annually from 2002 to 2007. OECD figures show that the contribution of foreign trade to GDP growth during those years was as high in Japan as in Germany. Some of the bumper profits of large exporters selling Lexus cars, video-game consoles and flat-screen TVs to Westerners during the cheap-credit era were also pumped back into building factories and investing in new technology at home, which further boosted growth. According to OECD estimates, export industries generated about a third of annual output during the pre-crisis years.

A current-account surplus that has persisted for almost all of the past three decades, whether the yen was strong or weak, suggests a structural issue rather than a cyclical one. A report on Asian imbalances by Morgan Stanley shows that throughout the boom-and-bust periods since the early 1980s, investment has consistently fallen short of savings (see Figure 8.21). Households, which used to be Japan's greatest hoarders, put less aside in the years before the financial crisis as a combination of low wage-growth and an ageing population took its toll: the household-saving rate fell from above 10% in the 1990s to about 2.2% in 2007. But the country continued to spend less than it earned because exporters squirrelled a chunk of their profits away.

A combination of factors kept domestic demand below par. Japanese workers benefited less from the recent export boom than they had previously: the OECD says their share of GDP fell from a peak of 73% in 1999 to 65% in 2007. Japan's ugly demography, with a shrinking working-age population and a growing grey-haired one, helped the

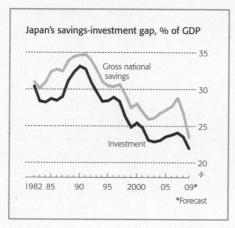

Japan's savings-investment gap, % of GDP

Gross national savings

Investment

35
30
25
20

1982 85   90   95   2000   05   09*

*Forecast

Source: IMF

FIG 8.21 Hoarding habits

downward pressure on wages. More high-paid workers were retiring and being replaced by lower-paid youngsters, which dragged down overall wages. The retirees did not spend as freely as they might because of uncertainty over the government's commitment to state pensions.

Two other features in the economy also held down pay, and hence consumer spending. First, Japan suffers from a glaring gap between large firms, which are highly profitable, and small ones. According to the IMF the latter continue to struggle with the legacy of Japan's 1990s debt crisis. Although they provide about 70% of jobs in Japan, they have meagre profits from which to fund wage increases (see Figure 8.22).

Second, within the manufacturing industry, there is a big disparity between unionised workers, who enjoy high pay, bonuses and job security, and "non-regular" workers. In the years before the crisis the latter grew to account for about one-third of the workforce, as firms sought to increase flexibility in the face of competition from low-wage rivals in Asia. That shift led wages to fall in 2007, even though the economy was near full employment. These wage pressures meant that the country's five-year growth spurt before the crisis – the longest in Japan's post-war history – had very little impact on the average household. Over the five years to 2007 real private consumption grew by 1.1% a year, about the same level as during the "lost decade" of the 1990s. That was higher than in Germany, but far lower than in America, where consumer spending grew almost three times as fast.

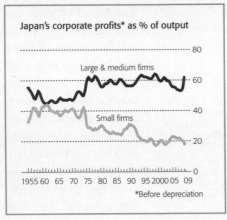

Japan's corporate profits* as % of output

Large & medium firms

Small firms

80

60

40

20

0

1955 60 65 70 75 80 85 90 95 2000 05 09

*Before depreciation

Source: Smithers & Co

FIG 8.22 Big money

Skew etiquette

Why is Japan such a lop-sided economy? Explanations for why the Japanese are serial exporters include government support of trade and industry (the links between big business, the ruling party and civil servants are known as the "iron triangle"), a strong sense of shared mission among firms' employees, and an obsession with detail that enables Japan to manufacture high-quality goods.

The aversion to spending is also deep-rooted. Richard Koo, chief economist at the Nomura Research Institute, believes that domestic demand is stunted by a respect for hard work, which chains people to their desks rather than unleashing them to enjoy themselves in shops or on holiday. A further structural problem is the way the Japanese save in order to rebuild their homes every 15 years or so. This is a legacy of centuries of earthquakes and fires in Japan, but it prevents an American-style culture of lavish home improvements.

There is also a reluctance to borrow. Consumers rarely shift credit-card debts from one card to another. Small businesses are still paying off loans from the previous crisis; banks are shy of lending because of the current one. Katsuyuki Hasegawa, chief market economist at Mizuho Research Institute, says the anti-debt culture is deeply entrenched. "People don't like borrowing. They just like paying back."

The crisis that has hit Japan since 2008, and which was expected to generate a decline of at least 5% of GDP in 2009, is only likely to make people more cautious. The export collapse that first hit Toyota and other big carmakers quickly spread down the supply chain to the domestic economy. As profits dived, so did business investment. Unemployment jumped from 3.8% in October 2008 to 5.4% in

June 2009 – not as high as in America and Europe, admittedly, but accompanied nonetheless by yet another onslaught on wages. In this context the sharp narrowing of the current-account surplus to 1.4% of GDP in the first quarter of 2009 is nothing to celebrate.

In the short term Japan's path out of the crisis is familiar. The government has stepped in with one of the most aggressive fiscal-stimulus packages in the rich world. Hopes are pinned on a pick-up in exports to China as it rebounds. On August 17th 2009 Japan was expected to report its first increase in quarterly GDP in five quarters.

But in the long term, rebalancing the economy is the best way to ensure higher growth. This is particularly important to Japan because it is saddled with the highest public-debt-to-GDP ratio in the rich world, at about 180%, the legacy of years of propping up a moribund economy.

The debt will rise even higher as spending on the elderly increases, raising the possibility of a fiscal crisis if ever the Japanese grow tired of funding their government's borrowing habit. (So far Japanese bond yields have risen less than in other crisis-hit countries such as America and Britain, partly because most of the debt is held at home, but the IMF warns that Japan would be very vulnerable if there were a loss of confidence in the sustainability of public debt.)

Eventually taxes will have to rise to reduce these debts. But the best way to ensure that does not throw the economy into another slump is to foster a more even-keeled recovery, with services playing a bigger part. Such businesses – retailers, builders, hairdressers and the like – are so inefficient that, according to the OECD, they have dragged down labour-productivity growth in the country as a whole from 4% in the boom years of 1976–89 to just 2% between 1999 and 2004. Only brothels appear to be doing well. A recent report from the Bank of Japan showed their numbers have mushroomed in the otherwise depressed northern city of Sapporo. Nearby eateries, by contrast, have shut down in droves.

The OECD in 2008 set out to explain why service industries were so poor in Japan. Research and development (R&D) in services was minuscule – one-quarter the level of America, as a share of total R&D. Competition among firms is stifled, with very high levels of concentration and high barriers to new entrants. Information technology in services is poor, an extraordinary weakness in such a tech-savvy country. Multinationals, meanwhile, find it unusually difficult to set up Japanese affiliates in fields such as telecoms and travel because of investment restrictions and regulatory barriers. But the outsiders' record, by and large, should encourage Japan to deregulate further: the OECD found that productivity growth among those foreign firms that did enter the market was 1.8 times the national average.

With the working-age population likely to shrink by 9% during the next decade, according to government estimates, the quest for higher productivity will become pressing. That search has costs of its own: restructuring would require job losses in some enterprises. But an unshackled service industry would eventually generate wage gains. Without one, overall living standards will suffer.

One of the most sensible ways to achieve higher productivity would be to slash the forest of regulations that surround service industries, protecting them from competition in the name of quality control. Farming could be liberalised, as could heavily protected bits of the economy such as energy, transport, health care and education. Policies to encourage investment, both foreign and domestic, would help.

Vote sinners

But in the run-up to general elections on August 30th 2009, a poll that marked the end of 54 years of almost unbroken rule by the Liberal Democratic Party, there was little talk of rebalancing the economy. Instead, politicians still seemed fixated by exports, this time geared towards fast-expanding but lower-margin regions such as China rather than America. There was also talk of re-regulating wages by restricting the hiring of non-regular workers in manufacturing.

None of the election rhetoric sounded enough to jump-start the juggernaut that Japan, still the world's second-largest economy, could be. Nor did it offer Japanese people much cause for optimism that the daily grind of hard work and modest pay would get any better. Despite the traffic jams, spending a few of their seven days' annual holiday venerating the past is more fun than contemplating the future.

The material on pages 212–74 was first published in *The Economist* in October 2010 (pages 212–50), July 2009 (pages 251–6) and August 2009 (pages 257–74).

PART 3

Flaws and remedies: the future of economics

Any list of the many casualties of the worst recession since the Great Depression must include the reputation of economics as a discipline and the credibility of its practitioners. The fall from grace was swift. Almost overnight, it seemed, economics went from being something that could explain virtually every aspect of human life to something that most people considered not just useless but downright dangerous. The articles in this chapter consider whether the discipline of economics – the "imperial social science", as some had begun to call it – had something to answer for. Did the emperor really have no clothes?

It should not be surprising that *The Economist*'s broad conclusion was that at their crudest, the attacks against economics were misguided. "If ignorance allowed investors to exaggerate the virtues of economics," the first article in Chapter 9 argues, "it now blinds them to its benefits. Economics is less a slavish creed than a prism through which to understand the world." Hopefully the preceding chapters demonstrate the truth of this statement.

But the broad utility of economics ought not to blind us to its failings and limitations. In particular, as the second and third articles in Chapter 9 argue, the financial crisis laid bare the flaws at the heart of macroeconomics and financial economics, making it clear that these areas of economics needed some serious rethinking. Macroeconomists were often content to develop elegant models where the system's financial plumbing was simply assumed to work. This made them less than adept at spotting the flaws in the financial system that eventually brought the global economy to its knees. And while some of their colleagues who studied finance spent considerable time poking holes in the idea that markets could always be relied upon to be efficient, they spent far too little in trying to disseminate their scepticism to the wider world. Too often, the profession cheered along – or was conspicuously silent – as its subtler insights were ignored.

The articles here lay out what is needed and what is happening as these fields struggle to regain their relevance. But they also make a broader point, which is that the crisis has exposed the shortcomings of economists becoming too narrow in their focus, arguing: "Economists need to reach out from their specialised silos: macroeconomists must understand finance, and finance professors need to think harder about the context within which markets work."

One of the most interesting things about contemporary economics is the extent to which this has been happening in other parts of economics – particularly development economics and microeconomics. Most of this has little to do with the crisis: economics is in a constant state of flux, as economists find new puzzles to explain and are sometimes led to explore new ways of looking at the world as a result. While Part 1 of this book tried to give the reader a sense of economics' fundamental concerns, Chapter 10 consists of articles that explore the ways in which the discipline is evolving. It describes how development economists have adopted some of the tools and vocabulary of the field of medical testing and how others are incorporating insights from psychology and neuroscience into their work.

This book began with accounts of the lives and works of some of those who defined the discipline in the 20th century. It ends with profiles of some who, in *The Economist*'s judgment, will shape the subject in the present one.

9 The failings of economics

What went wrong with economics

And how the discipline should change to avoid the mistakes of the past

OF ALL THE ECONOMIC BUBBLES that have been pricked, few have burst more spectacularly than the reputation of economics itself. A few years ago, the dismal science was being acclaimed as a way of explaining ever more forms of human behaviour, from drug-dealing to sumo-wrestling. Wall Street ransacked the best universities for game theorists and options modellers. And on the public stage, economists were seen as far more trustworthy than politicians. John McCain joked that Alan Greenspan, then chairman of the Federal Reserve, was so indispensable that if he died, the president should "prop him up and put a pair of dark glasses on him".

In the wake of the biggest economic calamity in 80 years that reputation has taken a beating. In the public mind an arrogant profession has been humbled. Though economists are still at the centre of the policy debate – think of Ben Bernanke or Larry Summers in America or Mervyn King in Britain – their pronouncements are viewed with more scepticism than before. The profession itself is suffering from guilt and rancour. In a lecture given in June 2009, Paul Krugman, winner of the Nobel prize in economics in 2008, argued that much of the past 30 years of macroeconomics was "spectacularly useless at best, and positively harmful at worst". Barry Eichengreen, a prominent American economic historian, says the crisis has "cast into doubt much of what we thought we knew about economics".

In its crudest form – the idea that economics as a whole is discredited – the current backlash has gone far too far. If ignorance allowed investors and politicians to exaggerate the virtues of economics, it now blinds them to its benefits. Economics is less a slavish creed than a prism through which to understand the world. It is a broad canon, stretching from theories to explain how prices are determined to how economies grow. Much of that body of knowledge has no link to the financial crisis and remains as useful as ever.

And if economics as a broad discipline deserves a robust defence, so does the free-market paradigm. Too many people, especially in Europe, equate mistakes made by economists with a failure of economic liberalism. Their logic seems to be that if economists got things wrong, then politicians will do better. That is a false – and dangerous – conclusion.

Rational fools

These important caveats, however, should not obscure the fact that two central parts of the discipline – macroeconomics and financial economics – are now, rightly, being severely re-examined. There are three main critiques: that macro and financial economists helped cause the crisis, that they failed to spot it, and that they have no idea how to fix it.

The first charge is half right. Macroeconomists, especially within central banks, were too fixated on taming inflation and too cavalier about asset bubbles. Financial economists, meanwhile, formalised theories of the efficiency of markets, fuelling the notion that markets would regulate themselves and financial innovation was always beneficial. Wall Street's most esoteric instruments were built on these ideas.

But economists were hardly naive believers in market efficiency. Financial academics have spent much of the past 30 years poking holes in the "efficient market hypothesis". A recent ranking of academic economists was topped by Joseph Stiglitz and Andrei Shleifer, two prominent hole-pokers. A newly prominent field, behavioural economics, concentrates on the consequences of irrational actions.

So there were caveats aplenty. But as insights from academia arrived in the rough and tumble of Wall Street, such delicacies were put aside. And absurd assumptions were added. No economic theory suggests you should value mortgage derivatives on the basis that house prices would always rise. Finance professors are not to blame for this, but they might have shouted more loudly that their insights were being misused. Instead many cheered the party along (often from within banks). Put that together with the complacency of the macroeconomists and there were too few voices shouting stop.

Blindsided and divided

The charge that most economists failed to see the crisis coming also has merit. To be sure, some warned of trouble. The likes of Robert Shiller of Yale, Nouriel Roubini of New York University and the team at the Bank for International Settlements are now famous for their prescience. But most were blindsided. And even worrywarts who felt something was amiss had no idea of how bad the consequences would be.

That was partly to do with professional silos, which limited both the tools available and the imaginations of the practitioners. Few financial economists thought much about illiquidity or counterparty risk, for instance, because their standard models ignore it; and few worried about the effect on the overall economy of the markets for all asset classes seizing up simultaneously, since few believed that was possible.

Macroeconomists also had a blindspot: their standard models assumed that capital markets work perfectly. Their framework reflected an uneasy truce between the intellectual heirs of Keynes, who accept that economies can fall short of their potential, and purists who hold that supply must always equal demand. The models that epitomise this synthesis – the sort used in many central banks – incorporate imperfections in labour markets ("sticky" wages, for instance, which allow unemployment to rise), but make no room for such blemishes in finance. By assuming that capital markets worked perfectly, macroeconomists were largely able to ignore the economy's financial plumbing. But models that ignored finance had little chance of spotting a calamity that stemmed from it.

What about trying to fix it? Here the financial crisis has blown apart the fragile consensus between purists and Keynesians that monetary policy was the best way to smooth the business cycle. In many countries short-term interest rates are near zero and in a banking crisis monetary policy works less well. With their compromise tool useless, both sides have retreated to their roots, ignoring the other camp's ideas. Keynesians, such as Mr Krugman, have become uncritical supporters of fiscal stimulus. Purists are vocal opponents. To outsiders, the cacophony underlines the profession's uselessness.

Add these criticisms together and there is a clear case for reinvention, especially in macroeconomics. Just as the Depression spawned Keynesianism, and the 1970s stagflation fuelled a backlash, creative destruction is already under way. Central banks are busy bolting crude analyses of financial markets onto their workhorse models. Financial economists are studying the way that incentives can skew market efficiency. And today's dilemmas are prompting new research: which form of fiscal stimulus is most effective? How do you best loosen monetary policy when interest rates are at zero? And so on.

But a broader change in mindset is still needed. Economists need to reach out from their specialised silos: macroeconomists must understand finance, and finance professors need to think harder about the context within which markets work. And everybody needs to work harder on understanding asset bubbles and what happens when they burst. For in the end economists are social scientists, trying to understand the real world. And the financial crisis has changed that world.

The other-worldly philosophers

Although the crisis has exposed bitter divisions among economists, it could still be good for economics.

ROBERT LUCAS, one of the greatest macroeconomists of his generation, and his followers are "making ancient and basic analytical errors all over the place". Harvard's Robert Barro, another towering figure in the discipline, is "making truly boneheaded arguments". The past 30 years of macroeconomics training at American and British universities were a "costly waste of time".

To the uninitiated, economics has always been a dismal science. But all these attacks come from within the guild: from Brad DeLong of the University of California, Berkeley; Paul Krugman of Princeton and the *New York Times*; and Willem Buiter of the London School of Economics (LSE), respectively. The macroeconomic crisis is also provoking a crisis of confidence in macroeconomics. In the last of his Lionel Robbins lectures at the LSE on June 10th 2009, Mr Krugman feared that most macroeconomics of the past 30 years was "spectacularly useless at best, and positively harmful at worst".

These internal critics argue that economists missed the origins of the crisis; failed to appreciate its worst symptoms; and cannot now agree about the cure. In other words, economists misread the economy on the way up, misread it on the way down and now mistake the right way out.

On the way up, macroeconomists were not wholly complacent. Many of them thought the housing bubble would pop or the dollar would fall. But they did not expect the financial system to break. Even after the seizure in interbank markets in August 2007, macroeconomists misread the danger. Most were quite sanguine about the prospect of Lehman Brothers going bust in September 2008.

Nor can economists now agree on the best way to resolve the crisis. They mostly overestimated the power of routine monetary policy (ie, central-bank purchases of government bills) to restore prosperity. Some now dismiss the power of fiscal policy (ie, government sales of its securities) to do the same. Others advocate it with passionate intensity.

Among the passionate are Mr DeLong and Mr Krugman. They turn for inspiration to Depression-era texts, especially the writings of John Maynard Keynes, and forgotten mavericks, such as Hyman Minsky. In the humanities this would count as routine scholarship. But to many high-tech economists it is a bit undignified. Real scientists, after all, do not leaf through Newton's "Principia Mathematica" to solve contemporary problems in physics.

They accuse economists like Mr DeLong and Mr Krugman of falling back on antiquated Keynesian doctrines – as if nothing had been learned in the past 70 years. Messrs DeLong and Krugman, in turn, accuse economists like Mr Lucas of not falling back on Keynesian economics – as if everything had been forgotten over the past 70 years. For Mr Krugman, we are living through a "Dark Age of macroeconomics", in which the wisdom of the ancients has been lost.

What was this wisdom, and how was it forgotten? The history of macroeconomics begins in intellectual struggle. Keynes wrote the "General Theory of Employment, Interest and Money", which was published in 1936, in an "unnecessarily controversial tone", according to some readers. But it was a controversy the author had waged in his own mind. He saw the book as a "struggle of escape from habitual modes of thought" he had inherited from his classical predecessors.

That classical mode of thought held that full employment would prevail, because supply created its own demand. In a classical economy, whatever people earn is either spent or saved; and whatever is saved is invested in capital projects. Nothing is hoarded, nothing lies idle.

Keynes appreciated the classical model's elegance and consistency, virtues economists still crave. But that did not stop him demolishing it. In his scheme, investment was governed by the animal spirits of entrepreneurs, facing an imponderable future. The same uncertainty gave savers a reason to hoard their wealth in liquid assets, like money, rather than committing it to new capital projects. This liquidity-preference, as Keynes called it, governed the price of financial securities and hence the rate of interest. If animal spirits flagged or liquidity-preference surged, the pace of investment would falter, with no obvious market force to restore it. Demand would fall short of supply, leaving willing workers on the shelf. It fell to governments to revive demand, by cutting interest rates if possible or by public works if necessary.

The Keynesian task of "demand management" outlived the Depression, becoming a routine duty of governments. They were aided by economic advisers, who built working models of the economy, quantifying the key relationships. For almost three decades after the second world war these advisers seemed to know what they were doing, guided by an apparent trade-off between inflation and unemployment. But their credibility did not survive the oil-price shocks of the 1970s. These condemned Western economies to "stagflation", a baffling combination of unemployment and inflation, which the Keynesian consensus grasped poorly and failed to prevent.

The Federal Reserve, led by Paul Volcker, eventually defeated American inflation in the early 1980s, albeit at a grievous cost to employment. But victory did not restore the intellectual peace. Macroeconomists split into two camps, drawing opposite lessons from the episode.

The purists, known as "freshwater" economists because of the lakeside universities where they happened to congregate, blamed stagflation on restless central bankers trying to do too much. They started from the classical assumption that markets cleared, leaving no unsold goods or unemployed workers. Efforts by policymakers to smooth the economy's natural ups and downs did more harm than good.

America's coastal universities housed most of the other lot, "saltwater" pragmatists. To them, the double-digit unemployment that accompanied Mr Volcker's assault on inflation was proof enough that markets could malfunction. Wages might fail to adjust, and prices might stick. This grit in the economic machine justified some meddling by policymakers.

Mr Volcker's recession bottomed out in 1982. Nothing like it was seen again until 2008. In the intervening quarter-century of tranquillity, macroeconomics also recovered its composure. The opposing schools of thought converged. The freshwater economists accepted a saltier view of policymaking. Their opponents adopted a more freshwater style of modelmaking. You might call the new synthesis brackish macroeconomics.

Pinches of salt

Brackish macroeconomics flowed from universities into central banks. It underlay the doctrine of inflation-targeting embraced in New Zealand, Canada, Britain, Sweden and several emerging markets, such as Turkey. Ben Bernanke, chairman of the Fed since 2006, is a renowned contributor to brackish economics.

For about a decade before the crisis, macroeconomists once again appeared to know what they were doing. Their thinking was embodied in a new genre of working models of the economy, called "dynamic stochastic general equilibrium" (DSGE) models. These helped guide deliberations at several central banks.

Mr Buiter, who helped set interest rates at the Bank of England from 1997 to 2000, believes the latest academic theories had a profound influence there. He now thinks this influence was baleful. On his blog, Mr Buiter argues that a training in modern macroeconomics was a "severe handicap" at the onset of the financial crisis, when the central bank had to "switch gears" from preserving price stability to safeguarding financial stability.

Modern macroeconomists worried about the prices of goods and services, but neglected the prices of assets. This was partly because they had too much faith in financial markets. If asset prices reflect economic fundamentals, why not just model the fundamentals, ignoring the shadow they cast on Wall Street?

It was also because they had too little interest in the inner workings of the financial system. "Philosophically speaking," writes Perry Mehrling of Barnard College, Columbia University, economists are "materialists" for whom "bags of wheat are more important than stacks of bonds." Finance is a veil, obscuring what really matters. As a poet once said, "promises of payment/Are neither food nor raiment".

In many macroeconomic models, therefore, insolvencies cannot occur. Financial intermediaries, like banks, often don't exist. And whether firms finance themselves with equity or debt is a matter of indifference. The Bank of England's DSGE model, for example, does not even try to incorporate financial middlemen, such as banks. "The model is not, therefore, directly useful for issues where financial intermediation is of first-order importance," its designers admit. The present crisis is, unfortunately, one of those issues.

The bank's modellers go on to say that they prefer to study finance with specialised models designed for that purpose. One of the most prominent was, in fact, pioneered by Mr Bernanke, with Mark Gertler of New York University. Unfortunately, models that include such financial-market complications "can be very difficult to handle," according to Markus Brunnermeier of Princeton, who has handled more of these difficulties than most. Convenience, not conviction, often dictates the choices economists make.

Convenience, however, is addictive. Economists can become seduced by their models, fooling themselves that what the model leaves out does not matter. It is, for example, often convenient to assume that markets are "complete" – that a price exists today, for every good, at every date, in every contingency. In this world, you can always borrow as much as you want at the going rate, and you can always sell as much as you want at the going rate.

Before the crisis, many banks and shadow banks made similar assumptions. They believed they could always roll over their short-term debts or sell their mortgage-backed securities, if the need arose. The financial crisis made a mockery of both assumptions. Funds dried up, and markets thinned out. In his anatomy of the crisis Mr Brunnermeier shows how both of these constraints fed on each other, producing a "liquidity spiral".

What followed was a furious dash for cash, as investment banks sold whatever they could, commercial banks hoarded reserves and firms drew on lines of credit. Keynes would have interpreted this as an extreme outbreak of liquidity-preference, says Paul Davidson, whose biography of the master has just been republished with a new afterword. But contemporary economics had all but forgotten the term.

Fiscal fisticuffs

The mainstream macroeconomics embodied in DSGE models was a poor guide to the origins of the financial crisis, and left its followers unprepared for the symptoms. Does it offer any insight into the best means of recovery?

In the first months of the crisis, macroeconomists reposed great faith in the powers of the Fed and other central banks. In the summer of 2007, a few weeks after the August liquidity crisis began, Frederic Mishkin, a distinguished academic economist and then a governor of the Fed, gave a reassuring talk at the Federal Reserve Bank of Kansas City's annual symposium in Jackson Hole, Wyoming. He presented the results of simulations from the Fed's FRB/US model. Even if house prices fell by a fifth in the next two years, the slump would knock only 0.25% off GDP, according to his benchmark model, and add only a tenth of a percentage point to the unemployment rate. The reason was that the Fed would respond "aggressively", by which he meant a cut in the federal funds rate of just one percentage point. He concluded that the central bank had the tools to contain the damage at a "manageable level".

Since his presentation, the Fed has cut its key rate by five percentage points to a mere 0–0.25%. Its conventional weapons have proved insufficient to the task. This has shaken economists' faith in monetary policy. Unfortunately, they are also horribly divided about what comes next.

Mr Krugman and others advocate a bold fiscal expansion, borrowing their logic from Keynes and his contemporary, Richard Kahn. Kahn pointed out that a dollar spent on public works might generate more than a dollar of output if the spending circulated repeatedly through the economy, stimulating resources that might otherwise have lain idle.

Today's economists disagree over the size of this multiplier. Mr Barro thinks the estimates of Barack Obama's Council of Economic Advisors are absurdly large. Mr Lucas calls them "schlock economics", contrived to justify Mr Obama's projections for the budget deficit. But economists are not exactly drowning in research on this question. Mr Krugman calculates that of the 7,000 or so papers published by the National Bureau of Economic Research between 1985 and 2000, only five mentioned fiscal policy in their title or abstract.

Do these public spats damage macroeconomics? Greg Mankiw, of Harvard, recalls the angry exchanges in the 1980s between Robert Solow and Mr Lucas – both eminent economists who could not take each other seriously. This vitriol, he writes, attracted attention, much like a bar-room fist-fight. But he thinks it also dismayed younger scholars, who gave these macroeconomic disputes a wide berth.

By this account, the period of intellectual peace that followed in the 1990s should have been a golden age for macroeconomics. But the brackish consensus also seems to leave students cold. According to David Colander, who has twice surveyed the opinions of economists in the best American PhD programmes, macroeconomics is often the least popular class. "What did you learn in macro?" Mr Colander asked a group of Chicago students. "Did you do the dynamic stochastic general equilibrium model?" "We learned a lot of junk like that," one replied.

It takes a model to beat a model

The benchmark macroeconomic model, though not junk, suffers from some obvious flaws, such as the assumption of complete markets or frictionless finance. Indeed, because these flaws are obvious, economists are well aware of them. Critics like Mr Buiter are not telling them anything new. Economists can and do depart from the benchmark. That, indeed, is how they get published. Thus a growing number of cutting-edge models incorporate one or two financial frictions. And economists like Mr Brunnermeier are trying to fit their small, "blackboard" models of the crisis into a larger macroeconomic frame.

But the benchmark still matters. It formalises economists' gut instincts about where the best analytical cuts lie. It is the starting point to which the theorist returns after every ingenious excursion. Few economists really believe all its assumptions, but few would rather start anywhere else.

Unfortunately, it is these primitive models, rather than their sophisticated descendants, that often exert the most influence over the world of policy and practice. This is partly because these first principles endure long enough to find their way from academia into policymaking circles. As Keynes pointed out, the economists who most influence practical men of action are the defunct ones whose scribblings have had time to percolate from the seminar room to wider conversations.

These basic models are also influential because of their simplicity. Faced with the "blooming, buzzing confusion" of the real world, policymakers often fall back on the highest-order principles and the broadest presumptions. More specific, nuanced theories are often less versatile. They shed light on whatever they were designed to explain, but little beyond.

Would economists be better off starting from somewhere else? Some think so. They draw inspiration from neglected prophets, like Minsky, who recognised that the "real" economy was inseparable from the financial. Such prophets were neglected not for what they said, but for the way they said it. Today's economists tend to be open-minded about content, but doctrinaire about form. They are more wedded to their techniques than to their theories. They will believe something when they can model it.

Mr Colander, therefore, thinks economics requires a revolution in technique. Instead of solving models "by hand", using economists' powers of deduction, he proposes simulating economies on the computer. In this line of research, the economist specifies simple rules of thumb by which agents interact with each other, and then lets the computer go to work, grinding out repeated simulations to reveal what kind of unforeseen patterns might emerge. If he is right, then macroeconomists, like zombie banks, must write off many of their past intellectual investments before they can make progress again.

Mr Krugman, by contrast, thinks reform is more likely to come from within. Keynes, he observes, was a "consummate insider", who understood the theory he was demolishing precisely because he was once convinced by it. In the meantime, he says, macroeconomists should turn to patient empirical spadework, documenting crises past and present, in the hope that a fresh theory might later make sense of it all.

Macroeconomics began with Keynes, but the word did not appear in the journals until 1945, in an article by Jacob Marschak. He reviewed the profession's growing understanding of the business cycle, making an analogy with other sciences. Seismology, for example, makes progress through better instruments, improved theories or more frequent earthquakes. In the case of economics, Marschak concluded, "the earthquakes did most of the job."

Economists were deprived of earthquakes for a quarter of a century. The Great Moderation, as this period was called, was not conducive to great macroeconomics. Thanks to the seismic events of

2007–09, the prestige of macroeconomists is low, but the potential of their subject is much greater. The furious rows that divide them are a blow to their credibility, but may prove to be a spur to creativity.

Efficiency and beyond

The efficient-markets hypothesis has underpinned many of the financial industry's models for years. After the crash, what remains of it?

IN 1978 MICHAEL JENSEN, an American economist, boldly declared that "there is no other proposition in economics which has more solid empirical evidence supporting it than the efficient-markets hypothesis" (EMH). That was quite a claim. The theory's origins went back to the beginning of the century, but it had come to prominence only a decade or so before. Eugene Fama, of the University of Chicago, defined its essence: that the price of a financial asset reflects all available information that is relevant to its value.

From that idea powerful conclusions were drawn, not least on Wall Street. If the EMH held, then markets would price financial assets broadly correctly. Deviations from equilibrium values could not last for long. If the price of a share, say, was too low, well-informed investors would buy it and make a killing. If it looked too dear, they could sell or short it and make money that way. It also followed that bubbles could not form – or, at any rate, could not last: some wise investor would spot them and pop them. And trying to beat the market was a fool's errand for almost everyone. If the information was out there, it was already in the price.

On such ideas, and on the complex mathematics that described them, was founded the Wall Street profession of financial engineering. The engineers designed derivatives and securitisations, from simple interest-rate options to ever more intricate credit-default swaps and collateralised debt obligations. All the while, confident in the theoretical underpinnings of their inventions, they reassured any doubters that all this activity was not just making bankers rich. It was making the financial system safer and the economy healthier.

That is why many people view the financial crisis that began in 2007 as a devastating blow to the credibility not only of banks but also of the entire academic discipline of financial economics. That verdict is too simple. Granted, financial economists helped to start the bankers' party, and some joined in with gusto. But even when the EMH still seemed fresh, economists were picking holes in it. A strand of sceptical thought, behavioural economics, has been booming. There are even signs of a synthesis between the EMH and the sceptics. Academia thus moved on, even if Wall Street did not. Nonetheless, the extent to which politicians and regulators trying to reform finance can trust financial economists is an open question.

The EMH, to be sure, has loyal defenders. "There are models, and there are those who use the models," says Myron Scholes, who in 1997 won the Nobel prize in economics for his part in creating the most widely used model in the finance industry – the Black-Scholes formula for pricing options. Mr Scholes thinks much of the blame for the recent woe should be pinned not on economists' theories and models but on those on Wall Street and in the City who pushed them too far in practice.

Financial firms plugged in data that reflected a "view of the world that was far more benign than it was reasonable to take, emphasising recent inputs over more historic numbers," says Mr Scholes. "Apparently, a lot of the models used for structured products were pretty good, but the inputs were awful." Indeed, the vast majority of derivative contracts and securitisations have performed exactly as their models said they would. It was the exceptions that proved disastrous.

Mr Scholes knows whereof he speaks. Long-Term Capital Management (LTCM), a hedge fund he founded with, among others, Robert Merton, a fellow Nobel laureate, skidded off the road in 1998. Since then, he has been pointing out dangers ignored or underestimated in the finance industry, such as the risk that liquid markets can dry up far faster than is typically assumed. (That did not stop Platinum Grove, the latest hedge fund in which he is involved, taking a big hit during the recent meltdown.)

He has also been "criticising for years" the "value-at-risk" (VAR) models used by institutional investors to work out how much capital they need to set aside as insurance against losses on risky assets. These models mistakenly assume that the volatility of asset prices and the correlations between prices are constant, says Mr Scholes. When, say, two types of asset were assumed to be uncorrelated, investors felt able to hold the same capital as a cushion against losses on both, because they would not lose on both at the same time. However, as Mr Scholes discovered at LTCM and as the entire finance industry has now learnt for itself, at times of market stress assets that normally are uncorrelated can suddenly become highly correlated. At that point the capital buffer implied by VAR turns out to be woefully inadequate.

Even as financial engineers were designing all sorts of clever products on the assumption that markets were efficient, academic economists were focusing more on how markets fall short. Even before the 1987 stockmarket crash gave them their first real-world reminder of markets' capriciousness, some of them were examining the flaws in the theory.

In 1980 Sanford Grossman and Joseph Stiglitz, another subsequent winner of a Nobel prize, pointed out a paradox. If prices reflect all information, then there is no gain from going to the trouble of gathering it, so no one will. A little inefficiency is necessary to give informed investors an incentive to drive prices towards efficiency. For Mr Scholes, it is the belief that markets tend to return prices to their efficient equilibrium when they move away from it that gives the EMH its continuing relevance.

Economists also began to study "institutional frictions" in markets. For instance, the EMH's devotees had assumed that smart investors would be able to trade against less well-informed "noise traders" and overwhelm them by driving prices to reflect true value. But it became clear that there were limits to their ability to arbitrage folly away. Andrei Shleifer, a Harvard economist, among others, pointed out that it could be too costly for informed investors to borrow enough to bet against the noise traders. Once it is admitted that prices can move away from fundamentals for a long time, informed investors may do best by riding the trend rather than fighting it. The trick then is to get out just before momentum shifts the other way. But in this world, rational investors may contribute to bubbles rather than preventing them.

In the early years of the EMH, researchers spent little time worrying about the workings of financial institutions – a weakness of macroeconomics too. In 2000, in his presidential address to the American Finance Association, Franklin Allen, of the University of

Pennsylvania's Wharton School, asked: "Do financial institutions matter?" Lay people, he said, "might be surprised to learn that institutions play little role in financial theory." Indeed they might. Mr Allen's explanation was partly that the dominant theories had been shaped at a time when America, especially, was spared financial crises.

In the past decade or so, financial economists have been paying more attention to institutional questions, such as how bankers should be paid. Many of these researchers broadly accept the EMH, but see their role as uncovering sources of inefficiency that can be addressed to make markets more efficient.

However, a second branch of financial economics is far more sceptical about markets' inherent rationality. Behavioural economics, which applies the insights of psychology to finance, has boomed in the past decade. In particular, behavioural economists have argued that human beings tend to be too confident of their own abilities and tend to extrapolate recent trends into the future, a combination that may contribute to bubbles. There is also evidence that losses can make investors extremely, irrationally risk-averse – exaggerating price falls when a bubble bursts.

Behavioural economists were among the first to sound the alarm about trouble in the markets. Notably, Robert Shiller of Yale gave an early warning that America's housing market was dangerously over-valued. This was his second prescient call. In the 1990s his concerns about the bubbliness of the stockmarket had prompted Alan Greenspan, then chairman of the Federal Reserve, to wonder if the heady share prices of the day were the result of investors' "irrational exuberance". The title of Mr Shiller's latest book, "Animal Spirits" (written with George Akerlof, of the University of California, Berkeley), is taken from John Maynard Keynes's description of the quirky psychological forces shaping markets. It argues that macroeconomics, too, should draw lessons from psychology.

"In some ways, we behavioural economists have won by default, because we have been less arrogant," says Richard Thaler of the University of Chicago, one of the pioneers of behavioural finance. Those who denied that prices could get out of line, or ever have bubbles, "look foolish". Mr Scholes, however, insists that the efficient-market paradigm is not dead: "To say something has failed you have to have something to replace it, and so far we don't have a new paradigm to replace efficient markets." The trouble with behavioural economics, he adds, is that "it really hasn't shown in aggregate how it affects prices."

Yet EMH-ers and behaviouralists are increasingly asking the same questions and drawing on each other's ideas. For instance, Mr Thaler concedes that in some ways the events of 2007–09 have strengthened the EMH. The hypothesis has two parts, he says: the "no-free-lunch part and the price-is-right part, and if anything the first part has been strengthened as we have learned that some investment strategies are riskier than they look and it really is difficult to beat the market." The idea that the market price is the right price, however, has been badly dented.

Mr Thaler also says that only some of the recent problems were behavioural. Many were due to things that are open to non-behavioural economics, "like better risk analysis, how we identify hidden correlations." It will be no surprise if, thanks to the catalytic power of the bubble and market meltdown, the distinctions between the two camps disappear and a new paradigm emerges.

One economist leading the effort to define that new paradigm is Andrew Lo, of the Massachusetts Institute of Technology, who sees merit in both the rational and behavioural views. He has tried to reconcile them in the "adaptive markets hypothesis", which supposes that humans are neither fully rational nor psychologically unhinged. Instead, they work by making best guesses and by trial and error. If one investment strategy fails, they try another. If it works, they stick with it. Mr Lo borrows heavily from evolutionary science. He does not see markets as efficient in Mr Fama's sense, but thinks they are fiercely competitive. Because the "ecology" changes over time, people make mistakes when adapting. Old strategies become obsolete and new ones are called for.

The finance industry is in the midst of a transformative period of evolution, and financial economists have a huge agenda to tackle. They should do so quickly, given the determination of politicians to overhaul the regulation of financial markets.

One task, also of interest to macroeconomists, is to work out what central bankers should do about bubbles – now that it is plain that they do occur and can cause great damage when they burst. Not even behaviouralists such as Mr Thaler would want to see, say, the Fed trying to set prices in financial markets. He does see an opportunity, however, for governments to "lean into the wind a little more" to reduce the volatility of bubbles and crashes. For instance, when guaranteeing home loans, Freddie Mac and Fannie Mae, America's giant mortgage companies, could be required to demand higher down-payments as a proportion of the purchase price, the higher house prices are relative to rents.

Another priority is to get a better understanding of systemic risk, which Messrs Scholes and Thaler agree has been seriously underestimated. A lot of risk-managers in financial firms believed their risk was perfectly controlled, says Mr Scholes, "but they needed to know what everyone else was doing, to see the aggregate picture." It turned out that everyone was doing very similar things. So when their VAR models started telling them to sell, they all did – driving prices down further and triggering further model-driven selling.

Several countries now expect to introduce a systemic-risk regulator. Financial economists may have useful advice to offer. Many of them see information as crucial. Data should be collected from individual firms and aggregated. The overall data should then be published. That would be better, they think, than a system based solely on the micromanagement of individual institutions deemed systemically significant. Mr Scholes favours relying less on VAR to calculate capital reserves against losses. Instead, each category of asset should have its own risk-capital reserves, which could not be shared with other assets, even if prices had not been correlated in the past. As experience shows, correlations can change suddenly.

Financial economists also need better theories of why liquid markets suddenly become illiquid and of how to manage the risk of "moral hazard" – the danger that the existence of government regulation and safety nets encourages market participants to take bigger risks than they might otherwise have done. The sorry consequences of letting Lehman Brothers fail, which was intended to discourage moral hazard, showed that the middle of a crisis is not the time to get tough. But when is?

Mr Lo has a novel idea for future crises: creating a financial equivalent of the National Transport Safety Board, which investigates every civil-aviation crash in America. He would like similar independent, after-the-fact scrutiny of every financial failure, to see what caused it and what lessons could be learned. Not the least of the difficulties in the continuing crisis is working out exactly what went wrong and why – and who, including financial economists, should take the blame.

Twin peaks

George Soros has left his mark on many economies. Can he do the same for economics?

IN 1996, DAVID COLANDER of Middlebury College, in Vermont, expressed his dissatisfaction with decades of economics by invoking a lofty analogy. He felt macroeconomists had clawed their way up a mountain, only to discover, when they broke through the clouds, that a neighbouring mountain would have taken them higher. On April 8th–10th 2010 Mr Colander joined many disgruntled economists at King's College, Cambridge, for the inaugural conference of the Institute for New Economic Thinking (INET). The Institute is sponsored by the renowned investor George Soros. He has promised to spend $50m spread over ten years to help economists climb the right mountain.

The conference rehearsed many familiar complaints, bashing the rational-expectations hypothesis (which holds that the people in an economic model all share the modeller's view of how the economy works), the efficient-markets hypothesis (which assumes that asset prices reflect all available information), and the use of representative agents (a kind of economic Everyman, whose behaviour mimics the macroeconomy in microcosm). The event was a coming-out party for misfits, mavericks and pioneers, as well as open-minded members of the mainstream.

There was gentle resistance from some well-adjusted economists. Mr Colander's analogy does not imply that economists are getting nowhere: they can make progress up their chosen peak, even if other, higher mountains beckon. Mainstream models of the macroeconomy, for example, are more sophisticated than they were, allowing for different kinds of shocks, better statistical testing and a variety of dramatis personae beyond the economic Everyman of yore. This progress is the result of hard theoretical work in response to successive rounds of criticism. The critics, who don't think the climb is worth the effort, may not always appreciate quite how far the leading economists have ascended.

The twin peaks image has a further, unsettling, implication. To get from one peak to the other, economists will have to lose a lot of altitude first. To tackle questions in a fresh way, they may have to set aside many of their favourite techniques and methods. This prospect probably explains a lot of the resistance to new economic thinking. Economists tend to cling to whatever assumptions are required to use the techniques they favour.

For example, the presumption that economic life repeats itself, eventually reverting to the mean, makes statistical work easier. Even the much-maligned figure of rational economic man, maximising his utility, is less an article of faith than an excuse to use calculus. When behavioural economists packaged emotion into equations, mainstream economists were mostly happy to entertain them. But they worry about descending into a valley of imprecision and ineloquence before they master the alternative tricks and tactics required by any new ascent.

Some attendees wondered how economists would ever get out of this valley. If the economy is governed by historical happenstance, not timeless laws, and subject to imponderable contingencies, not calculable risks, then the economist may have precious little to say. One speaker argued that economists should give up on prediction and settle for explanation, identifying where earthquakes might strike, if not when, and how they might be withstood, if not prevented. They may have to hang up their ropes and carabiners and settle for rambles in the foothills.

But the optimists think it is possible to avoid losing altitude by building a bridge between where they are and where they would like to be. Markus Brunnermeier of Princeton University, who is on INET's advisory board, is trying to incorporate a richer model of financial breakdowns into a fairly standard macroeconomic model with the help of Yuliy Sannikov of the University of California, Berkeley. For all his radical airs, Joseph Stiglitz, who is also on the board, is keen to conserve as much of the canon as possible (especially the bits he contributed). He argues that you can explain a lot of what went wrong during the crisis in a model with rational expectations, but without "common knowledge": a model, in other words, in which everyone knows how the economy works, but not everyone knows that everyone knows.

Publish or be damned

Before launching the institute, its director, Robert Johnson, studied the incentives that govern the profession. Success depends on publishing in a handful of prestigious journals, which can be too narrow in their preoccupations. One Nobel prizewinner, who sits on INET's board, told him that he ceased teaching macroeconomics to graduate students because he thought his unconventional approach would damage their job prospects.

Mr Colander thinks the imperative to publish frequently forces young economists to tackle bite-sized problems, rather than asking big questions with distant, uncertain answers. One student who wanted to work on a book was told that one book might not hurt him, but he definitely shouldn't do two. Ambitious young economists must prove that they are better climbers than their rivals. What they climb is a secondary concern.

Mr Soros hopes his pledge can change these incentives. Is the money enough to make a difference? America's National Science Foundation, which dispenses federal research grants, spends about 20 times as much on the social sciences as a whole. The University of Chicago spent $19.6m on research in the social sciences in 2007, excluding outside bequests. In 1988 Raymond Sauer of Clemson University calculated that a publication in a leading journal adds about $3,600 (in today's prices) to an economist's annual salary. So over a young economist's career of, say, 30 years, each article makes them $108,000. By that standard, the Soros pledge is big enough to persuade 463 young economists to take a break from their next shot at getting a paper into a journal and spend some time rethinking economics instead. But that would assume that economists are only in it for the money.

The material on pages 277–99 was first published in *The Economist* in July 2009 (pages 277–96) and April 2010 (pages 297–9).

10 An evolving field

Do economists need brains?

A new school of economists is controversially turning to neuroscience to improve the dismal science

FOR ALL THE UNDOUBTED WIT of their neuroscience-inspired concept album, "Heavy Mental" – songs include "Mind-Body Problem" and "All in a Nut" – The Amygdaloids are unlikely to loom large in the annals of rock and roll. Yet when the history of economics is finally written, Joseph LeDoux, the New York band's singer-guitarist, may deserve at least a footnote. In 1996 Mr LeDoux, who by day is a professor of neuroscience at New York University, published a book, "The Emotional Brain: The Mysterious Underpinnings of Emotional Life", that helped to inspire what is today one of the liveliest and most controversial areas of economic research: neuroeconomics.

In the late 1990s a generation of academic economists had their eyes opened by Mr LeDoux's and other accounts of how studies of the brain using recently developed techniques such as magnetic resonance imaging (MRI) showed that different bits of the old grey matter are associated with different sorts of emotional and decision-making activity. The amygdalas are an example. Neuroscientists have shown that these almond-shaped clusters of neurons deep inside the medial temporal lobes play a key role in the formation of emotional responses such as fear.

These new neuroeconomists saw that it might be possible to move economics away from its simplified model of rational, self-interested, utility-maximising decision-making. Instead of hypothesising about *Homo economicus*, they could base their research on what actually goes on inside the head of *Homo sapiens*.

The dismal science had already been edging in that direction thanks to behavioural economics. Since the 1980s researchers in this branch of the discipline had used insights from psychology to develop more "realistic" models of individual decision-making, in which people often did things that were not in their best interests. But neuroeconomics had the potential, some believed, to go further and to embed economics in the chemical processes taking place in the brain.

Early successes for neuroeconomists came from using neuroscience to shed light on some of the apparent flaws in H. *economicus* noted by the behaviouralists. One much-cited example is the "ultimatum game", in which one player proposes a division of a sum of money between himself and a second player. The other player must either accept or reject the offer. If he rejects it, neither gets a penny.

According to standard economic theory, as long as the first player offers the second any money at all, his proposal will be accepted, because the second player prefers something to nothing. In experiments, however, behavioural economists found that the second player often turned down low offers – perhaps, they suggested, to punish the first player for proposing an unfair split.

Neuroeconomists have tried to explain this seemingly irrational behaviour by using an "active MRI". In MRIs used in medicine the patient simply lies still during the procedure; in active MRIs, participants are expected to answer economic questions while blood flows in the brain are scrutinised to see where activity is going on while decisions are made. They found that rejecting a low offer in the ultimatum game tended to be associated with high levels of activity in the dorsal striatum, a part of the brain that neuroscience suggests is involved in reward and punishment decisions, providing some support to the behavioural theories.

As well as the ultimatum game, neuroeconomists have focused on such issues as people's reasons for trusting one another, apparently irrational risk-taking, the relative valuation of short- and long-term costs and benefits, altruistic or charitable behaviour, and addiction. Releases of dopamine, the brain's pleasure chemical, may indicate economic utility or value, they say. There is also growing interest in new evidence from neuroscience that tentatively suggests that two conditions of the brain compete in decision-making: a cold, objective state and a hot, emotional state in which the ability to make sensible trade-offs disappears. The potential interactions between these two brain states are ideal subjects for economic modelling.

Already, neuroeconomics is giving many economists a dopamine rush. For example, Colin Camerer of the California Institute of Technology, a leading centre of research in neuroeconomics, believes that incorporating insights from neuroscience could transform economics, by providing a much better understanding of everything from people's reactions to advertising to decisions to go on strike.

At the same time, Mr Camerer thinks economics has the potential to improve neuroscience, for instance by introducing neuroscientists to sophisticated game theory. "The neuroscientist's idea of a game is rock, paper, scissors, which is zero-sum, whereas economists have focused on strategic games that produce gains through collaboration." Herbert Gintis of the Sante Fe Institute has even higher hopes that breakthroughs in neuroscience will help bring about the integration of all the behavioural sciences – economics, psychology, anthropology, sociology, political science and biology relating to human and animal behaviour – around a common, brain-based model of how people take decisions.

Mindless criticism

However, not everyone is convinced. The fiercest attack on neuroeconomics, and indeed behavioural economics, has come from two economists at Princeton University, Faruk Gul and Wolfgang Pesendorfer. In an article in 2005, "The Case for Mindless Economics", they argued that neuroscience could not transform economics because what goes on inside the brain is irrelevant to the discipline. What matters are the decisions people take – in the jargon, their "revealed preferences" – not the process by which they reach them. For the purposes of understanding how society copes with the consequences of those decisions, the assumption of rational utility-maximisation works just fine.

But today's neuroeconomists are not the first dismal scientists to dream of peering inside the human brain. In 1881, a few years after William Jevons argued that the functioning of the brain's black box would not be known, Francis Edgeworth proposed the creation of a "hedonimeter", which would measure the utility that each individual gained from his decisions. "From moment to moment the hedonimeter varies; the delicate index now flickering with the flutter of the passions, now steadied by intellectual activity, low sunk whole hours in the neighbourhood of zero, or momentarily springing up towards infinity," he wrote, poetically for an economist.

This is "equivalent to neuroeconomics' brain scan," notes David Colander, an economist at Middlebury College in Vermont, in an article last year in the *Journal of Economic Perspectives*, "Edgeworth's Hedonimeter and the Quest to Measure Utility". Later economists such as Irving Fisher, Frank Ramsey (who proposed a utility-measuring machine called a "psychogalvanometer") and Friedrich von Hayek would discuss the role of the complex inner workings of the brain. Hayek cited early advances in neuroscience to explain why each individual has a unique perspective on the world.

The reason why economists in the late 19th century and much of the 20th put the rational utility-maximising individual at the heart of their models was not that they thought that economics should avoid looking into the brain, but because they lacked the technical means to do so, says Mr Colander. "Economics became a deductive science because we didn't have the tools to gather information inductively. Now, better statistical tools and neuroscience are opening up the possibility that economics can become an abductive science that combines elements of deductive and inductive reasoning."

The big question now is whether the tools of neuroscience will allow economics to fulfil Edgeworth's vision – or, if that is too much to ask, at least to be grounded in the physical reality of the brain. Studies in the first decade of neuroeconomics relied heavily on active MRI scans. Economists' initial excitement at being able to enliven their seminars with pictures of parts of the brain lighting up in response to different experiments (so much more interesting than the usual equations) has led to a recognition of the limits of MRIs. "Curiosity about neuroscience among economists has outstripped what we have to say, for now," admits Mr Camerer.

A standard MRI identifies activity in too large a section of the brain to support much more than loose correlations. "Blood flow is an indirect measure of what goes on in the head, a blunt instrument," concedes Kevin McCabe, a neuroeconomist at George Mason University. Increasingly, neuroscientists are looking for clearer answers by analysing individual neurons, which is possible only with invasive techniques – such as sticking a needle into the brain. For economists, this "involves risks that clearly outweigh the benefits," admits Mr McCabe. Most invasive brain research is carried out on rats and monkeys which, though they have similar dopamine-based incentive systems, lack the decision-making sophistication of most humans.

One new technique being used by some neuroeconomists is transcranial magnetic stimulation, in which a coil held next to the head issues a low-level magnetic pulse that temporarily disrupts activity in a certain part of the brain, to see if that changes the subject's preferences – for example, for a particular food and how much he is willing to pay for it. However, this tool, too, has only limited applicability, as it cannot get at the central temporal node of the brain where much basic reward activity takes place.

Still, Mr Camerer is confident that neuroeconomics will deliver its first big breakthroughs within five years. Likewise, Mr McCabe sees growing sophistication in neuroeconomic research. Since 2005, a group of leading neuroeconomists and neuroscientists has met to refine questions about the brain and economic behaviour. Researchers trained in both neuroscience and economics are entering the field. They are asking more sophisticated questions than the first generation "spots on brains" experiments, says Mr McCabe, such as "how these spots would change with different economic variables". He expects that within a few years neuroeconomics will have uncovered enough about the interactions between what goes on in people's brains and the outside world to start to shape the public-policy agenda – though it is too early to say how.

The success of neuroeconomics need not mean that behavioural economics will inevitably triumph over an economics based on rationality. Indeed, many behavioural economists are extremely pessimistic about the chances that brain studies will deliver any useful insights, points out Mr Camerer with regret.

However, Daniel Kahneman, a Princeton University psychologist who in 2002 won the Nobel prize in economics for his contribution to behavioural economics, is an enthusiastic supporter of the new field. "In many areas of economics, it will dominate, because it works," says Mr Kahneman.

Even so, "we are nowhere near the demise of traditional neoclassical economics," he argues. Instead, insights from brain studies may enable orthodox economists to develop a richer definition of rationality. "These traditional economists may be more impressed by brain evidence than evidence from psychology," he says; "when you talk about biology either in an evolutionary or physical sense, you feel they have greater comfort levels than when you start to talk about psychology."

In this respect, Mr Kahneman's Princeton colleagues and neuro-science-bashers may be making a mistake in bundling behavioural economics – soft mind science – and neuroeconomics – hard biology – together. "It is far easier to argue for mindless economics than for brainless economics," he says.

Cause and defect

Instrumental variables help to isolate causal relationships. But they can be taken too far

"LIKE ELABORATELY PLUMED BIRDS ... we preen and strut and display our t-values." That was Edward Leamer's uncharitable description of his profession in 1983. Mr Leamer, an economist at the University of California in Los Angeles, was frustrated by empirical economists' emphasis on measures of correlation over underlying questions of cause and effect, such as whether people who spend more years in school go on to earn more in later life. Hardly anyone, he wrote gloomily, "takes anyone else's data analyses seriously". To make his point, Mr Leamer showed how different (but apparently reasonable) choices about which variables to include in an analysis of the effect of capital punishment on murder rates could lead to the conclusion that the death penalty led to more murders, fewer murders, or had no effect at all.

In the years since, economists have focused much more explicitly on improving the analysis of cause and effect, giving rise to what Guido Imbens of Harvard University calls "the causal literature". The techniques at the heart of this literature – in particular, the use of so-called "instrumental variables" – have yielded insights into everything from the link between abortion and crime to the economic return from education. But these methods are themselves now coming under attack.

Instrumental variables have become popular in part because they allow economists to deal with one of the main obstacles to the accurate estimation of causal effects – the impossibility of controlling for every last influence. Mr Leamer's work on capital punishment demonstrated that the choice of controls matters hugely. Putting too many variables into a model ends up degrading the results. Worst of all, some relevant variables may simply not be observable. For example, the time someone stays in school is probably influenced by his innate scholastic ability, but this is very hard to measure. Leaving such variables out can easily lead econometricians astray. What is more, the direction of causation is not always clear. Working out whether deploying more policemen reduces crime, for example, is confused by the fact that more policemen are allocated to areas with higher crime rates.

Instrumental variables are helpful in all these situations. Often derived from a quirk in the environment or in public policy, they affect the outcome (a person's earnings, say, to return to the original example) only through their influence on the input variable (in this case, the number of years of schooling) while at the same time being uncorrelated with what is left out (scholastic ability). The job of instrumental variables is to ensure that the omission of factors from an analysis – in this example, the impact of scholastic ability on the amount of schooling – does not end up producing inaccurate results.

In an influential early example of this sort of study, Joshua Angrist of the Massachusetts Institute of Technology (MIT) and Alan Krueger of Princeton University used America's education laws to create an instrumental variable based on years of schooling. These laws mean that children born earlier in the year are older when they start school than those born later in the year, which means they have received less schooling by the time they reach the legal leaving-age. Since a child's birth date is unrelated to intrinsic ability, it is a good instrument for teasing out schooling's true effect on wages. Over time, uses of such instrumental variables have become a standard part of economists' set of tools. *Freakonomics*, the 2005 bestseller by Steven Levitt and Stephen Dubner, provides a popular treatment of many of the techniques. Mr Levitt's analysis of crime during American election cycles, when police numbers rise for reasons unconnected to crime rates, is a celebrated example of an instrumental variable.

Two papers – one by James Heckman of Chicago University and Sergio Urzua of Northwestern University, and another by Angus Deaton of Princeton – are sharply critical of this approach. The authors argue that the causal effects that instrumental strategies identify are uninteresting because such techniques often give answers to narrow questions. The results from the quarter-of-birth study, for example, do not say much about the returns from education for college graduates, whose choices were unlikely to have been affected by when they were legally eligible to drop out of school. According to Mr Deaton, using such instruments to estimate causal parameters is like choosing to let light "fall where it may, and then proclaim[ing] that whatever it illuminates is what we were looking for all along".

IV leagues

This is too harsh. It is no doubt possible to use instrumental variables to estimate effects on uninteresting subgroups of the population. But the quarter-of-birth study, for example, shone light on something that was both interesting and significant. The instrumental variable in this instance allows a clear, credible estimate of the return from extra schooling for those most inclined to drop out from school early. These are precisely the people whom a policy that sought to prolong the amount of education would target. Proponents of instrumental variables also argue that accurate answers to narrower questions are more useful than unreliable answers to wider questions.

A more legitimate fear is that important questions for which no good instrumental variables can be found are getting short shrift because of economists' obsession with solving statistical problems. Mr Deaton says that instrumental variables encourage economists to avoid "thinking about how and why things work". Striking a balance between accuracy of result and importance of issue is tricky. If economists end up going too far in emphasising accuracy, they may succeed in taking "the con out of econometrics", as Mr Leamer urged them to – only to leave more pressing questions on the shelf.

Control freaks

Are "randomised evaluations" a better way of doing aid and development policy?

DOCTORS STUDY DISEASES from several vantage points. Laboratory scientists peer into microscopes to observe the behaviour of bugs. Epidemiologists track sickness in populations. Drug-company researchers run clinical trials. Economists have traditionally had a smaller toolkit. When studying growth, they put individual countries under the microscope or conduct cross-country macroeconomic studies (a bit like epidemiology). But they had nothing like drug trials. Economic data were based on observation and modelling, not controlled experiment.

That is changing. A tribe of economists, most from Harvard University and the Massachusetts Institute of Technology (MIT), have begun to champion the latest thing in development economics: "randomised evaluations" in which different policies – to boost school attendance, say – are tested by randomly assigning them to different groups. In one celebrated example, researchers looked at what happened in 20 antenatal clinics in western Kenya when some gave away insecticide-treated bednets, an anti-malaria therapy, and others sold them for different prices. Their conclusion was that free distribution is far more effective in getting people to use bednets than charging even a nominal sum would be.

Such trials are not unprecedented in economics. America's welfare reform of 1996 was based partly on controlled experiments. But they have been rare enough for today's upsurge to count as a revolution in thinking about development. In 2007 the Spanish government gave the World Bank €10m ($16m) – the institution's largest trust fund – to spend on evaluating projects. The fund's first criterion calls for randomised trials. This will spread their influence further.

But are such trials all they are cracked up to be? In May 2008 randomistas gathered at the Brookings Institution, a think-tank in Washington, DC, to discuss that.[1]

Randomised evaluations are a good way to answer microeconomic questions such as how to get girls to go to school, and teachers to turn up for work. They cannot tell you much about macro questions like the right exchange-rate or budget policy. But often, they provide information that could be got in no other way. To take bednets: supporters of distributing free benefits say that only this approach can spread the use of nets quickly enough to eradicate malaria. Supporters of charging retort that cost-sharing is necessary to establish a reliable system of supply and because people value what they pay for. Both ideas sound plausible and there was no way of telling in advance who was right. But the trial clearly showed how people behave.

So evidence from randomised trials is good. But is it better than other economic data? That is what many randomistas believe. Abhijit Banerjee, the co-founder of the Abdul Latif Jameel Poverty Action Laboratory (J-PAL), argues that "the quality of the evidence that informs much of the macro-growth debates is significantly worse than the quality of the data that bears on many of the micro-policy questions". He adds: "The beauty of randomised evaluations is that the results are what they are." In other words, they provide hard evidence, resting on a solid empirical base. Aid and development policy, concludes Mr Banerjee, should take more account of that evidence.

But is the evidence really incontrovertible? On its own terms, yes. As Mr Banerjee says, the evidence is what it is. But policymakers do not want to know whether something works in a few villages. They want to know whether it will work nationwide. Here, randomised trials may not be quite so helpful.

Go back to the bednets once more. You might conclude that the trial showed that they should always be given away. Yet it turns out that millions of nets were already in use in the part of Kenya where the field trial took place, so their value was known. The experiment guaranteed supplies, so it did not test the assertion that you need to charge something to encourage reliable suppliers. And the recipients were pregnant women, whereas the point of giving bednets away is to provide anti-malaria treatment universally. The evidence from western Kenya was clear. But it hardly settled the question of whether the government should give bednets away across the country.

Questions like that may still have to be made on the basis of the soft evidence that randomistas turn up their noses at.

Randomistas rule?

Mr Banerjee doubts whether randomistas and other development economists will ever get along. The differences over research methods and what counts as evidence are too great. Economists do not know enough about growth, he says, to justify their obsession with it, however important it may be. Following the law of comparative advantage, they should do much more of what can be done best – randomised testing.

But given doubts about how widely applicable such tests are, it may be better to think of them not as a new, superior form of development economics but as one more technique – admittedly a useful one – for finding out what works, filling in gaps in knowledge, testing policy ideas, and puncturing conventional wisdom. Dani Rodrik of Harvard University argues that differences in research methods between randomistas and other economists are in danger of reopening a split between macro- and micro-economists that is starting to heal. Over the past few years, he claims, both groups have converged on a more experimental approach to development, eschewing lists of standard prescriptions and stressing the importance of context. That approach may be bearing fruit. It would be a shame if triumphalist claims by randomistas were to limit their contribution to it.

Note

1 Papers available at www.brookings.edu/events/2008/0529_global_development.aspx

An economic bestiary

Macroeconomists need to apply some new lessons and relearn
some old ones

NO TWO ECONOMIC CRISES are identical. But the same questions recur. How did we get into this mess? How can we get out
of it? How do we avoid another? Some answers repeat themselves
too. You can be pretty sure that sooner or later someone, quite possibly an anguished economist, will declare that economics itself has
gone astray. The wisdom of some past master, whether celebrated
(John Maynard Keynes, for example) or neglected (Hyman Minsky,
perhaps), has been forgotten, and the economy is paying the price.

A book,[1] "Animal Spirits", by George Akerlof of the University of
California, Berkeley, and Robert Shiller of Yale, follows this rule to the
letter. The authors seek to answer the first of those three old questions and thus to provide some pointers about the other two. They
do indeed believe that economics has lost its way. And their chosen
economist is Keynes.

So far, so familiar. But this book is rather more than the usual
lament about the failings of economics. Its authors are two of the
discipline's leading lights. Mr Akerlof won a Nobel prize in 2001, in
part for a classic paper explaining how, if sellers know more than
buyers, markets may fail. (It was turned down by three leading journals before finding a home.) Mr Shiller sounded a warning about the
"Irrational Exuberance" of the tech-boom stockmarket in a book of
that name – and did the same for the housing market in a second
edition. With a collaborator, Karl Case, he drew up a widely cited set
of indices of American home prices.

The lesson that Messrs Akerlof and Shiller draw from Keynes is
not just the standard one, of the usefulness of deficit finance in recessions. They borrow their title from "The General Theory of Employment, Interest and Money":

Most, probably, of our decisions to do something positive, the full consequences of which will be drawn out over many days to come, can only be taken as a result of animal spirits – of a spontaneous urge to action rather than inaction, and not as the outcome of the weighted average of quantitative benefits multiplied by quantitative probabilities.

Too much economics, say Mr Akerlof and Mr Shiller, has been built on the premise that humans are rational calculators. That is not a new criticism, even from economists. Over the past couple of decades *Homo economicus* has evolved into a being more like *H. sapiens*, as economics has drawn on psychology, biology and even neuroscience. "Behavioural" economics has shaped public policy – for instance, in encouraging people to save or in shaping the choice of investments in their pension pots. Behavioural economists have earned Nobel prizes. Mr Akerlof and Mr Shiller, however, complain that this evolution has been confined mainly to microeconomics. It is time for macroeconomics to catch up.

One, two, three, four, five

Keynes mentioned animal spirits only twice, in a paragraph on what motivates people to invest and speculate. From this single thread, Messrs Akerlof and Shiller spin five classes of spirit. First and closest to the original is confidence. This goes beyond a rational estimate of next week's share price, or the price in ten years' time of what a new factory might produce. And confidence, or the lack of it, builds on itself – in a way similar to Keynes's multiplier, but defying easy quantification. Second is fairness. Even if economists know that fairness matters, too little of their work reflects it. Third is corruption, or bad faith: what explains a Charles Ponzi or an Enron? Fourth is money illusion: economists have come to assume that people see through inflation, but they don't, especially when it is low. The fifth they call "stories". Economists are loth to suppose that people are irrational enough to latch onto plausible tales and forecasts – for example, that house prices will never go down. So their models won't spot the consequences of misplaced belief until it is too late.

Messrs Akerlof and Shiller list eight questions which, they say, cannot be well explained without an appeal to animal spirits – but can be tackled with them. These range from why markets for housing and shares swing wildly (a combination of confidence, stories and bad faith) to why, contrary to standard theory, there appears to be a long-run trade-off between inflation and unemployment (mainly, a mix of money illusion and fairness).

The most topical of the eight, however, is the power of central banks. The animal-spirits version of the credit crisis is a mixture of bad faith, a collapse of confidence and a change from a happy economic "story" to a thoroughly miserable one. Credit has dried up – so that applying the fiscal and monetary stimulus consistent with full employment is not enough. The Federal Reserve should also have a target for credit. Unless credit flows again, fiscal and monetary measures will not suffice: companies can't borrow to build factories and consumers can't borrow to buy cars. The Fed was set up, Messrs Akerlof and Shiller point out, to maintain confidence after the financial crisis of 1907. That, rather than the fine-tuning of interest rates in steady times, is its most important task.

How much do animal spirits help? Most of the time, the unrealistic assumption of rationality serves economists fairly well. They should, however, be more prepared to depart from it, especially in times like these – even if that makes behaviour more difficult to describe in elegant equations. Messrs Akerlof and Shiller have therefore done their profession a service.

Yet their ideas carry risks too. To a politician seeking to rein in free markets, animal spirits are a gift. The authors sum up their view of the role of government thus: "The role of the parent is to create a *happy home*, which gives the child freedom but also protects him from his animal spirits." For liberals (in the European sense) that is not a wholly comforting thought.

Note

1 "Animal Spirits: How Human Psychology Drives the Economy, and Why It Matters for Global Capitalism", Princeton University Press, March 2009.

Freud, finance and folly

Human intuition is a bad guide to handling risk

PEOPLE MAKE BARMY DECISIONS about the future. The evidence is all around, from their investments in the stockmarkets to the way they run their businesses. In fact, people are consistently bad at dealing with uncertainty, underestimating some kinds of risk and overestimating others. Surely there must be a better way than using intuition?

In the 1950s and 1960s, a group of researchers at American universities set out to find a more scientific method. They created a discipline called "decision science" which aimed to take the human element out of risk analysis. It would offer a way of making soundly based decisions for a future fraught with uncertainties. This would involve using computer models for forecasting, estimating the probabilities of possible outcomes and determining the best course of action, thus avoiding the various biases that humans brought to decision-making. Such models, the researchers thought, would provide rational answers to questions such as whether to build a factory, how to combat disease and how to manage investments.

Business schools soon adopted their teachings, and even some policymakers were persuaded. Decision science's heyday may have been the Vietnam war when Robert McNamara, then America's defence secretary, used such techniques to forecast the outcome of the conflict (though, as it turned out, without much success). But mostly the approach did not quite catch on. Decision-makers, whether in business or politics, were loth to hand over their power to a computer. They preferred to go with their gut instincts.

Think like a machine

Daniel Kahneman, now a professor at Princeton, noticed as a young research psychologist in the 1960s that the logic of decision science was hard for people to accept. That launched him on a career to show just how irrationally people behave in practice. When Mr Kahneman and his colleagues first started work, the idea of applying psychological insights to economics and business decisions was considered quirky. Since the 1990s the fields of behavioural finance and behavioural economics have blossomed, and in 2002 Mr Kahneman shared a Nobel prize in economics for his work.

Today he is in demand by organisations such as McKinsey and PartnerRe, and by Wall Street traders. But, he says, there are plenty of others that still show little interest in understanding the roots of their poor decisions. The lesson from the analyst's couch is that, far from being random, these mistakes are systematic and predictable:

- **Over-optimism**. Ask most people about the future, and they will see too much blue sky ahead, even if past experience suggests otherwise. Surveys have shown that people's forecasts of future stockmarket movements are far more optimistic than past long-term returns would justify. The same goes for their hopes of ever-rising prices for their homes or doing well in games of chance. In a study of Dutch game-show contestants, people's estimates of their odds on winning were around 25% too high. Americans are perhaps the most optimistic: according to one poll, around 40% of them think they will end up among the top 1% of earners.

   Such optimism can be useful for managers or football players, and sometimes turns into a self-fulfilling prophecy. But most of the time it results in wasted effort and dashed hopes. Mr Kahneman's work points to three types of overconfidence. First, people tend to exaggerate their own skill and prowess; in polls, far fewer than half the respondents admit to having below-average skills in, say, love-making or driving. Second, they overestimate the amount of control they have over the future, forgetting about luck and chalking up success solely to skill. And third, in competitive pursuits such as betting on shares, they forget that they have to judge their skills against those of the competition.

- **The anchor effect**. First encounters tend to be decisive not only in judging the character of a new acquaintance but also in negotiations over money. Once a figure has been mentioned, it takes a strange hold over the human mind. The asking price quoted in a house sale, for example, tends to become accepted by all parties as the "anchor" around which negotiations take place, according to one study of property brokers. Much the same goes for salary negotiations or mergers and acquisitions. If nobody has much information to go on, a figure can provide comfort – even though it may lead to a terrible mistake.

■ **Stubbornness.** No one likes to abandon a cherished belief, and the earlier a decision has been taken, the harder it is to give up. In one classic experiment, two groups of students were shown slides of an object, say a fire hydrant or a pair of spectacles. The slides started out of focus and were gradually made clearer until the students could identify the object. Those who started with a very blurry image tried to decide early and then found it difficult to identify it correctly until quite late in the process, whereas those who started less out of focus kept a more open mind and cottoned on more quickly.

The same sort of thing happens in boardrooms or in politics. Drug companies must decide early to cancel a failing research project to avoid wasting money, but find it difficult to admit they have made a mistake. Bosses who have hired unproductive employees are reluctant to fire them. Mr Kahneman cites the example of Israel's failure to spot growing threats in the lead-up to its 1973 war with its Arab neighbours. Part of the explanation was that the same people who had been watching the change in political climate had to decide on Israel's response. Similar problems have arisen in counter-terrorism work in America. In both cases, analysts may have become wedded early to a single explanation that coloured their perception. A fresh eye always helps.

■ **Getting too close.** People put a lot of emphasis on things they have seen and experienced themselves, which may not be the best guide to decision-making. For example, many companies took action to guard against the risk of terrorist attack only after September 11th 2001, even though it was present long before then. Or somebody may buy an overvalued share because a relative has made thousands on it, only to get his fingers burned.

In finance, too much emphasis on information close at hand helps to explain the so-called "home bias", a tendency by most investors to invest only within the country they live in. Even though they know that diversification is good for their portfolio, a large majority of both Americans and Europeans invest far too heavily in the shares of their home countries. They would be much better off spreading their risks more widely.

■ **Winning and losing.** Fear of failure is a strong human character-istic, which may be why people are much more concerned about losses than about gains. Consider the following bet: with the flip of a coin, you could win $1,500 if the coin turns up heads, or lose $1,000 on the tails. Now describe it in another way: with heads, you keep all the money you had before the bet, plus $1,500; with tails, you also keep everything, except $1,000. The two bets are identical, and each one, on average, will make you richer by $250 (although that average will be little consolation to the punter who has just lost $1,000). Even so, people will usually prefer the second bet.

Behavioural economists say that is because the prospect of losses seems far more daunting in isolation, rather than in the context of looking at your entire wealth, even if the average outcome is the same. This sort of myopia in the face of losses explains much of the irrationality people display in the stockmarket.

■ **Misplaced priorities**. More information is helpful in making any decision but, says Mr Kahneman, people spend proportion-ally too much time on small decisions and not enough on big ones. They need to adjust the balance. During the boom years, some companies put as much effort into planning their Christ-mas party as into considering strategic mergers.

■ **Counterproductive regret**. Crying over spilled milk is not just a waste of time; it also often colours people's perceptions of the future. Some stockmarket investors trade far too frequently because they are chasing the returns on shares they wish they had bought earlier.

Mr Kahneman reckons that some types of businesses are much better than others at dealing with risk. Pharmaceutical companies, which are accustomed to many failures and a few big successes in their drug-discovery programmes, are fairly rational about their risk-taking. But banks, he says, have a long way to go. They may take big risks on a few huge loans, but are extremely cautious about their much more numerous loans to small businesses, many of which may be less risky than the big ones.

Pensions by default

Behavioural finance offers a tempting alternative to voluntary and forced saving for old age

GOVERNMENTS AROUND THE WORLD want workers to save more for their pensions. Alarmed at the impending strains on public budgets as the post-war baby-boom generation nears retirement, they are anxious to limit the load on already stressed tax-financed pay-as-you-go pension systems.

But in turning this policy goal into reality they face an awkward dilemma. Left to their own devices, many workers do not save enough for their retirement, if they save at all. Exhortation falls on deaf ears; even generous tax incentives are ignored. But if the voluntary approach is ineffective, compulsion is an invidious alternative. Although individuals will control the savings they are forced to make, many will resent mandatory contributions and regard them as a tax increase.

Politicians would love to avoid this dilemma. Fortunately for them, economists are now offering them a way to do that: simply make enrolment into funded pension schemes automatic. At present, most workers have to opt in to retirement-saving plans. With automatic enrolment, they have to opt out. This flick of the switch makes pension saving the default option while retaining the voluntary principle.

The simplicity of the policy is deceptive. It is grounded in some quite subtle findings of behavioural finance. This branch of economics, which draws upon psychology and experiments, shows that people are not always rational, especially when it comes to saving. Although they may want to save for old age, they never get around to it because they lack the self-control to put their good intentions into effect in the short term.

The economic interpretation of this tendency to procrastinate is that in trading off present and future consumption people apply a higher discount rate in the short term than in the long term, rather than the same rate assumed in mainstream economics. Given the choice between $1,000 now and $1,100 next year, an individual may well take the money at once. But, asked to choose between $1,000 in 2025 and $1,100 in 2026, the same person might choose to wait a little longer for the larger sum.

Behavioural finance also shows the surprising extent to which people are swayed by the way that choices are framed. If, when they come to invest, most of the funds offered by the retirement plan are equities, then they will put most of their savings into stocks. If, on the other hand, most of the funds offered are bonds, then they will put most of their money into bonds.

What this suggests is that reframing decisions about retirement saving through better-designed default rules can be surprisingly effective. Automatic enrolment puts the onus on the worker to opt out rather than to opt in. This is a change of form rather than substance. Yet in one American firm, this switch raised the enrolment rate into its 401(k) plan – the main vehicle for employer-sponsored retirement saving – from 49% of newly eligible employees to 86%.

Save more today

Once workers are enrolled, pre-commitment can be used to raise saving rates. For example, Richard Thaler, of the University of Chicago, and Shlomo Benartzi, of the University of California, Los Angeles, have proposed a programme (called "Save More Tomorrow") that makes use of the lower discount rates people apply to future saving decisions than to those in the present. A study of one firm by Mr Thaler and Mr Benartzi has shown that pre-commitment by workers to allocate a portion of their future pay rises to their pensions raised their average contribution rate from 3.5% of pay to 13.6% over a 40-month period.

The success of such private-sector schemes is prompting interest among government reformers too. New Zealand is leading the way. From April 2007, all new employees will be automatically enrolled into "KiwiSaver", a retirement-saving scheme run by the tax authority, at a default contribution rate of 4% of pay. Workers have three weeks to opt out. If they stay in, they can take contribution breaks. They can save at a higher rate of 8% and choose a fund manager, although there will also be a default option for their investments.

Britain may follow New Zealand's lead. An independent commission reviewing the country's troubled pension system has been considering compulsory savings. However, the government is already taking steps to encourage automatic membership of company pension schemes. A more ambitious national programme, along the lines of New Zealand's reform, could be a politically alluring alternative to compulsion.

There are potential snags. American companies that put new employees automatically into 401(k) plans generally choose a low contribution rate and a safe but low-return investment fund. This is because they want to avoid blame if things go wrong. If governments press for retirement saving by default, they will have to wrestle with this conundrum as well.

Furthermore, it is uncertain whether individuals will respond to a national scheme with the same readiness that they do to corporate plans. One interpretation of workers' responsiveness to employer-sponsored automatic enrolment is that they see it as an endorsement by the company – which is, of course, precisely the worry that many firms have about it. But the evidence, in Britain at least, is that employees in occupational schemes are much more likely to trust employers about pensions than they are governments.

These snags are unlikely to put politicians off. After all, in formulating pension policy they are also susceptible to the psychological flaws highlighted by behavioural economics. The temptation is always to procrastinate. Not the least of the attractions of automatic enrolment is that the policy addresses the politics as well as the economics of pension reform.

The material on pages 300–22 was first published in *The Economist* in July 2008 (pages 300–5), August 2009 (pages 306–8), June 2008 (pages 309–11), March 2009 (pages 312–14), January 2004 (pages 315–19) and August 2005 (pages 320–2).

11 Emerging economists

International bright young things

The next generation of economists do their best work somewhere between the field clinic and the dissection room

IN 1998 *The Economist* wrote about eight young economists who were making a big splash in their discipline and beyond. One of them, Paul Krugman, won the Nobel prize for his models of international trade and economic geography. Ten years later we tried to repeat the trick, identifying another eight young stars, many of whom were taking their discipline far off-piste. One has since achieved even greater fame than anticipated. Steven Levitt of the University of Chicago became a household name as co-author of "Freakonomics", a bestselling book published in 2005.

"Freakonomics" owed its origins to a profile of Mr Levitt in the *New York Times* magazine in 2003. Its success has won a new readership for economists, beyond the business section and the opinion columns, in the glossier pages of the weekend supplements. The best young economists, as a consequence, have already attracted plenty of attention. That leaves us in a bit of a quandary. We feel like lonely prospectors, who, returning to a favourite stream, find it overtaken by a gold rush.

Undeterred, we have given the prospecting pan another shake. We asked leading authorities in the discipline to name the best young economists in the world. Between them, they proposed over 50 researchers, but several names recurred on many lists. We have sifted the 50 down to eight, all of whom received their PhDs after 1998.

The family tree

Several of the scholars in 2009's batch trace their intellectual ancestry back to those we picked ten years earlier. For example, **Jesse Shapiro** of the University of Chicago and **Roland Fryer** of Harvard are recognisably the intellectual heirs of Mr Levitt. They share the same knack for finding ingenious ways to answer unlikely questions, often by plundering forgotten troves of data.

At just 29, Mr Shapiro can already boast a collection of eye-catching findings worthy of a sequel to "Freakonomics". He has shown that some judgments are best made without too much information: people are better at predicting the winner of American gubernatorial elections when they watch the candidates with the sound turned off. Harsher jail conditions do nothing to deter prisoners from reoffending. If anything they encourage recidivism. Preschoolers who watch television do better academically than children who don't, especially if their parents have little education or poor English.

Mr Fryer's ambition is to unravel the causes of black under-achievement in America, especially in education. His search for explanations extends beyond racism and poverty to contemplate the role of a self-defeating culture. He calculates that a black student who earns straight A grades will have 1.5 fewer friends from his ethnic group than an equally swotty white student.

Michael Kremer, another of those we cited in 1998, can also claim an intellectual relative in 2009's cohort. **Esther Duflo** of the Massachusetts Institute of Technology (MIT) received more recommendations than any other economist. Some who didn't nominate her thought she was too established to count as "new".

With her colleague, Abhijit Banerjee, Ms Duflo and Mr Kremer have remade development economics, nudging it away from its concern with policies, towards a preoccupation with projects. They study economic development as seen from the field, clinic or school, rather than the finance ministry. They might be called the "peace corps" of economists, bringing the blessing of their investigative technique to the neglected villages of India or the denuded farms of western Kenya.

Ms Duflo has made her name carrying out randomised trials of development projects, such as fertiliser subsidies and school recruit-ment. In these trials, people are randomly assigned to a "treatment" group, which benefits from the project, and a "control" group, which does not. By comparing the average outcome of each group, she can establish whether the project worked and precisely how well.

In one study, Ms Duflo and her colleagues showed that mothers in the Indian state of Rajasthan are three times as likely to have their chil-dren vaccinated if they are rewarded with a kilogram of *daal* (lentils) at the immunisation camp. The result is useful to aid workers, but puzzling to economists: why should such a modest incentive (worth less than 50 cents) make such a big difference? Immunisation can save a child's life; a bag of lentils should not sway the mother's decision either way.

Randomised trials "give you the chance to be surprised", Ms Duflo says. Had they arrived at this result using some other method, she and her colleagues would have assumed they had made a mistake. But randomisation removes such doubts, showing that it was indeed the lentils that made the difference. The result cannot be dismissed; it must be explained.

The approach has its critics. A randomised trial can prove that a remedy works, without necessarily showing why. It may not do much to illuminate the mechanism between the lever the experimenters pull and the results they measure. This makes it harder to predict how other people would respond to the remedy or how the same people would respond to an alternative. And even if the trial works on average, that does not mean it will work for any particular individual.

The randomistas, as Ms Duflo and her comrades are called, liken their studies to the clinical trials that prove the efficacy of new drugs. But the ultimate ambition of economics is for something more akin to anatomy. Researchers hope to dissect the underlying physiology of an economic problem, revealing how the leg bone is connected to the thigh bone. With a full anatomy of behaviour – what economists call a structural model – they can determine if a policy or project will work even before it has been attempted.

The early anatomists of the human body suffered from a short-age of fresh cadavers to work on. Medical students would trek long distances to watch a dissection performed. Economists often find themselves in a similar predicament. Short of good empirical meat, they have to rely on elaborate theory and guesswork to fill in what they cannot observe.

Amy Finkelstein, also of MIT, the fourth of our young stars, has anatomised the market for annuities in Britain. The industry suffers from "asymmetric information": customers may know more than the provider about their chances of dying. Unfortunately, this private information is as hidden from economists as it is from the annuity company. Ms Finkelstein and a colleague, James Poterba, have shown how to infer the cost of this unseen problem from what can be observed, namely the kind of annuities people choose and the length of their life after retirement.

Like Ms Finkelstein, **Raj Chetty**, recently hired by Harvard from the University of California, Berkeley, is a promising young "public economist": a student of tax and spend. He has great respect for structural models. But in a 2008 paper he makes the case for judicious short cuts. Often you don't need to dissect a whole body; a few choice incisions are enough.

For example, he wanted to know whether policymakers should raise unemployment benefits. To answer this question, a structural model would need to specify how much a dollar is worth to a person on the dole, as compared with someone in work. It would also need to quantify the burden a job hunt imposes. This isn't easy to find out. But Mr Chetty argues it is unnecessary.

He gleans all the information he needs by looking at the time it takes unemployed people to find a new job. Unsurprisingly, they take longer when their benefits are more generous. This is usually attributed to "moral hazard" – people take less care to escape a danger, such as joblessness, if they are insured against it. But Mr Chetty shows that skewed incentives account for only 40% of the delay.

The rest is due to what he calls a "liquidity effect". The unemployed typically have few liquid assets to fall back on and little chance of a loan from the bank. This forces them to rush their job search. If they had savings to dip into or credit to tap, they might search with greater deliberation. This kind of dallying is, in a sense, optimal. The unemployed decide that an unhurried job search is worth the extra cost of depleted savings or heavier loan repayments.

Higher benefits ease this liquidity problem. Raising benefits by $1 a week would do as much social good as raising American GDP by $290m, Mr Chetty calculates, although government loans to the unemployed might do better still.

In 1998 macroeconomists dominated our list of the best young thinkers, but they are under-represented in 2009's batch. We found plenty of agreement about the three or four young macro thinkers most likely to succeed, but surprisingly little confidence that they would. One leader in the field suspected their work represented a moment of beauty, not truth. Another complained that the youngsters lacked the "vision thing" that distinguished the greats of the past.

Ramsey revisited

If so, perhaps they can blame the times that produced them. They came of age during the Great Moderation, a period of macroeconomic tranquillity and intellectual consensus. They are in thrall not to John Maynard Keynes, sage of the Depression, but to his Cambridge contemporary, Frank Ramsey, a precocious polymath who made his contributions in the prelapsarian 1920s. Ramsey was interested in how much of its income a nation should save so as to maximise its prosperity now and in the future. His work underpins much of modern macroeconomics, in which agents act today with an eye on tomorrow. But the framework is best suited to analysing steady accumulation, not violent cycles of speculation and liquidation. So it is not the obvious place to start to explain the world economy's present predicament.

The macroeconomist nominated most often for our list was **Iván Werning** of MIT. Mr Werning is an economist's economist; an elegant theorist, whose early contributions provided streamlined proofs that other thinkers could make use of. One of Mr Werning's ambitions is to unite Ramsey's work with that of another elegant theorist, Sir James Mirrlees. Sir James won the Nobel prize in 1996 for exploring how best to set taxes when people can disguise their true worth from the revenue collector. Mr Werning asks the same question, but in the forward-looking, macroeconomic setting provided by Ramsey.

Mr Werning and his co-authors have so far derived at least two theoretical results of note. The first is to show that the unemployed have sufficient incentive to find work, even if they receive unemployment benefits indefinitely. The second is that bequests from one generation to the next should be subsidised by the government, with smaller inheritances receiving higher rates of subsidy. Mr Werning and his co-author, Emmanuel Farhi (a young Harvard macroeconomist), point out that the biggest roll of the dice in life is the family you are born into. Their system of subsidies would take the edge off this uncertainty.

Two of the economists we highlighted in 1998 – David Laibson of Harvard and Matthew Rabin of Berkeley – were exponents of "behavioural economics", incorporating the insights of psychology into the dismal science. The sub-discipline has continued to flourish in the decade since, seeping so far into the mainstream that its disciples no longer constitute a self-contained school. The randomistas, for example, often invoke behavioural explanations for their experimental results.

Xavier Gabaix of New York University, our seventh pick, is another example of someone who is au fait with behavioural economics but not defined by it. He has written papers with Mr Laibson, including one that explains why hotels can get away with overpricing the mini-bar. But his interests extend beyond the behavioural.

He has, for example, shown a fascination with "power laws": tantalising statistical patterns that seem to crop up wherever you look hard enough. The size of cities, the pay of executives and the performance of the stockmarket all seem to follow such laws. For cities, the law can be crudely expressed as the "rank-size rule". The second-biggest city will have roughly half the population of the biggest; the population of the third-ranked city will be one-third of the first's, and so on. The relationship between executive pay and company size also obeys a power law: companies twice the size tend to pay their chief executives roughly 25% more.

These curious regularities have more than numerological appeal. They give clues about what can and cannot explain the size and growth of the things they describe. For example, the rank-size rule could not hold if small cities grew systematically faster than big ones, or vice versa. The power law of executive pay also requires a particular kind of economics to explain it. Mr Gabaix thinks the "economics of superstars", invented by Sherwin Rosen, fits the bill.

Top executives may differ only slightly in their talents, just as sports champions differ only slightly from runners-up. But the better managers nonetheless get hired by the bigger firms, just as the best entertainers sing to the largest audience. This means an executive's small edge in managerial skill is amplified, because his talents go to work on a bigger canvas. Mr Gabaix made a splash in 2006 when he concluded that the "excessive" pay of chief executives was not necessarily excessive. Compensation may have grown sixfold from 1980 to 2003 not because managers were six times greedier, but because the firms they ran were six times bigger.

If the size of firms obeys a power law, economies will comprise some very big firms and a long tail of small ones. The fortunes of the biggest companies might then stir the whole economy, Mr Gabaix conjectures. The $24 billion dividend paid by Microsoft in December 2004, for example, added 3% to America's personal income that month. Mr Gabaix calls for a more "granular" approach to macroeconomics, which would weigh the contribution of big firms to national aggregates.

This granular view is already taking hold in studies of international trade. Countries, after all, do not trade with each other; companies do. A few firms usually account for the lion's share of a country's exports: in America, the top 10% of exporters account for 96% of the country's foreign sales, and only 4% of firms export at all.

These observations (drawn from work by Andrew Bernard of Dartmouth College among others) demand a theory to explain them. That gap has been filled by **Marc Melitz**, a trade economist at Princeton University and our final new star.

Mr Melitz is a pioneer of the "new, new trade theory", which succeeds the "new" trade theory propounded by Mr Krugman over 30 years ago. The source of its novelty is its recognition that firms differ, and only the best firms export. In America, for example, exporting factories are more than twice as big as plants that do not sell beyond their shores, and they squeeze 14% more out of their workers.

In Mr Melitz's theory firms first prove themselves at home, discovering their own limits and abilities. Only the best then venture overseas. Entering a foreign market is an expensive endeavour, he points out, even before firms encounter the tariffs or transport costs that preoccupy most trade models. An exporter must find and introduce itself to distant customers, comply with alien regulations and set up distribution channels abroad. One study found that it cost Colombian chemical factories over $1m to enter a foreign market.

The gains from trade also differ in Mr Melitz's model. In the new trade theory that preceded it, international commerce raises the productivity of firms by enlarging their market, allowing them to reap economies of scale. In Mr Melitz's model, trade raises the productivity of industries, not by allowing firms to grow bigger, but by giving the better firms a bigger share of the market. Foreign competition sifts and sorts firms, winnowing out the weakest firms and leaving a greater share of the market to their stronger rivals.

Just as Mr Krugman found a clean way to account for economies of scale, Mr Melitz handles the heterogeneity of firms without spoiling the lines of his model. It now serves as a pliant workhorse for lots of "granular" thinking in the field.

Bodice rippers

Over 60 years ago Paul Samuelson laid down "the foundations of economic analysis" in his seminal work of that name. In the introduction, he describes his dawning realisation of the underlying unity of the subject. As he laboured in each field – consumer behaviour, public finance, international trade, business cycles – he encountered similar problems, which yielded to the same set of mathematical techniques. Mr Samuelson's book squeezed a shapeless body of economic knowledge into a tight corset.

In the decades since, the laces have been unpicked. It is not just that economists are nosing into new fields of social behaviour. They have been doing that at least since Gary Becker of the University of Chicago wrote about crime and the family in the 1960s and 1970s. But today's economists show no great attachment to the rational model of behaviour that guided Mr Becker. Economic theory has become so eclectic that ingenious researchers can usually cook up a plausible model to explain whatever empirical results they find interesting.

Economics is now defined neither by its subject matter nor by its method.

What, then, unites these eight young stars and the discipline they may come to dominate? Economists still share a taste for the Greek alphabet: they like to provide formal, algebraic accounts of the behaviour they explain. And they pride themselves on the sophistication of their investigative methods. They are usually better at teasing confessions out of data than their rivals in other social sciences. What defines economics? Economics is what economists do – the best of them, anyway.

The material on pages 323–31 was first published in *The Economist* in January 2009.

Index